GUIDED BY Divine Love

An Inspiring True Story of a Young Man's
Journey Out of the Darkness of Oppression and
Discovery of the Inner Light That Was There All Along

David K. Haaland

Ordering Information:

For orders and inquiries, please contact:
1-888-404-1388
www.goldtouchpress.com
book.order@goldtouchpress.com

Printed in the United States of America

Dedication

*This book is dedicated
to those whom I have loved from my earliest days.*

My dear mother, who not only brought me into this world, but in our few years together before her very early passing, instilled in me what others cannot do in a lifetime. Mother, you were always a beautiful angel to me, and it is not surprising to know that you are an angel now helping all needy people beyond the veil as you did on earth. You are always in my heart and soul and you are truly my divine overseer who has always guided me with love.

My dear father, who always instilled in all his children the value of high ethics, morals, and education. Father, I saw you time and time again make big transactions signed and sealed by only a handshake. I learned from you to trust people and to stand behind my words, even absent any legal contracts. I thank you for teaching me ethics and the value of hard work.

My dear siblings, especially brothers Jamel (handsome in Arabic) and Jamal (beauty in Arabic), who were jailed by Saddam Hussein after deporting our entire family and later gassed and killed for no apparent reason other than being Kurds. May you rest in peace, my dear brothers.

Sister Layla, you were always so kind to me, and despite your young age, you were always so much like our mother whom we lost so soon. I hope to see all of you someday in this lifetime, heaven or both.

My sweet daughters, Nadia and Miranda. Thank you for the times we were able to spend together. I am so sorry that those times were often interrupted by the times you were taken away from me by your mother against God and your wishes. The love I have always had for both of you made me a very strong person, both emotionally and spiritually. I pray that those times were lessons for you to make a brighter future for yourselves. This book is my small gift to both of you. I hope you will accept it with love.

Lastly, this book is dedicated to my first love, Nadia, wherever you are. My pure love for you was never about "what's in it for me." I truly loved you without any expectation and held your love true to my heart, regardless of the thousands of miles and the passing of time that has kept us apart. You are the one who made me prove to myself that love is eternal and has no limits.

I really wish you could see this with me Mother and Father as I know you are seeing it behind the veil.

Contents

Preface

You are about to read my true, life story exactly as it happened and be a witness to the details of many of its events. I was guided to begin writing down my story in this book while I was going through the darkest days of my life. As you will probably be able to see for yourself when you read it, until that time I never truly cared for anything literary or even related to any kind of writing. My focus was always math, physics, and numbers in general. Being a creator of literature was never truly an issue for me when I began writing, and it is still not my primary concern.

I finished writing the book in midsummer 2013. Since that time, all editing, re-editing, page design, page formatting, and all other needed steps to make my writing an actual book have happened. In truth, when I had to revisit parts of what I had written for editing or formatting purposes, I had a difficult time reliving all the tragedies and my mental and physical condition as they had occurred. I simply could not bring myself to reread any more than I absolutely had to.

Tuesday, October 15, 2013, marked a glorious day, a moment I will never forget, when I opened a box and found a review copy of my book inside. In truth, I was not able to open the book for nearly two days. I handled it with great care and was even afraid to leave any fingerprints. It was beyond beautiful. For those two days all I could do was admire the combined efforts of my book design team at 1106 Design and myself. Once I came back to Earth and began looking for any errors, I got a repeated sense of "not having done my best" in terms of some of the words I had used. I did find a few small errors. But even after I had submitted the corrections, I was still feeling and hearing a still, small voice inside of me saying "Halt everything! Major rewriting needed!"

I was very confused, and while hearing that voice I became even more confused when a louder voice came in: "Don't you dare rewrite anything. You were writing from your soul while going through those difficulties. If you rewrite anything, you will be dishonoring your soul and feelings." I totally agreed with the louder voice. I made a quick decision to put all the misgivings to rest and keep on moving forward.

Amazing coincidences began to occur within a day or two as I was re-reading various online articles. I came across a few quotes that were very fitting to that louder voice that I had already agreed with. I remembered having taken notice of those quotes at an earlier time and wondering what were the odds of actually getting back to these online articles and having the time to read them. I pondered over and over again, and concluded that God, the angels, and my mother were behind my coming back to those messages, and I truly wanted to honor them by making them a part of this book. And so that is when I decided to give my readers those feelings and thoughts in this Preface. The first quote was from the author Arthur Plotnik:

We write to communicate to the hearts of others what's burning inside of us, and editing lets the fire be seen through the smoke. Edit everything, but don't remove your soul from what you say because then it will sound like writing. And if it sounds like writing, then it needs to be rewritten.

The second quote was from a North American Indian proverb:

Tell me a fact and I'll learn.
Tell me the truth and I'll believe.
But tell me a story and it will live in my heart forever.

I knew that adding this Preface might delay my receiving the second book proof. To me, that was a very insignificant price to pay in the overall scheme of everything. I have made the final decision to not rewrite, to not remove my soul from my writing, because I am not here to show you my excellent literary skills, only to share my true story told from my heart. My only wish is that it will reach your heart as well.

Prologue

Often, we do not realize, acknowledge, or believe that everything has happened, is happening, or will happen in divine order and timing.

Of course, if we believe that, we also believe the saying "everything is happening for a reason." Regardless of whether we understand or even agree with this, sometimes when certain things happen we hear someone to our pleasure or displeasure repeating this mantra. Case in point: a horrible accident that results in the passing of a child. Regardless of whether we believe in God or believe that God has a master plan for all of us, including the child, we often question God as to the reason for this child to pass on so soon. We often, in the moment of sadness, grief, or anger, fall into the trap of questioning divine order. Many of us, myself included, have done that all the time.

As I finished my life story to date and was ready to write this part, I had to think deeply and be completely honest with myself and answer some of the questions that presented themselves to me. They might present themselves to you also, but for a long time I had no honest answer for them. I was finally guided to those answers by God and the angels. I am not about to go back and rewrite what I have already put forth, because that would not be my true honesty. I also believe that there was a reason for me not to get those answers sooner than now.

When you finish reading my story, I hope you will realize the type of love I had, and still have, for Nadia. When Nadia, fearing rumors that might destroy her reputation, asked me to at least get engaged to her (be aware that it was unheard of at that time and in that type of society for any woman to ask a man to do that), I did not go along with her request because I was afraid of creating a family like my own, a stateless family, lacking any proof of citizenship, which meant for me a life sentence in a big prison called Iraq. It is clear that I had a hard time accepting the fact that my father and our family would almost certainly never get that proof of citizenship. I never knew that there was a divine order behind all of that. By not accepting or even knowing the divine order, I attempted to somehow change or stop the pattern by refusing to get engaged to the one I loved. It never crossed my mind to trust that God and the angels would find a way to help. I threw away the one thing that was certain, Nadia's love, for what I thought of as a bigger prize. I now and only now realize that I will be searching my entire life for the one thing that I threw away years ago. Will I ever find it? Only God and the angels know.

I repeated the same mistake once I arrived in my mother's "promised land." My Iraqi family endured deportation to a foreign land stripped of everything they owned, including their beautiful home. Again, instead of becoming aware of and accepting the divine order that allowed these things to happen, I dismissed such thoughts and became very angry. These events made me determined to not think of getting married, even remotely, before getting my citizenship. As it turned out, I got engaged only a few days after getting my citizenship. Yes, I got engaged without even being in love, even though I had known love with a few before my citizenship. Why did I do that? I know I am not stupid, so why? Again, I dismissed everything in the face of getting the citizenship, thinking that would be the answer for everything.

The fact is, I saw how my father loved his family, and I witnessed the deportation and the killing, for no reason, of my brothers. Out of anger and the dismissal of divine order for everything, I was going to create the "perfect" family and stop the drama. The irony was that I was going to be the "superman" and put an end to this pattern that I was not accepting or agreeing with.

It was clear that I had not learned the lessons that "everything happens for a reason," and the universe was going to teach me these lessons one way or another. The universe might have said, "David, yes, you are a U.S. citizen now and no one will deport you or take your freedom because you are a Kurd, but let me show you what I can do." The universe made my own family the teacher, and it was going to teach me the lessons I had dismissed all along.

My wife, the mother of our children, showed me how my freedom could be taken away and I could be stripped of my own children, for no reason. She did this over, over, and over again, and I refused to learn the lesson while mistakenly trying to protect this "perfect" family. The more I tried to keep my family, the more lessons my wife showed me. I could not even imagine at the time that when the mother of our children was doing all those horrible things, she could not have even remotely loved me. This would have gone on forever if I had not finally learned the lessons. My amazing journey and connection with God and the angels finally taught me about divine timing and order. When I finally accepted that all of this heartache was in divine order, only then did I decide to trust God and the angels, realize that there were better things waiting for me, and find the courage to stand on my own. Standing on my own while my children were taken away from me was the easy part, but having the courage to write honestly without any omissions about my life was a completely different story. Writing this story is my first proof to myself that I accept and trust in divine timing and order for everything. I have not intentionally bypassed anything or any story just because I thought it was shameful or not appropriate. I am very proud of myself and my story, and I am fully aware now that my mother behind the veil, God, and the angels were helping me write what you are about to read.

Acknowledgements

I would like first and foremost to thank my parents for being the loving, extraordinary human beings they always were, always acting with God's love and light shining on their way no matter the situation. I am so sorry, Mother, that you had to leave us so early. Your passing forever left a hole in our hearts. I am so sorry, dear Father, that you had to go through what you went through just because you were a Kurd. You were also stripped of your children just like I have been, for no reason at all. Not only that, but you were robbed of everything you worked so hard for. I recall how excited you were when you bought a young palm tree and planted it in our beautiful garden. I hope someone is now enjoying that palm tree and all the orange trees you planted. I am so sorry, Father, I was not there for your funeral. I promise to visit you as soon as I possibly can, when all the political nonsense allows me.

To my sister Layla who was and still is like a mother despite her younger age. You always sensed my feelings without expressing anything to you.

To my first love Nadia. Nadia, I loved you very pure love while we were together and I stayed faithful to your love despite all the miles between us. I was very happy for you when I learned that you were safe and living a "normal" life.

To the official in the West German Embassy who knew I was not coming back, but gave me the visa to enter West Germany anyway. Oh, how I wish I knew your name.

To Dr. Amir and his wife, Maria, for all the help you gave me and for putting up with me. I knew how hard it was to host someone for so long, but you did. I forever thank you for your hospitality, and I would be so happy if I could somehow find you and reconnect with you again.

To the Lutheran Social Services organization, wherever you are operating. You never asked me what church I belonged to, nor did you ask me to belong to anything. You just helped without any expectation, and I am forever thankful for what you did for me.

To Charles Hoffman, thank you for all your help. You walked and walked to come see us just to help, without expecting anything in return. May you rest in peace, Mr. Hoffman.

To Mr. Olaf Haaland, his wife, and their family for all the help and generosity. May you rest in peace, Mr. Haaland.

To Patty Francis of Minot, wherever you are and whatever your last name may now be. I thank you for seeing something in me and my story and creating that "buzz" when you wrote about me in the *Red & Green*.

To my friends, Ken and Linda Erhardt—Linda, I forever thank you for being such a great friend. When I think of my U.S. citizenship, you immediately come to mind. Thank you for coming to the courthouse to be with me and to take those pictures. I had no one else, and you took time off from your job just to be with me. I think of you both every time I hear Neil Diamond.

To my friend, Denise—I am truly sorry I never had the courage to open up and tell you how I felt about you. I am also very sorry that we are not friends anymore. That was not my choice, and regardless of what might have happened, I am thankful for knowing you.

To Dee Dee, for everything you did. I truly thank you for "forcing" us to find heaven on earth.

To Kathryn Harwig—thank you for your friendship. You helped me and opened my eyes to my interest in intuition. I will always be grateful to you for connecting me with my parents and helping me know that they are always with me.

To the one and only, my dearest friend, Insiah Beckman and her husband Gary. Dear Insiah, you are the one who led the way to my new journey and made me aware of the archangels. That awareness has been nothing but amazing. For that I am forever grateful to you. Everything I came to know and learn has been because of you and your inspiration. Gary, you have asked me many times when I will have my own booth at one of your Expos. The answer is—very soon.

To all my beloved archangels, especially St. Michael and Gabriel. Thank you for protecting me and guiding me, St. Michael, as I learned to call upon you in my comings and goings. I am well aware of your guidance. To Gabriel, I thank you for igniting my creativity and for being with me. You were there whenever I needed you.

To the amazing Deborah King: It is very hard to say enough about you and your teachings. As I write this, it is doubly amazing the kind of impact you continue to make on me, even before I have met you in person. That meeting is next in line for me to manifest. I cannot wait for that day.

To my mentor, Dr. Wayne W. Dyer: What can I say and how can I thank you enough for being you? I have always liked you, listened to you, even before my awareness of the angels. You and Doreen Virtue were my primary reason for going to Vancouver—and the beginning of my journey. It was you who made my first angel encounter possible, and that is something I will never forget. I am very sure that we will see each other many more times.

To my dear mentor and spiritual guide, Doreen Virtue. Right from the beginning, I was guided to follow you and your teaching, even though I cannot explain why this happened the way it did. I have never said or written this anywhere before, but I have had many people wanting to be friends on Facebook with this message: "I was looking for Doreen and the angels led me to you. Can you please accept my friendship?" I heard this in one way or another many times, and frankly, I did not know what to make of it. Whatever is the message behind all those requests and regardless of how I feel right now about some of the things I have witnessed, I am forever thankful to you.

To Hay House and the amazing Louise Hay: You are an inspiration for millions, Ms. Hay. Thank you for being you.

I would like to also thank Caroline Myss, Marianne Williamson, Greg Braden, Dr. Brian Weiss, and Cheryl Richardson.

Finally, I must apologize if I have missed anyone who has been an inspirational force to me. I want to thank you here, too.

Part 1:

A Mother's Love Beyond the Veil (1955–1979)

CHAPTER ONE

Devoted Family

M y name is David Kariem Haaland. (More detail about the "Haaland" later.) I was born in Baghdad, Iraq. My birth year was noted as 1955, but the month and the day are questionable at best. In those days, documentation of birth dates was not accurate, and issuing birth certificates was not important. There was a time where all my friends were documented as being born on July 1. Birthdays were not celebrated at all—people had many survival issues to worry about before celebrating birthdays. At that time and in that society, being born was an event as ordinary as eating and drinking. Of course, if the government and social services had required accurate birth dates for registration, people would have done a better job of noting them. Unfortunately, there was no government or social services at that time. The country was still under the administration of the British Empire, which had come in after the end of World War I, and the country was called the Kingdom of Iraq. The Kingdom ended in July 1958 when Abdal Kariem Qasim (known as al-Zaim, "the leader" in Arabic) became the president/prime minister of Iraq by means of a military coup d'état against King Faisal II. It was said that this action was inspired by the coup d'état in Egypt in 1952 by Nasser. I am a Kurd from Kurdish parents who lived in a very populated area in Baghdad called El Sadrya. Most Kurds lived in the northern regions of the country, but there were many, like us, who were big-city dwellers. The Kurdish community of Baghdad was, and still is, the biggest minority among the Arab majority. During that time, and maybe because I was very young, I did not see any discrimination by the Arab majority. Arabs, Kurds, and other minorities seemed to live in peace and mutual

respect, and religions did not follow lines of nationality. An Arab or Kurd could have been Muslim, Christian, or any other religion. Although Islam was the official and main religion for Iraq, I do not recall any religious persecution or disharmony. People with different religions and nationalities were living side by side as one.

My father's name was Kariem, and my mother's name was Fatima. My father was a wholesaler of rice, and my mother, like most mothers during that time, was a housewife. My father was one of the hardest-working people I have ever known.

An old and only picture in my possession of my father

4

He really cared about providing for his family, and he did very well. The other thing that I remember about him, and have the utmost respect for, is the way he cared about our education. He always wanted us to be high achievers. I have always wanted to be like my father and make him proud of me. One of my strongest early memories from when I was only five or six years old is my mother's happiness at seeing President Qasim in his convertible motorcade waving to the masses. Qasim was much loved in the area where I grew up. He had charisma. But Qasim's presidency was haunted by assassination attempts. It has been said that because of that earlier second chance, Saddam Hussein chose to kill anyone and everyone who was against him. Hussein never gave anyone a second chance, even his own family. I also vividly remember the eventual successful assassination of Qasim in February 1963 via military coup d'état under the leadership of Abdul Salam Arif. It was said that Nasser of Egypt was behind his assassination.

We were living in a very big, old two-story home—the house, actually, where I was born. We did not have a television and neither did anyone we knew; we had only a big tube radio, which brought in only one or two stations. We had to wait for it to warm up before hearing anything. That was our only possible indoor entertainment. All activities for a young boy like me were outside the house, and one of the major ways I had of socializing and spending time was playing with a little wooden car made by hand out of four or five pieces of wood and three wheel bearings.

For several days after the coup, we were under curfew law and could not leave our homes. It was not safe at all, and the sounds of gunfire were heard everywhere. During those curfew days, I grew very bored and longed to go outside, but we could not even walk on the sidewalk. One day I decided to take my kite to the roof to enjoy killing some time. (All houses in those days had flat roofs that were fenced in.

People used to sleep on their roofs in the summer to stay cool. In many ways, I miss sleeping under the stars without actually camping.) I peeked out at the street to see if there was any moving life but saw only military vehicles and a few soldiers or rebels (unorganized fighters) with their machine guns not far from our house. I ignored all that, as I really did not know much about it, and started flying my kite. It took me a while, but I was able to fly it higher and higher until I reached the end of my long string.

Flying kites and keeping them flying requires, like many things, a lot of practice and skill. You must move in a lot of different directions to keep the kite where it needs to be. So that day I completely forgot about everything else, including the curfew. I was in "the zone." The open roof of our big house was very large, but in attempting to control the kite, I came very close to the fence. Actually, my back was completely against the fence, and the fence was not very high, so my head and shoulders were very visible to those below or on the street.

Something happened to me then, but it did not make much of an impression on me at the time. Somehow the image of that event is more vivid in retrospect, coming back to me from nowhere and for no apparent reason. Standing next to the fence, I felt the sensation of a big insect or small bird buzzing past my right ear forcefully enough that I felt the pressure there. It only stopped me for a second before I went back to flying my kite, which had started to fall from the sky. The image of the event I received many years later was much clearer and appeared to me like a video taken of me and my surroundings by someone else. It showed me, much to my surprise, that the object I felt buzz past my ear was not a big insect or small bird. It was a bullet, fired by one of the rebels I had seen earlier. It also told me that the rebels thought I was flying the kite to let the opposition group, whoever they were, know the location of these rebels. As a result, one of them decided to shatter my head. He missed, but not by much at all. The vacuum I felt in my ear created by the traveling bullet was an indication of how close it was. To my knowledge, this was my first "close brush with death" or "escape from death" experience. I was seven years old.

In spite of the unrest, life was pleasant enough. Our parents were kind to all of us. I was the third child of nine, with two older brothers and two younger, and four sisters who were all younger than me. I was attending a private school in Baghdad, getting that good education my father wanted so much. The country was almost getting used to seeing a military coup d'état every few years.

I did not spend all my time studying. I was enchanted with sparrows for some reason. Even at a young age, if I saw another young boy playing with a sparrow that had fallen from its nest or was injured, I would do anything to get enough money so I could exchange it for the sparrow. I would take care of the sparrow day after day until I was sure it was able to be on its own. Once I did, I would let it fly, and then I would search for another sparrow to take care of. I had no idea what I was doing at the time, but I literally had my own sparrow rehabilitation center.

After school one day, I ran home to my hospital to check on a certain little injured bird. My mother asked me to go and deliver a message to my father at his shop before he closed up, so I put the sparrow in a little cage, and off we went. When I arrived, he was drinking late afternoon tea with friends, as he often did. As I opened the door to the cage to give the sparrow a few crumbs, he fluttered his wings just enough to escape, landing on a roof across the street. I knew the sparrow was not quite healed yet, and I became very concerned. I knew I had to go to him. I had no idea my father and his friends were watching. I found a ladder to the roof and crept within seven feet of the bird. The bird recognized me and moved toward me until I was able to hold it again. I brought it down to my father's shop and returned it to the cage. My father's friend, without any hesitation, pointed at me and told my father, "This son of yours will realize high achievements, and I can see he will be financially secure." At the time, I did not clearly understand what this man was saying.

My mother worked very hard all day and every day without ever asking for anything special. She rose before anyone else to make sure that everyone in the family had a good breakfast. Then she did the dishes. That task was not anything like we know today. We had plumbing, but it was only cold water. She had to heat washing water on a kerosene burner. After that, she would go to the market early enough to get first choice of meats and vegetables for our dinner. We did not buy frozen meat or chicken. I don't think we even knew what a refrigerator or freezer was. Our chickens were live and processed by us on the same day they were consumed. Once shopping was done, she cut up the food and prepared to cook. We did not have a Jenn-Air cooktop; it was just the kerosene burner and very hard labor. While the food was cooking, she did all the cleaning and dusting. The morning process repeated itself at dinner as my mother made sure that the big family had enough to eat; then it was on to clean the dishes again.

My mother, depicted by Spirit Artist Rita Berkowitz

My mother was about five-five, with beautiful features, and she always looked like an angel. Her hair was a light color that seemed to me sandy or golden. She had a narrow nose with beautiful cheekbones. Her skin was like peaches and cream. Her most beautiful features, which she passed on to all of her children, were her long eyelashes. Her eyes were bluish-green, and her favorite color was lavender. My mother, despite our financial well-being, never cared about fancy clothes or jewelry. She was very gentle and a beautiful soul, inside and out. She wanted to help everyone, was very patient, and was always able to be the peacemaker in any heated situation.

My mother taught me one of my biggest life lessons without my even knowing it. In fact, I can say I hated getting that lesson when it was being delivered, mostly because of the street darkness and the stray dogs. You have to know that there were no streetlights then, and many stray dogs that came out only at night to hunt for food. They ran in packs and were very dangerous. Many days I saw my mother cooking all day, more food than I knew our family could ever eat. She sometimes had two sets of very large cookware going at the same time, pots easily ranging eighteen to twenty-four inches in diameter and twelve inches deep. She usually cooked a favorite fragrant and savory dish, and always rice. My father was well known for selling the best rice, and we enjoyed it almost every day.

In the evening after our family dinner, my mother would come to me and my older brother, give us some money, and ask us to take the extra dishes to a family whom she knew did not have enough to eat. Shivering with fear, we tried to find any excuse, but we ended up doing it every time. I once asked her why she waited until dark to send the food. I somehow knew even then that she wasn't telling me what she truly had in her mind and heart, and it took me many years to know the real reason. At that time, not having enough to feed your family was looked down on by most people. My mother did not want anyone to know that she was helping another family, and most importantly, she did not want anyone to know that these people were in need. She made similar arrangements to retrieve the cookware, and this too was never during the day. It took me many years after my dear mother had passed to realize her powerful message and teaching by example. My mother was doing what God wanted us to do. She was helping without any expectations. She used to tell us when we were very young that

God knows everything and knows what we do. She always told us to do what pleases God. That is how she raised us.

I only remember her working hard for her family and friends, never doing anything for herself. It seems as though that was her happiness. When I was in fifth or sixth grade, she went into labor with my new baby brother. I was young and busy with my life and myself, so I do not recall the details, but I know she was taken into a very nice hospital in an upscale neighborhood of Baghdad called El Karada. After a couple of days, we were told that she must undergo a caesarean section in order to have a healthy child. My father agreed, and the surgery went well. Of course, my mother and brother would have to be kept in the hospital a little longer. Everything seemed normal. My father and I went to visit her and enjoyed walking through the hospital's very nice garden filled with many flowers and fruit trees and a huge statue of the Virgin Mary. (One thing you must know is that this was not in any way a religious hospital.) People in Baghdad respected each other and respected other religions, as God had intended. They shared the general belief that God sent his messages through different messengers and that people on earth created these differences, not God. God is one. Were there any extremists? Of course there were, but they were the minority. My mother seemed healthy and recovered from the surgery, so my father and I left quickly, eager for my mother to come home with our baby brother. My brothers and sisters and I cleaned and swept the house to make it just as clean as she had left it.

―――

Our world was flipped upside down with the shocking news of my mother's passing away. The suddenness of her passing ignited many rumors and assumptions that went on for many years. There was speculation about who might have been behind it, especially since she had been seemingly doing so well. My mother had several half-sisters from a different mother. All along, there was some perceived jealousy from these half-sisters because my mother was doing so well financially. For years many in my family, including myself, suspected that these half-aunts of mine had somehow been involved.

Recently, when I connected to my mother through the well-known medium and artist known as Spirit Artist—Rita Berkowitz, I learned that the doctor who operated on her had used surgical instruments that were not sterilized, which immediately caused an infection and made her lungs fill with fluid. I have been very grateful to receive many messages from my mother in recent years, and through this medium was able to get a beautiful drawing of my mother, especially welcome because it was the first picture I ever had of her.

We were a newly enlarged family with no one to care for us, especially my one-week-old brother. My father carried out the traditional burial ceremonies. My mother was buried in Najaf, Iraq, a Shi'a Muslim holy city about 160 kilometers south of Baghdad. (For Shi'a Muslims, the Imam Ali Mosque in Najaf is the third holiest shrine in the Muslim region after Mecca and Medina of Saudi Arabia.)

After my mother's burial, the family was in hardship and thrown into an ultimate dilemma. There was nothing even close to what we now know as day care. My sisters were too young to provide any type of help. In those days, 1964 or 1965, there were strong social taboos against my father even thinking of getting remarried before at least a full year had passed. The choices were very limited. My father burdened most of our relatives by asking them to care for the baby for days at a time during his working hours. I would take the baby over and bring him home in the evenings. None of our relatives ever said anything, but it was very obvious that it was all a bit much for some of them. Many of them pushed my father to find a new wife. I was old enough to realize what was going on, and I feel my father did not want to marry purely out of respect to our mother's memory. I could be wrong, but it's possible that if it had not been for the new baby, my father would not have considered getting remarried at all. But he did.

CHAPTER TWO

· · · · · · · · · · · · · · · · · · · ·

Mother's Promise and Coming of Age

The angels and the universe have reminded me to go back and mention a few more things about my dear mother. The first thing is something I had totally forgotten until those visions came. My mother used to come to wake me up for school. As we walked down the two flights from the roof, she would tell me to remember to squeeze my nose in the morning many times to make it more slim and pointy, like the noses of the rest of my brothers and sisters. Obviously, she loved me and wanted me to have what she thought was a "nice" nose. She also often told me to not to sleep on my stomach, because that would flatten my nose even more. When I think back on those comments, I realize the kind of love my mother had for me. Of course, I realize now that no matter how much I squeeze my nose, it will not change the shape at all, but when I make the squeeze motion, for whatever reasons, I do recall my mother's advice.

The other thing that I will never forget and that was truly life-altering for me is my mother's promise to send me to the United States as soon as I graduated from high school. I was maybe in third or fourth grade when she was opening my eyes and making these promises. I do not think that they meant much to me at the time. I was only worried about passing the grade I was in. I did not even have a goal about what to be when I grew up. But my mother, without even trying very hard, planted those seeds of a huge goal in my young mind for the days and years to come.

My father did find a new wife, and the entire family moved into a big story-and-a-half house in a brand-new suburb called Gamila ("pretty" in Arabic) within a year. I think he must have done it out of respect for my mother's memory. By this time, I had graduated from private elementary school. I registered to attend an intermediate school (grades seven through nine) that was about forty-five minutes each way on foot; that was the only transportation other than bicycling.

The new home and all surrounding homes gave us the feeling we had moved into a new era or generation. It had a garden full of flowers and fruit trees like orange trees. The kitchen was semi-modern, even by today's standards. We had an oven fueled by gas cylinders delivered to our house by truck. Of course, by this time, the country was ready for a regime change. In 1966, President Abdul Salam Arif was killed or, as announced, "killed in an accident." His brother, General Abdul Rahman Arif, assumed power immediately. People in general had become so used to military coups d'état that it was a non-event when it happened, and they hardly even saw it as news.

Life at home was different now. Our next-door neighbors, who lived in a very nice home, were my uncle and his family. My uncle was very rich and drove nice cars like Mercedes. My father was not rich on my uncle's level, but he was well-off regardless. As a young man, I did sense some sort of competition between my father and my uncle. One of the perks of the competition for my brothers and me was that one day my father bought us boys brand-new bicycles. You have to remember that bicycles were not priced as they are now, where a trip to Walmart can result in buying a bicycle without any major expense. It was not like that at all—it represented an investment for our father. But with our bikes, getting to school became just a little easier.

Grade seven was somewhat strange. At that time, intermediate school determined your future as a student. The higher your grade scores, the higher the next level you could apply for. For medical or engineering schools, you had to achieve high scores, especially in ninth grade. Since I had always wanted to be an engineer, I knew I had to take school very seriously, and I did. It took time to get adjusted to a new home, new location, new school, new friends, and a stepmother. My older brother never came to like my stepmother, and he led a charge against her by pushing the rest of us to not like her or even give her a chance. It all seemed a lot to absorb. The first year went by like a dream, and before you knew it, I had passed seventh grade, and it was spring of 1967.

During June, I witnessed the Arab-Israeli conflict known as the Six Days' War. This was a major event, as you probably know, and the Iraqis were involved in some way. However, as a preteen, I did not understand or even care about the conflict between the Arabs and Israel. I did care about the result of the war. Everything American was banned as soon as the war started. Things like cars, television programming, and electronics became very hard to find. The tragic thing for me was that before the war I had become completely hooked on the TV series *The Fugitive*. I anxiously awaited each new episode to see how Richard Kimble was going to escape yet another time. I was feeling for Richard Kimble and still remember how much I disliked Lt. Gerard. All regular TV programming was disrupted. Of course, the sad news was that after the TV went back to regular programming, there were no more episodes of *The Fugitive* because it was an American product. Needless to say, I never got to see the ending. Years later, I did see the movie, but not the original TV series with David Janssen.

Sometime in 1968, when I was in eighth grade, the country saw another military coup d'état against President Abdul Rahman Arif. This time, the coup seemed bolder than it needed to be and resulted in the Ba'ath party taking power. Ahmad Hassan al-Bakr became the president, and Saddam Hussein became the secretary general. Hussein was the second man in power after the president, but I got the feeling, even as a young boy, that it was just a matter of time before Saddam Hussein was the president. Even someone like me could see the body language of Hussein's desires. But the president was not smart enough to see that. Hussein was already acting as if he were the president in making many of the decisions. Something about Hussein, even in his early days, sent fear by just watching him on television.

During this time, politics became part of everyday life, regardless of who you were or whether you liked it. Saddam Hussein created party cells throughout the country. The Ba'ath party was in schools, markets, communities—everywhere. Day by day, Iraq was becoming a police state. Day after day, people had to watch what they were saying in public and soon even in their own homes. The Ba'ath party knew everything about every home and business via those party cells. They knew how big or small each family was and their political views. If anyone was reported, even by mistake, to be "pro-West," that person's life usually came to an end by means of an "accident."

Also during this school year, I developed my first attraction to a beautiful girl; her name was Sabah, meaning "morning" in Arabic. Sabah actually lived not too far from where I lived, and her school was very near mine. My school went only from grades seven through nine, but hers was intermediate through high school (seventh through twelfth grade). At that time, male-female segregated schools were the only option. Only in college or university could males and females attend together. (They would probably have been segregated there, too, if there had been enough colleges and/or universities to make that possible.)

Since Sabah's school went up to grade twelve, I had no idea how old she was or what grade she was in. Sabah used to walk the long trip home from school with a girlfriend who would catch another bus at Sabah's house to get home. The amazing coincidence is that I also had a best friend with whom I spent most of my time and walked home with, even though I had a bicycle. He even lived in the same area where Sabah's friend lived, and he also needed to catch a bus by my house to get home. Sabah, our two friends, and I were in the very same situation. On top of that, my friend developed an attraction to Sabah's girlfriend. My friend and I would pretty much time our walk to be at the same time as Sabah's walk with her girlfriend. The girls definitely recognized that we were attracted to them, but which one of us liked which one of them? That was the question on their minds.

Of course, the first thing you might say is, "What's the big deal? Just stop and talk to her." However, that was not even remotely possible. The culture was such that I could have caused Sabah a lot of trouble—and, of course, eventually trouble for myself—if one of her parents, relatives, or friends saw us talking. A woman's reputation could have easily been tarnished for the rest of her life by a small "rumor." So day after day my friend and I would walk either in front of or behind Sabah and her girlfriend. I used to turn around every now and then if we were ahead of them and give Sabah a dazzling smile. That was the most I could do. My friend and I tried to think of a way to somehow be able to confess to Sabah my feelings, but there were no answers. If only Sabah would walk alone and find a way to meet me secretly, but that day never came. I ended the school year with a strong wish that she was also in eighth grade in order to have another year together. That was my only hope.

Life went on and other things happened, such as the day the math/ geometry teacher went above and beyond to humiliate me in front of all my friends in class when I did not know the answer for a question at hand. I think that he did not like me personally and took every opportunity to humiliate me. I did not know that I was "not good" in math and geometry until that moment. I have no idea how, but that was a turnaround moment for me. In no time, I was on top of the class in math and geometry. I even started to tutor my friends in geometry. The teacher had somehow ignited the power within me without even trying.

During the months we were out of school, I did ride my bicycle a few times around Sabah's house, but I never, ever saw her. Every house had a fence, and people would hardly ever be seen socializing outside, especially women. My brother was also falling in love with a girl who lived across the street from our house. Our house had two rooftops because it was a story and a half. Most of us slept on the lower rooftop. My brother used to wait until everyone was ready to go to sleep, including all neighbors, and then played romantic songs very loudly to make sure his girl could hear them. What he did not realize or care about was that the entire neighborhood could also hear his songs.

I used to raise homing pigeons on the upper rooftop, as many people did at that time. I had always loved birds, and flying the pigeons was something I enjoyed. My brother told me many times that he did not like me doing that. It must have had something to do with the impression it made on the girl he liked across the street. One day as

I went to feed and fly my pigeons, I found the door to the top rooftop was locked. This door had never been locked before. I asked everyone about it, including my brother. No one had any idea why it was locked or where the key was. Of course, no one admitted to locking the door either. The weather was very hot, and I needed to feed my pigeons and, most importantly, give them water. They were trained not to go anywhere, and they were my responsibility. I was running out of options.

The distance from the lower rooftop to the top of the upper roof was more than fifteen feet. I found a ladder, but it was only about ten feet long. I kept thinking of ways to make up the difference to reach the top of the roof. I finally found a three-foot-high table and put the ladder on top of it. I believed that when I reached the last step, I could somehow climb to the top of the roof. I did not consider or care about any danger—I just wanted to care for the helpless pigeons. The ladder was becoming more unstable with every step as I went higher. As I made the leap from the top step, the table under the ladder collapsed, and the ladder went down violently. If the ladder had gone a little more to the left, I would have smashed down all the way to the cement driveway. But it came down straight. I hit the top of the lower roof very hard and was quite shaken, but not hurt. That was the second "close brush with death" or "escape from death" encounter of my very young life, and I often remember it. Later that evening my father was able to take the locking mechanism off, allowing me to care for my pigeons. The amazing thing is that a year or so later, when we moved from that house and my older brother asked me to help him move his furniture, I found the key hidden in his dresser. I have never confronted him about it.

September 1968 finally arrived, and it was time to start the ninth grade—my last year in that school. I started the year full of promises to myself to make more attempts to talk to Sabah. How? I really had no idea, but thought I must try anyway. Much to my surprise and shock, I did not see her anymore. I waited and waited day after day for several weeks—no Sabah. There were two possibilities: either she had gotten married and decided to take a break from school, or she had graduated from grade twelve and was now in college. I was at a loss and angry at myself for never having made any moves. I started riding my bicycle again every day, but I was now going by Sabah's house every morning instead of going straight to school. It was not really too far out of my way, but it was out of my way nonetheless. One morning I saw Sabah leaving her house, and I guessed that she was going to school or college. I slowed down and kept my eye on her to see where she was heading. I was surprised to see her go to wait at the nearby bus stop. I went on to my school, happy. The same thing happened several more times. I told myself that the time had come to plan something.

One day I decided to skip school to try to find out what school Sabah was going to. I went to the bus stop very early and let several buses go by without boarding them until I saw Sabah coming. I was so nervous to be standing in the same bus stop with Sabah. I do not think I dared to look at her directly. Soon the bus came, and we both got on. The buses were the same kind of two-story buses that you see in England. I seated myself in such a way to make sure that I would be able to see when she got off. I did not get off with her, as I did not want to look like I was watching her; instead, I memorized her stop.

Several days later I repeated the same thing, but this time I decided to get off the bus at her stop and act as if I had also reached my destination. I followed her to the El Mostenseria University. Of course, now I was developing some huge self-doubt. If she really was at the university, she would have no time for a high school boy. But I was not going to give up that easily, even though it seemed an impossible task. One idea I had was to write her a letter and somehow give it to her. I wrote and rewrote the letter until I was finally happy with it. I carried it to the bus stop, but I could never find the right way, or the courage, to pass the letter without anyone noticing.

The year was 1969, and the country was becoming more and more like a military state. The Ba'ath party developed more cells everywhere, and it was becoming more difficult to speak one's mind. The cells were becoming very noticeable, even in schools. In reality, most people and students joined the party, not because they liked it, but because they were seeking recognition and avoiding any trouble.

The final test of the essential grade nine was a national test called the Bakaloria. The results of this test determined eligibility for high school fields of study. The students who were interested in becoming doctors or engineers had to score high to be allowed to attend science high school. Lower scorers had to attend economic high school, where math and physics were not heavily demanded. Since I was aiming for electrical engineering, I needed to score high, and I had no doubt that I was going to do so.

As the school year was winding down, I wrote another desperate letter to Sabah, and one day I came up with a different plan. I decided to follow her from the university as she was heading home. I didn't accomplish anything on the bus but jumped off quickly and ran to her home so that I could turn around and casually come face to face with her as she approached and somehow hand her the letter. Well, everything worked out except handing over the letter. I was so nervous passing her on the sidewalk that I was just happy I did not stumble to the ground.

I went home with very mixed emotions. One was fear—what if one of her parents had seen me that close to Sabah? There were too many what-ifs. The other emotion was self-blame for being a coward and failing to accomplish what I had planned. Torn between these two emotions, I went to my room and turned on love music. I listened mostly to Abdel Halim Hafez of Egypt in those days. Several weeks later, I wrote another letter to Sabah and followed the same plan as before. Unfortunately, the results were the same.

The last few months of the school year were gearing up to the Bakaloria. There was no time to waste or to try anything else to make contact with Sabah. I really had no idea where she would end up in school and how it was even possible to find out. I had no control over any of these issues, so I spent my time worrying about the things at hand. I locked myself in my room many days and nights to study. It was a marathon. I knew how much my future depended on this exam. Finally it began, and of course, it did run many days. Each subject was on a different day. Then it was finally over, and the waiting game for the scores began. I passed with grades good enough to go to the high school of my desire. I immediately applied to a very well-known academic high school called El Nidhal, or "struggle" in Arabic. (It was usual then to have names of streets, bridges, and schools reflecting the era of military and forcible regime change.)

One night in the summer of 1969, just before freshman year, I heard megaphone speaker music coming from the direction of Sabah's house. I rode my bicycle to investigate, and sure enough, it was her house. People were coming and going, and there were many light strings all over the yard similar to what many do at Christmas. It appeared to be a wedding. I went closer and asked a man who was getting married. "Sabah," he said. I know I could have easily gone inside, as parties like this were usually like an open door for everyone, but I did not. I went home, lay down on my bed, and was very sad. I put on an appropriate album to play over and over—one by an Egyptian singer, Nagat. I loved Nagat as much as I loved Abdul Halim Hafez. She sang "Sakeen Ousaddy We Bahabou," meaning "living next door to me, and I love him." It was about Nagat being in love with a boy and finding out one day that he was getting married. Her emotions were the same as mine. That was my first love, which started from nowhere, lived only in my heart, and ended before it even started.

Our two-story home in Baghdad taken during my high school years

Just a few weeks later, almost as if he sensed my hurt, my father surprised us by purchasing two (not just one) adjacent lots in a newly developed area closer to Baghdad. By this time, our family was even larger, with two half-brothers. My father designed and built our new two-story home. It was beautiful, even by today's standards. Now my father was an owner, no longer a renter. I was sad to leave Al Jamila, because I knew that I might never see Sabah again, even accidentally. I did not know anything about her or where to even attempt to see her.

Soon we moved into our new home, and I was getting ready to start my first year at Al Nidhal high school in the heart of Baghdad. My room was on the second level. The lot next to our home was undeveloped, so that gave me more freedom to play my favorite music, Abdel Halim Hafez and others, as loudly as I liked. My older brother was even unhappier than I, because, for some reason, he'd had to repeat the ninth grade three times in three years, so all of sudden we were in the same grade, though in different schools. My brother's grades were not high enough to follow the science route in high school, so he was limited to economics. He was very jealous of me, because he had always wanted to be a doctor. My goal had always been electrical engineering. He commandeered half of the entire second level for himself in a manner that was very disrespectful to my peace-loving father, who never wanted to escalate anything. My brother was a real bully who created problems for all of us, even my step-mother. I did not understand why he needed all that space. My regular-sized room with its bed, two tables, and cabinet to hold all my cassettes and LPs was plenty for me. Later, I found out that my brother had been dreaming of getting married someday and not moving anywhere. So he was just ahead of himself, I guess. Getting married and still living with your parents was not uncommon at all.

CHAPTER THREE
. . . .

Storm Clouds Gather

By January 1969, the country had become truly militarized, and everything was under the watch of Saddam Hussein and the Ba'ath party. Our prosperous country was no more. Given the history of our frequent military coups d'état, it seemed as though Hussein and the Ba'ath party had decided to keep people's minds off politics with various distractions.

One day our entire school was forcibly gathered to join a mass rally in support of the Ba'ath party, whether we liked it or not. We all realized that if we refused to go and somehow the party found out, it could have meant the end. The news media outside Iraq was either not aware of the fact that people had been forced to go or just simply ignored it in their reports. We were led shouting to Sahet El Tahreer (Freedom Square in Arabic) in the center of Baghdad. Thousands of people had already arrived, and the distance this created for our group from the center of activity turned out to be a blessing. I could from a far distance just make out a display of wooden blocks, and from the center of each block hung a dead person with a rope around his neck. I was shocked, and if the intent had been to spread fear, it certainly worked for me. That image was burned into my brain.

Another way to control the country was by harshly restricting all simple consumables. Before we knew it, we had to stand in long lines for a dozen eggs, soap, bread, everything—and only on certain days. This, too, was copied from the Communist tactic of keeping the masses so busy with details of daily life that they are not able to get involved in politics. My father's business, along with everyone else's, was getting worse and worse, and it was very difficult for him to make his accustomed living. Slowly, the entire country became monitored by local agents of the Ba'ath party. It is not an exaggeration to say that the party knew something about each home—how many children lived there, or how the people thought, or whether they were pro-West or pro-East. People did not trust their friends, their next-door neighbors, even their own children. No one knew who was reporting what to whom.

I was able to stay clear of any politics and concentrated on my own schooling. The first year in any school is usually tougher, it seems, because of the time it takes to make new friends, get to know new teachers, and get used to a new system. By the time I was feeling comfortable, the school year was almost half over. At that point, I noticed that I was ahead of most students in certain subjects, such as geometry, physics, and math in general, though not so much in chemistry, history, or geography. I took this as a clear indication that I was correct in my original goal of being an electrical engineer. I wanted to graduate as quickly as possible, as I wanted to fulfill my mother's desire to send me to the United States of America.

Sahet El Tahreer where I saw the hanging bodies

I received a big surprise one day in early spring 1970 when my sister Layla brought me a letter from one of her friends in school. Layla told me the girl's name was Nadia and that she lived just behind us—so close that the corners of our houses touched. I ran upstairs to my room and quickly opened it. It was a love letter. Nadia told me that she had been listening to my Abdel Halim Hafez songs and that she had been trying to get my attention, unsuccessfully thus far, and so had resorted to writing a letter. I wrote back to Nadia welcoming this friendship and saying I hoped to see her someday. Layla delivered my reply. Much to my pleasant surprise, I could see

My dear sister Layla

Nadia's room from my second-story window, and I could even see her if she elected to open the curtains and look in my direction. This turned out to be the major means of communication between us for some time.

For weeks and months, Nadia and I waited for the evenings where she was in her room and I was in mine. I closed the curtains in such a way that no one could see me except Nadia. The distance was too far for us to communicate by voice, and we couldn't meet because of the fear of any rumors that might be created, so we quickly developed our own sign language. The summer before eleventh grade passed quickly in this way, and I was excited when school started again. Now my sister, Layla, could be my messenger to Nadia, as they attended the same school. My sisters all knew about our messages, and they were fine with it.

⁓

The country was growing even more militarized, and secrets were everywhere. It was becoming clear that no one could trust anyone. There was news that some parents were killed because their children had told someone at school that their parents did not like what was going on with the country. A simple statement like that, without investigation or verification, was enough to get someone killed. When news of the killings spread, it created enormous fear, and no one was the same as before. We all had to act as if we liked the Ba'ath party and make that liking visible in case someone was checking on us. So it appeared that everyone loved or belonged to the Ba'ath party, even though many actually hated it.

My only true interests were my school and my love, except maybe the passing of Jamal Abdel Nasser, the president of Egypt. The songs of my beloved Egyptian Abdel Halim Hafez had taught me to love Nasser, and I listened to his speeches whenever I had a chance. This was my first political emotion, and I cried as I walked around in front of the

Egyptian Embassy. I even wished I could fly to Egypt and take part in the ceremonies. It seems as if I felt a far greater connection to Egypt than my connection to Iraq.

Soon I suggested to Nadia the idea of coming to visit our house. I told her I believed that no one would ever think anything of it because she was my sister's schoolmate. Layla and my stepmother and I soon had a plan for Nadia's first visit. My stepmother initially did not know that the plan was for me to meet Nadia—she thought it was a friend coming to visit my sister. It took several weeks before my stepmother realized that I was in love with Nadia. We agreed that when Nadia came to visit, they would leave the two of us alone in the living room. I was so nervous when I saw Nadia for the first time! Of course, it was clear that Nadia was nervous, too. We greeted each other, and soon the others left us sitting on the couch.

We spent more than two hours on very general talk, just like any host and guest. Neither of us was courageous enough to talk about love, relationships, or anything other than school, family, and other ordinary subjects. But I know the love was implied. (I found out in this meeting that Nadia was from a mixed family. Nadia's father was a Kurd, and her mother was an Arab. Why is this worth mentioning? Because it illustrates how people were living before the politics changed everything. Arabs, Kurds, and others were living side by side in peace. Muslims, Christians, and Jews were respecting each other's faiths. The altercations and problems began only after politicians ruined the country and used people against people solely for their own advantage.)

Soon it was time for Nadia to leave. Traditionally, you would walk your guest to the outside door. I could not do that, because I did not want to give anyone a chance to see us together outside the house, which they could have easily done over the low fence around our garden. Instead, I let my sister walk her out. How could I ever forget this day? I stayed home for a while, happier than happy, and eventually left the house to go about my business. But the whole time, my mind was on getting back to my window to see Nadia. She was just as anxious to get back to our signing conversations as I was. I like to say that this was the beginning of a great love that I want to call "forever"—a pure love relationship without any ulterior motives.

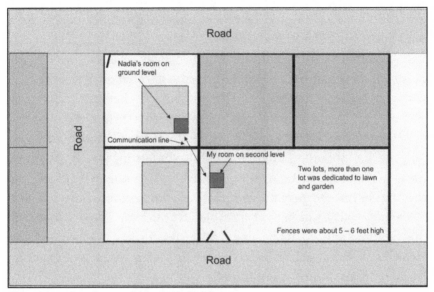

Illustration of our home relative to Nadia's home

Just one year away from graduation, I still had no idea of how to go about fulfilling my mother's dream of sending me to the United States. I figured it must be easy, like riding the bus, so why worry about it? I began to utilize my time very wisely, as I needed to keep up with my studies and also make time to stand by the window to see Nadia for hours every day, up until spring of 1971. Nadia came to visit us several times. Each time was a duplicate of the first visit. I borrowed a camera and took many pictures of Nadia in our garden. The amazing thing is that we had yet to even hold hands or kiss or even talk love talk. Nadia and I kept our relationship at the purest form. I pictured Nadia as my soul mate and future partner, and we both respected the traditions and customs, even when we were together alone.

As time went by, Nadia's mother became aware of our relationship, and I know she approved, though she never said a word. One day my sister, Layla, told me that Nadia's mother would visit me at home at a certain time. I did not know what to make of that and had no choice other than saying I would be home. I had not met her before then, but I knew what she looked like. When the doorbell rang, I let her in. She immediately turned around and ran away, as a child would. We never even exchanged a word. I wondered about it until the next day when Layla said that Nadia told her that as soon her mother saw me, she liked my eyes, did not know how to handle her emotions, and had to run away. I took that as a compliment, but more importantly, I felt relieved, as I thought I might have done something wrong. That was the only connection I ever had with Nadia's mother. Of course, the real thanks have to go to my own mother, who gave me those eyes and eyelashes. Nadia's father was completely different. I have always felt that he somehow did not like me at all. I think he had the intuition that I was seeing his daughter, even though he had never seen us together. He never gave me any friendly looks.

Only once did Nadia and I try to meet outside the house in an area far away from our houses to prevent anyone that we might know from seeing us. We agreed to meet in the heart of Baghdad, where most movie theaters were, at a particular bus stop. I was very excited and left early to make sure I would not be late. When I arrived, Nadia was with an older woman. I was very surprised, and I made eye contact, wondering what might be the story. Because of our window sign language, we were able to communicate without talking. I quickly understood that she could not be free from the woman she was with, so I moved on, very disappointed. You could also say that I was a bit angry. This was the first letdown involving Nadia, so I did not know how to react. I must admit that even though I watched from my window as usual that evening, I did not turn the lights on in my room. I saw Nadia several times, and I know she was wondering where I might have been. That was my way of showing Nadia that I was angry. It seems very silly now, but it is true and that is what I did.

Nadia later explained in a letter through Layla that when her father found out she was going to downtown Baghdad, he must have suspected that she might be meeting me, so he made one of his relatives accompany her. That was the only time we ever tried to meet like lovers do.

I was moving with ease through eleventh grade, happily anticipating my final year. By this time, it seemed as if the entire neighborhood was aware of my love for Nadia. It was not in a bad way at all. I believe they all respected my wishes and knew I had the highest intentions.

That summer, things became more serious. Keep in mind that to that point, Nadia and I had never kissed, touched, or even held hands. Our feelings were solely from the heart, and none of those things mattered. The normal custom when it came to getting engaged or married was for the male's family (father and close male relatives on the first visit) to visit the female's family to ask for her hand. For me, this never crossed my mind, not because I did not love Nadia, but because I knew that I would be heading to the United States the following year. There were no doubts about fulfilling my mother's wishes. I really had not, to that point, shared with Nadia the thought of my leaving Iraq. I figured I had plenty of time and that I might be able to convince her to go with me. During a visit to our house, Nadia asked me to at least go to visit her family. She said that people were talking, and it might be best if we were engaged. It was something I had not even thought of, and it did surprise me. I am not sure exactly how I responded, but I know I did break the news about my intentions of going to the United States. I don't think she took it very well. I guess I was not happy with my response either. The rest of the visit became very awkward, and neither one of us knew how to react. After she left, I wondered if I would ever see her again. That was a sad day. All the next day I wondered anxiously if Nadia would be by her window. She was there, but I could feel the disappointment. Maybe Nadia doubted my love for her, or maybe she was afraid of the rumors that could easily ruin her life and reputation.

In the fall of 1971, I was very excited about entering my senior year. Of course, I knew that I would be facing another Bakaloria exam at the end of the term. It made me very nervous, but I was not entirely aware of the horrors building at that time that would make the Bakaloria look like a picnic. I did know that the country was getting worse and worse, which gave me further motivation to finish so I could get to the United States. Of course, I never really dared to tell anyone about my intentions, because the United States was on the blacklist, and knowledge of my pro-West leanings could have easily ended my life at the hands of Saddam Hussein and the Ba'ath party.

I did not know the logistics of how I was going to get to the United States or what I would need; I assumed that there was plenty of time, and I did not need to worry about anything other than graduating. I did realize that I would have to spend some time trying to learn the American English accent. We were taught that only the British accent was "correct." One way of getting my ears used to the American accent was to block the Arabic transliteration at the bottom of the screen when watching old American movies or cartoons. I must say that it did help me a great deal.

I also tuned in to a shortwave channel called Voice of America that broadcast from somewhere near Lebanon. It carried news and regional current affairs and worked clearly only at night. I listened carefully to a short program that taught the listener to speak English, and I even recorded it. These activities were very risky—I could have been labeled pro-West and lost my life. To do it, I practically hid in my own room in our big house with the volume turned low. I especially enjoyed following the actual English conversations. It is amazing what I did in secret just to learn a language. I wonder what one person could accomplish today with that kind of desire and the facilities available now!

Between school, Nadia, and my passion to learn the American English accent, I rarely had any time to spare. During family conversations, I learned that many Kurdish families were being deported without any notice or reasons by Hussein and the Ba'ath party. Some of these families were my relatives. They were loaded into trucks like animals, without any of their possessions, and driven to the Iranian borders. Their houses were then used as offices for the Ba'ath party. Mystified, I was told that the only reason was that they were Kurds. I hadn't realized until that moment that there were any differences between Kurds and Arabs. Apparently, the Ba'ath party considered the Kurds non-Iraqi, and they were not liked at all. The war against the Kurds in northern Iraq had been going on for years, as the Kurds sought their independence from Iraq. Apparently, until that point, my devotion to my schooling had made me oblivious to all that.

This deportation of innocent people had a major impact on me. I had many questions on my mind but no answers. Who am I? Do I even belong? The "regular" fear of being killed for being thought pro-West had just become bigger, and now I was afraid we might have to join the deportees. The bigger my fear became, the more I got into my books so I could graduate and leave for the "land of the free."

⁓

Nadia and I kept to our usual routine: talk or sign-talk at night and get a visit for an hour or so every several weeks. I took as many pictures as I could when Nadia came to visit. I didn't have a camera of my own; instead, I borrowed one from my friend Aala ("height" in Arabic). Aala was a common Arabic name. He lived nearby, and we went to school together. He was one of a small number of friends with whom I went out for a beer or a movie every now and then. Although

Aala was a friend, I kept many private things from him, just in case. I always thought of him as being part of the Ba'ath party, like many. I never tried to find out if he believed in the party or was just riding the waves to avoid trouble. His goal was to enter the very prestigious Iraqi Air Force. Uniformed Air Force pilots were treated like kings when they walked in the market, even as students. Aala wanted me to join up too, but I just ignored his request without telling him about my goal of going to the United States. The reality was that as a Kurd, I knew I would have no chance to enter the Air Force, even if I truly wanted to. I am not even sure if Aala knew that I was a Kurd.

CHAPTER FOUR
·····················

Lost Innocence

One seemingly normal day in early 1972, during my last term in high school, I came home thinking only about what song I should play. My sisters were all crying and seemed to have no idea of what to do. After I had calmed my sisters down a bit, they told me that a group of Ba'ath party members, headed by the Moukhtar ("chosen" in Arabic), had been at the house. Each area had its own Moukhtar, who was responsible for signing all needed legal documents for that particular community. Think of the Moukhtar as the leader of the entire township for each community. In many ways, this person's role was to keep an eye on the whole area and mark people for reporting to the Ba'ath party. His group was going around asking whomever they wanted about their "Shahadet El Genssea," which means "witness or proof of birth certificate." This was not just a birth certificate, but something that proved your citizenship. Not many had this certificate, especially the Kurds. The Iraqi government had made it very difficult for the Kurds to get one, thus making them subject to these types of attacks. The group had taken my younger brother, Jamel, with them. I only knew that I must go to help him. I knew the danger, but at that moment, I truly did not care.

Filled with anger, I headed to El Moukhtar's house. It took some time, but eventually I caught up to the group and their truck. I confronted them and asked what was going on. The response was very swift—two men grabbed me and asked me to board the truck. No questions were asked. I did not resist. Jamel was in the truck, along with a few other young men. I was very embarrassed and tried to comfort him. The weather was cool, and we were driving in the dark for a very long time. I was shaking uncontrollably. I never did figure out what roads we were taking. Finally, we were told to get out and were led into what looked like a military compound. We went through some simple processing and were finally led into a very large, jail-like, windowless room filled with people packed in like sardines. We had room only to sit on the floor, shoulder to shoulder. At night, we had barely two feet of sleeping space. I was happy to be with my brother and wondered what he would have done all by himself. The food was awful, and the restrooms were worse. I finally realized that we were actually in jail.

It was impossible to think clearly enough to figure out what was really going on. Though I was packed in with many people, I could not really relate to them. Would I ever be able to graduate? Would I ever get back home to my family? What was happening with Nadia? Most importantly, would I be able to fulfill my mother's dream and promise? I had many questions, but no answers.

I was very depressed. We had not even been questioned—just rounded up and thrown in jail. Day after day we sat there with no room to move freely or even look outside to know if it was raining or clear. Everyone thought we might be killed, and we wondered if we would ever see our families again. After about ten days, my father and some of my brothers and sisters came to visit us, though they had been trying to get to the prison since day one. I was not happy to see them, as I was very fearful for their safety. At that point I had already given up on Jamel and myself. I asked my father where we were being held, as no one knew the exact location. He replied, "Abu Ghraib." Yes, the very same prison where the U.S. soldiers would abuse the Iraqi detainees in 2004.

I had no idea where Abu Ghraib was and how far it was from home. I knew only that it was a very unpleasant experience. My father was trying hard to get us some help, but it was very difficult. We had not committed any crimes to be defended, and it almost seemed like we were being played with like toys by the authorities. I trusted my father, but I pleaded with him to not subject himself and our family to any unnecessary danger. My father was a very loving man, and he did not want any part of my plea. He was going to do what he needed to do. I desperately wanted to get back to school. I had never missed that many days, and this was not just any year—it was the year of the Bakaloria. I wanted to graduate with a high score, but so much time had gone by that I was losing confidence that I would even pass—if I ever got free.

What my father did and how he did it, I have no idea exactly, but after about three weeks, the special day finally came, and my brother and I were free. My father came to take us home. Two young boys had been taken away in broad daylight from their family, driven around while more innocent people were collected, dumped in prison for weeks, and finally freed without any criminal accusations ever having been presented or even a single question. I had learned a lesson that was very hard to swallow: No matter what, someone could come and crash everything right in front of your eyes and even kill you if they wanted, and you had no right to even ask, "Why?"

Riding home in my father's beautiful, one-of-a-kind 1966 Opel station wagon, all I could think about was school and what my classmates might say. *What am I supposed to tell everyone? Do I need to let the year go and try again next year just to avoid all these questions? What is Nadia thinking? Does she know where I was? Has she given up on me?* Too many questions! The first thing my brother and I did was run inside and each take a hot bath. I turned on the lights in my room and then decided to turn them off and look in the dark to see if Nadia was there. Sure enough, she was, and she had noticed the lights. I wanted to answer her questions but put that off for later in order to spend the evening with my family, especially my sister, Layla.

Though younger, Layla acted as a mother to me. She was always there for me and willing to do anything to comfort me. We had a great evening, but it was the first time I truly understood that we—like many Kurdish families—did not have that citizenship certificate so important to El Moukhtar and his men. Only then did it fully hit me: I was not going to be able to attend any university, I was not going to be able to get a passport to go anywhere—I couldn't, I couldn't, and I couldn't. I was *not* free. I was in a big prison called Iraq, with no future. How would I fulfill my mother's dream and go to the United States? Lying in bed that night was one of the toughest nights ever, even tougher than when I was in prison. I realized that everything I was dreaming of was just that—a dream. I was not even a citizen. Why? How? No one could answer my questions.

In the morning, I was overwhelmed with the thought of how behind I was in my schoolwork. Could I really complete the year? There was only one way to find out—go to school and face the music. I also had a great sense of shame, and I am not even sure why. Maybe the knowledge that I was not considered a citizen was very hard on my ego. I quickly conferred with all my teachers and explained that I was not a quitter and needed to know what I must do to catch up. I was very determined to put those dark days behind me. Not being a citizen and not being able to get a passport or travel did not hinder me. I have always trusted that for every problem there is a solution somewhere. I was not going to worry about the how.

I am not sure if I even tried to explain my absence to Nadia, maybe because I thought that what had happened was probably common knowledge given the state of the country. We just kept doing what we were doing, as if nothing had happened. My main worry and priority was graduating, but I had also begun to think about my options if I could not leave Iraq and go to the United States.

Soon it was time for the Bakaloria. I spent countless hours studying and memorizing to make up for the crucial missed weeks, but I had great difficulty focusing. Was all of this for nothing? I was not the same person anymore, but I still did my best and was more than willing to go through with the exam. It took a week, and each day covered a different subject. I passed. My scores were not what I was hoping for, but considering that I had been in prison for over three weeks, I was very grateful. Nadia was very happy for me also. I was not sure what to think and was asking myself, *Now what?*

Practical reality really hit after graduation. I could not even apply for or obtain a passport because I did not have the proof of my citizenship. I asked my father, somewhat angrily, why we did not have this proof. He explained to me that he had spent many hours, days, months, years trying, but when he would complete one requirement, the authorities would just want more and more. Instead of just denying his request, they sent him to chase a very moving target simply because he was a Kurd and not an Arab. I was shocked after all those years of thinking that there were no differences. It was the Ba'ath party's mission to divide the Iraqis, and this one was an easy step for them. My father also told me that if we had been born in Tikrit, we wouldn't have had any problems and would not have been required to present any documents. Tikrit was Saddam Hussein's birthplace, and he was often called Saddam El Tikriti.

These tragic facts only further ignited my desire to fulfill my mother's dream. How? I had no idea, but I was determined. I would pursue my proof of citizenship. My father agreed, though reluctantly, to give his approval. Young though I was, I made a list of important things to do.

Number one. Find out where the American Embassy was in Baghdad. I quickly found out that there was none. It had been closed after the 1967 war between the Arabs and Israel. There was only a small office in the Belgium embassy in Baghdad to take care of American-related issues. I went there and obtained many addresses of American universities.

Number two Find out what one must do to get the proof of citizenship. My friend, Aala, was ready to apply for the Air Force, and he had been putting a lot of pressure on me to join him. I never mentioned that I thought I wouldn't get in even if I were to pass the exams, but I decided to go with him anyway. He explained that the first thing was to go through many challenging physical exams, which would take weeks to complete. I figured that if I just went along, I would for sure fail the physical and medical exams and would not need to give him any more excuses.

I had another unpleasant realization at this time. If I did not enroll in a university soon, I would be drafted into the Army whether I liked it or not, and that would almost be a death sentence. For one thing, there were no rules or laws to limit your service—no maximum number of years. The other thing was that the war with the Kurds in northern Iraq was producing many casualties. And even if I survived, losing four or five years to military service would be a dream killer to me. My burning desire to find a way to leave the country intensified. Nadia was wondering why I had not entered any universities in Baghdad. I kept telling her that I was trying to go to the United States, when in fact I could not attend any universities in Iraq without the proof of citizenship. I had already tried that in my attempts to avoid the draft and failed. I did tell her that I was thinking of trying for the Air Force. She was excited about that. Maybe for her it was about the prestige rather than the profession.

When Aala and I went to the Air Force Academy, we first had to fill out many forms and stand in very long lines. Next were some very strict medical evaluations that would take several days. If an applicant passed those, he would then be subjected to simulated atmospheric pressure and flying conditions. We were told that there was less than a one percent chance of passing through it all. That percentage was not very comforting, but I felt little concern because I knew that it would soon be over, and even if I passed, I could not join.

After the first long day of standing in many lines (one for each medical exam), I was done with only three. Aala's ambitions ended right there. He had failed some of the early, basic exams. I was very sad for him, as I knew how much he had wanted this. I also thought of ending my own effort, because now I did not have my friend forcing me. But Nadia was excited. So, for that very reason, I decided to go back and see what the next days might bring.

My older brother, Jassim, was still working on his Bakaloria while I was going through the Air Force application. He had failed in several subjects and would have to repeat the exam. At that time, I was also applying to American universities and working on my proof of citizenship—so many things for a young man to worry about in a land where there was no respect for human lives in general. Each day at the Academy I completed more medical exams and was passing without any questions. The lines became shorter and shorter as other applicants were eliminated. Nadia was getting even more excited.

Iraqi movies about the Air Force were being aired on television quite frequently. I loved these movies and wished for the certificate of citizenship even harder. I was becoming convinced that it would be great to be in the Air Force uniform. After watching one of the movies, I ran upstairs to my room only to find Nadia waiting for me. Apparently she had seen it too and was excited for us. My confidence was getting stronger after I completed the medical exams with no issues. I started to wonder if I would be part of that elite one percent.

Then it was time for the many difficult physical exams and simulations. Young men were failing one after another before my eyes. Several exams truly impressed themselves upon my memory. The first one took place in a controlled chamber with only a few applicants at a time. They closed up the chamber very tightly, and there were many eyes outside of it looking at the applicants through windows. It was pressurized to simulate a high altitude, and the applicants were given instructions on what to do, such as pretending to swallow when they felt the pressure in their ears. Many fell down or got a bloody nose, but I passed without any trouble.

The other exam that impressed itself on me was horrible. I had a chance to view other applicants undergoing it in advance, and it scared me so much that I had to take off a day or two, wondering the entire time what exactly I needed to do to pass this one. The exam looked innocent at first. You simply sat in an ordinary chair with your hands clamped down on the chair handles. Then a rod ending with a V shape was fastened to the chair and in front of you. You would place your forehead in the V shape, which forced you to look down and you were unable to see anything around you. Then the chair would suddenly spin at a very high speed. After a few minutes, the tester slammed on the brakes to suddenly stop the chair. Applicants immediately lost their balance and were all over the floor like chickens without their heads. When I finally developed the courage, I went to this exam with an empty stomach to avoid any accidents. It was hard when the tester slammed on the brakes. I was disoriented, but I do remember someone examining my eyes immediately while I was on the ground. Once I regained my balance, I realized that I had just passed another exam. Was it still all for nothing? I was thinking that since only a few get to this point, maybe they would bend the citizenship rules. I had developed a love of flying and had not lost hope for that elite Air Force status and being a fighter jet pilot.

I soon learned that I had passed everything. I just needed to do some "minor" paperwork. Minor for a citizen, but it turned out to be much harder than climbing Mount Everest for me. I tried and tried to see if I could get some help or recommendations, but no one was listening. Rules were rules.

I quickly put this sad experience behind me. I did hang on to a card that was issued to me before starting the exams that was useful going from one exam into the next. At the time, I kept the card only for my memories, but it became useful later.

During my application process, I had visited the office of citizenship almost every day. I started to get to know some of the officers. It was always crowded. Sometimes I would wait all day in the summer heat and never get to see anyone. It was very demoralizing, especially if I had to stand in the hot sun. My father had been telling me the truth. There was a big folder for our family that my father had started many years ago. Apparently, it contained documentation of things that were impossible to overcome. Our folder was kept in the secure area, and it needed a special procedure for any officer to obtain it when they had to talk to me. I never knew the exact contents of this folder other than that it was treated differently. For weeks and days, I was given the same runaround as they gave my father years ago—before he gave up. But I had no choice but to continue if I was ever going to leave the country.

Time went very fast, and my brother passed the Bakaloria but was facing the same future as I. The only difference was that I was now trying every day to pursue the citizenship for our family, while my brother was just warming up the chair behind the desk in my father's business. My father was very proud of me for trying so hard. Because neither of us had enrolled in college or university by the fall of 1972, my brother and I were both up for the draft. I had a very difficult time with that fact. I had just passed an elite exam to join the Air Force but was not accepted because I was not a citizen. How is it that I must be drafted to defend the same country that was denying me citizenship? Both my brother and I refused to join and were thus breaking the law. If anyone reported us to the authorities, we would have faced a penalty. We were no longer free to move around, as there were many random checkpoints for people like us. I still saw Nadia once every few months or so, but there was some added pressure, as she did not understand why I was not in college or university or doing anything with my career. She knew I was going somewhere every day, but she had no idea that it was to pursue my citizenship. I did not tell her that I was basically running away from the government and the draft. It was hard to communicate anything subtle with our sign language. Even when we saw each other face-to-face, because it was such a rare hour or two, we did not really get into any heavy conversation at all.

CHAPTER FIVE

·················

The Whirlwind Descends

One day Nadia and I got into a loving disagreement about something very small during one of her visits. I left the living room and went next door into the formal living room to sit on the couch and pretend to pout. Nadia came up behind me and put her comforting hands on my shoulders. That was the first time we had come that close to each other. I can still feel her hands shaking on my shoulders. Without thinking, I pulled her down next to me and gave her one small kiss on the right cheek. I was very embarrassed, and Nadia was just as surprised, but in a loving way. After Nadia left, I left the house and boarded a bus to go to my father's business in kind of a daze. I felt like I was walking on the clouds. I had never ever looked at Nadia in a sexual way. My love was pure, old-fashioned romantic love. The innocent, loving kiss was natural and unplanned—and my very first. I have bottled that moment from 1973 in my memory bank forever.

I spent the rest of that year and most of the next pursuing our proof of citizenship, haunting the halls of the government agency for as many days and hours as anyone could ever handle. There was no other way. I was stopped several times at various checkpoints as a suspected draft dodger, but each time I presented the little Air Force exam card to the MPs and was let go. Those few moments always sent fear through my spine. The soldiers were mostly uneducated tough guys who did not know how to reason with anyone. To get away from them was a miracle. The only thing my older brother managed to do during that time was wait around for me to give him any potential good news regarding the citizenship. Once when I was passing through the market, a hand from nowhere grabbed my right wrist and held on tightly. It turned out to be an MP from one of the checkpoints who must have read the fear in my face. I was able to set myself free after presenting the Air Force card. Even today, I can still feel that hand clutching my young wrist.

As days went by and Nadia neared graduation from high school, I started to sense that she might be giving up on me. I knew she was impatient to be engaged and married, even though we had never even talked about that. Most of our neighbors knew that we were in love with each other.

During high school years, in my room

My brother and I were getting many applications from universities in the United States, which we filled out as if it were possible for us to just pick up and leave. Some days my brother would come to our father's shop just to wait for the mailman and collect the mail from America. He would then head home, as if that were the only mission he had every day. It seems almost like a meaningless hobby, but in reality, it did keep the hope alive for both of us and help us remember what we needed to do.

My brother and I also considered finding a way to escape to an "open" country such as Lebanon. Before the war, Lebanon was considered to be almost like heaven. The word was that in Lebanon we could easily reach out to the U.S. Embassy there and find a way to make it to the United States. The price for such an adventure was very heavy if we were caught. We could be killed without any questions if the Ba'ath party found out. We explored all ideas, but the main topic was our safety and chances of success. We knew people who went to Kuwait and Lebanon illegally to bring products to sell—for profit, of course. These people did not have as big a stake in safety considerations as my brother and I. Money or bribery could do almost anything in that part of the world. You just had to know whom to approach.

In the formal living room where I kissed Nadia

My father was feeling somewhat guilty about the situation the family was in. He would do anything for us and our education. He was definitely a very smart man, and even with his limited education, he had made a very successful businessman of himself. It was very difficult for him to see us struggling week after week. He did his part by talking to his friend about finding a way for us to somehow leave the country. He knew that if we did, we could not come back, because we would have left illegally. But our future meant even more to him than possibly not seeing us again. What a dilemma that must have been for him.

Many Iraqi soldiers were being killed in the line of duty fighting the Kurdish fighters in northern Iraq. The news was rapidly spreading that the Kurds were gaining the upper hand. The army seemed to have only one door, and that was going in. I continued my citizenship proof quest almost five days a week. I had become very familiar with many others with the same problem, and there was no way to give up. My relationship with Nadia was still there, but my negative views of my future and Nadia's loss of hope about our marriage were taking their toll. I did make it clear to Nadia that I would not get married in my current situation. I did not see myself having children who would have no future. I refused to even think about that, even if it meant spending the rest of my life alone. Life was unchanged as we moved into 1975. My brother did not even have the checkpoint problem, as he never did anything or went anywhere.

More and more troops were coming home every day from northern Iraq. There was funeral after funeral everywhere. Iran and its leader, the Shah of Iran, were helping and arming the Kurds to fight the Iraqi government. Ironically, the Shah of Iran did not even like the Kurds or want them to succeed. Iran, in fact, had its own problems with a large independence-seeking Kurdish community, though their movement was not quite as strong as the Kurdish movement in Iraq. The Shah helped the Kurds only because the Shah had his own conflict with the Ba'ath party in Iraq over borders and water rights for the Shatt-El-Arab ("Arabic River") waterway that formed the boundary between Iran and Iraq. The Shah saw that Iran could use the Kurds to its advantage. Kurdish fighters at that time could go in and out of Iran without any objections from the Iranian government, and the Shah supplied them with a lot of ammunition. These actions had several effects on the Ba'ath party. Most of all, it put them in defense mode, and their hatred for the Kurds increased.

Another school year ended in the spring of 1975, and many of our younger relatives were now graduating from high school, while my brother and I were standing still in relation to our futures and going nowhere. There was also news spreading like wildfire among the commons—Saddam Hussein and the Ba'ath party had countered all their losses against the Kurdish fighters by a devious tactic that aimed for one thing and one thing only, regardless of the price. Hussein and the Shah of Iran had met in Algiers and agreed that Iraq would give up many of the disputed water rights to Iran. The only thing Iraq demanded in return was that Iran would stop helping the Kurds and close its open border against them. This was the best deal for Iran and the Shah. The Shah easily got everything he had wanted from Iraq, and in addition, he could stop helping the Kurds, whom he had never liked to begin with. The Shah's tactics had worked far better than he ever expected.

The Shah then issued an ultimatum to his old "friends" (the Kurdish leaders), and everyone (especially the Kurdish population) soon became aware of it. Iran, after a specified time, would close the borders against what used to be free traffic. The Shah gave the Kurds a "choice": stay on the Iraqi side or come to the Iranian side before the borders shut down. It was tough, because the Kurds knew that without Iran's help and the open border, they would have a very difficult time against the Iraqi army and air force.

This news sent fear through the Kurdish population in general. Even the Kurds like us in Baghdad, who were far away from the fighting, were wondering what might happen next. Many considered joining the Kurds up north and moving to Iran, in accordance with the Shah's ultimatum. Many considered moving to Iran an opportunity to get away from the Ba'ath party rule. Someone suggested to my brother and me that we do this. It was not a secret that the Shah and Iran were supported by the United States. The idea was that if we made it to Iran, it would be as good as making it to the United States.

Because of the Shah's deadline, we did not have a whole lot of time to think about this idea, but we knew we had to consider it. My father was not one hundred percent sure, but he was willing to support us in whatever decision we made. He also said that if we decided to go, he would give us some helpful recommendations. He told us that we were close relatives of many Kurdish leaders, including Mustafa El

Barzani and one of his right-hand men. I was naïve and too young to pay close attention to names, but I did understand that if we just told El Barzani who our father was, we would be taken care of. At first I leaned toward the idea, but the more I thought about it, the more personal reservations developed. Ninety percent of my issues were about keeping the faith with Nadia. I had no problem with leaving her for a time, as I had been planning on doing that all along, but the idea of not being able to ever come back was very difficult. I had been thinking that once I got established in the United States, I could always come back and marry Nadia and take her with me. However, I might never be able to return from Iran. The other ten percent concerned what we already knew about the Shah of Iran. We had heard that the Shah was in many ways even worse on his own people than Hussein was in Iraq. The Shah had a brutal secret service worse than the Ba'ath party's secret service, called Savak.

There was not a lot of time to decide, and at the end of the day, I decided against going to Iran. My brother decided for it. My father and brother quickly prepared everything my brother would need for a trip to northern Iraq. The first leg was an internal trip from one Iraqi city to another, and we did not say anything about the master plan, which was to join up with other Kurdish populations in specific areas in the Kurdish-controlled northern cities. The rest would be taken care of as part of the plan. My brother was not happy with my decision, but I could not imagine leaving Nadia behind. The trip had its risks, but we were all hoping for the best. My father did not have an easy way at that time to connect to the family on their journey, so we had to wait for several days until the safe arrival of my father back home.

All I knew was that my brother was going to be handed to the right people and that he was expected to be safe. We did not hear from him for more than a month, which was very troubling for my father. My brother's brief letter didn't say much other than hello, he was okay, and he had joined many other Kurds and they had all gone to Iran. He knew very well that each and every letter was inspected before it was delivered. We did not know how he was living or where or how he was being treated. Knowing he was alive and safe seemed enough to us at that time.

A couple of weeks later, we received a package from my brother with some shirts and sweaters for my other brothers and sisters. He had selectively not sent anything for our half-siblings. He also forgot about me. I assumed that he was still angry at me for not going with him. Regardless, we were very happy that at least we had evidence that he was doing well enough to be able to send gifts.

—

By now, it was the fall of 1975, and Nadia would be starting at the university. Of course, I was very happy for her, but in truth, I was very sad that I had wasted so many years and would waste even more without knowing if there would be any light at the end of the tunnel. Our relationship had suffered from all of the uncertainty over my future. Soon I could not see Nadia from my window anymore. When I sent her messages through my sister to come and visit, the request was denied. I was very hurt and became ill. I had always been very healthy, healthy enough to pass the Air Force exams, but all of sudden I was lying in bed for days without knowing what was wrong with me. Nadia's curtains now were fully shut, signifying "not interested." Why hadn't I gone with my brother? What would I do with my life without Nadia? I felt ashamed and betrayed, blaming myself for everything. I was truly, and for the first time, at a complete loss.

After these major disappointments, there was a tiny bit of good news. The government announced an amnesty for all the people who had escaped the draft over the past several years. There would not be any penalties assessed on anyone who surrendered within a certain period of time to be drafted. I thought about this really hard. I had managed to escape so many close checkpoint encounters. At any time an MP could have ignored the card that I used so many times, and I could have ended up being punished as well as being drafted. Not having Nadia in my world helped me decide. I did not waste more time pondering. In many ways, this was my escape from my memories and from home. I went to the specified location, filled out the paperwork, and was given a date a few days later to report for duty. Those few in-between days were days when I sensed some type of freedom—not being scared of checkpoints. I tried and failed to get Nadia's attention before I surrendered to my fate. I had no doubts that I still loved her. My main problem was the self-blame that I was feeling. I was well aware that I was entering into the draft not knowing if I would come back alive. Would I be able to pursue my dreams of further education some day? No one could give me any answers.

The first day I reported to duty, we were taken like sheep from Baghdad to El Najaf in open military trucks. Nothing can describe my true feelings that day. A few months earlier, I had been among the elites passing the Air Force exams. Now I was among people who could not read or write and had no manners, and I was no different from any of them. We all had our hair buzzed off and had to quickly get used to the uniform and the thin, torn sleeping blankets. Getting used to the food and how it was served was something else completely. I had heard all the jokes about the "army bread," and now I actually had to eat it. For the first time, I realized that if you are hungry, you will eat almost anything. Basic training had very strict rules and regulations, and the physical training and exercises were very hard. It took us many days to begin to meet their standards. All ranked officers were very good at humiliating people, regardless of their background or education, for any reason or no reason. They knew how to break anyone's will in a big hurry. Physical abuse like slapping or kicking was common.

After a few days, I got severely homesick and wanted to be home even for one day, but I could not. My mind was on Nadia and my sisters and brothers. I often wondered if Nadia noticed my absence. I realized how much I loved her and wished I could reignite our relationship. Of course, I also wondered if she had found a new love at the university.

I was aware that this was the first year that males and females were not segregated in higher education. After about a month, we were allowed to go home for the weekend—such as it was. We were let go on Thursday evening, after all duties were completed properly. Then we had to walk the long distance from the camp to where the buses were fighting for our business. It was easily more than a three-hour trip to Baghdad, and we did not arrive at the central area where the local buses could pick us up until after eight o'clock in the evening. By the time I arrived home, it was nearly ten o'clock. My little "mother," Layla, got me something nice to eat while I took a long, hot bath—my first real bath since leaving home. The camp "baths" had been dreadful. After my bath, I ran to the window to see if Nadia's curtains were open. Unfortunately, the curtains were the same as when I had left. I asked Layla in private if she had heard anything from Nadia. Sadly, she had not. After dinner, I went to my room to listen to Abdel Halim Hafez. I had never been away from my music that long. My music had become an essential part of my soul diet. I was well aware Friday was my only full day at home. I had to report back to camp by Saturday afternoon, and most of that day would be travel time and looking for buses.

I took full advantage of Friday and went to the market feeling free, with no more checkpoint worries. Lack of hair was an issue, but the sense of freedom was greater than worrying about my hair. I enjoyed another dinner with my family and played my music as usual, maybe a little louder to get Nadia's attention, but there was no Nadia. On Saturday, I got up early to make sure I enjoyed every minute of my last morning. (The one thing that I must mention is that Friday is considered the end of the week. That is the only day off in Iraq, as in other Muslim countries. Saturday is a normal school and workday and is the beginning of the week.) It all went much too quickly.

Returning to camp was very difficult, as I was still adjusting to my limited quarters and surrounded by uneducated recruits. I developed some survival techniques very quickly, such as counting the days. Yes, I realized that there was probably no end in sight for any of us, but somehow adding up my service days gave me a good feeling. Soon we were done with our basic training and expected to be placed any day to serve somewhere in Iraq. I was praying for a location not far from Baghdad, although I did realize that we had to accept whatever came our way. I just did not want to end up in northern Iraq to have to fight the Kurds. Fighting against the Kurdish fighters was not something I was going to do, regardless of the consequences.

~~~

By 1976, I was very proud to have completed many months of service. I had come to accept my fate and what I needed to do. I never considered myself a failure, even in those days. I have always believed that there are reasons for any obstacles. I looked at my condition and convinced myself that I would be a stronger person once I completed my service and that it would help me in my later pursuits. Many of my mates asked me why I looked so happy. I would always say, "And if I am miserable, will that change anything?" Of course, the response was always, "No." Then I always ended the conversation with, "If how I feel will not change the facts, then I elect to be happy." They even laughed at me because I ironed my uniform at home whenever I had a chance. I was the subject of all kinds of jokes, but I never let that bother me. My answer was, "If knowing that I have a clean and ironed uniform makes me feel better about myself, then why not?" Looking back, it seems that I had a great attitude about life in general, with no exposure whatsoever to any spiritual books, movies, or anything at all of that nature. I somehow knew how to keep myself motivated in even the darkest places. I had no choice—if I did not motivate myself, nobody else would have or cared to at that time.

Several weeks after completing basic training, the day we all feared came—we were collected at a moment's notice to be told where we would serve our army time. To the uneducated, village-raised majority of us, the army was a "retreat." There were only a few high school graduates besides myself who, for whatever reason, had not continued on to higher education and were thus drafted. The majority were sent to what was called "walks battalion." These are the units that learn to use the hand/ shoulder-held ammunition to support any ground units. The high school graduates, including myself, were assigned to a tank unit. At first, I was scared to death. Why tanks? I just knew that we would end up in northern Iraq to fight the Kurds. Wisely, I kept all my fears and feelings to myself. Unit location was of great concern to us all. I had already learned that the farther we were from home, the fewer real time away we enjoyed because of increased travel time. I finally learned that my tank unit was in the city of Baqubah, about an hour and a half northeast of Baghdad. That was the only good news that day, because the idea of being in a tank unit was, in general, not comforting at all. In a few days, we were all in our new "homes." I quickly learned that we were no longer in basic training and that any wrong move received a punishment, even on-site jail. This was a whole new game. Threats and fear got our attention and respect no matter where we went.

We were given our assignments right away and broken up into teams. I was one of only two on my entire team who had gotten there by being drafted. The rest were professionals who had chosen the army as a career. That was a huge disadvantage in many ways. The two of us were considered by our professional teammates to have been born with silver spoons in our mouths. There was a lot of resentment toward us, leading, of course, to some of the worst and toughest assignments. I did not become bothered or shaken by any of the bad treatment. I always knew that we had to earn the respect of each and every teammate. I always kept my cool and had my final goal in mind, which was *not* to make a career out of the army. I just wanted to finish my service and move on to making it to the United States of America.

After a quick orientation, our service began. I despised the early morning training. Presented as exercise to get us into shape, it was more than that. I sensed a need on the part of the officers to humiliate soldiers for no reason other than they were higher ranking and could do what they pleased. The part I hated most passionately was climbing a high wall using a rope. Once atop the wall, we had to walk about twenty feet on a board no wider than four inches. On the ground below were strewn broken glass bottles. I could never bear to look down, knowing that falling would leave lifelong scars—if I even survived. I never did understand the logic behind it. Needless to say, I never fell.

I was able to communicate with my family only in thirty-six-hour visits once every two or three weeks. I missed everyone so much. During these precious times, we read letters from my brother that came, not from Iran, but from the United States. I was happy he had made it to our dream land and hoped that when I completed my service I would find a way to join him. The first few letters had not been addressed to me, and I wondered if my brother was still angry that I hadn't joined him in his escape to Iran. Nevertheless, because I was the oldest in the family at home now and my other brothers were not interested in writing, I took the responsibility of composing our replies. His letters never gave any details about how he got to the United States, because he knew that all letters were monitored in Iraq and read before delivery. All we knew was that he was in a state called North Dakota. We had a hard time finding information on North Dakota. The only U.S. locations we were familiar with were California, Florida, Detroit, Texas, and Chicago.

Besides connecting with my family, my other main mission at home was to reconnect with Nadia. Unfortunately, I was never successful. All I knew was that she was studying at the university. At times I just felt angry, probably for being ignored by her. Other times I was sad because I felt that I must have hurt her or her reputation somehow. I had many questions on my mind but no answers. I was feeling only hopelessness, frustration, and discouragement.

Back at service, we began training on assembling and disassembling our assigned Russian-made machine guns. Everything we had seemed to have been made in Russia. This training was taken very seriously, and we spent many hours on it. I had never liked guns, but I had to obey orders.

We were constantly cleaning, oiling, and polishing them. The next steps were a few days of classroom teaching on how to aim, hold, and shoot followed by shooting range practice. It was not a true range but rather an open, scenic area full of trees and hills. This was the real deal, with very strict routines and live ammo. I had never seen live ammo before. Watching how awkwardly my service mates went to the ground into the shooting position, I resolved to not make any mistakes when it was my turn. There were many targets. Some were pretty far away, and for those, we were trained to aim higher. Four or five soldiers were all shooting at different targets at the same time. Seeing all the bullets flying was very disturbing, and I always hoped that no sparrows or other birds were in their way. Finally, it was my turn to take a position. Everything seemed fine to me until we were given the order to start shooting.

The top officer apparently did not think everything was so fine with me. I'd only had very limited encounters with him, but something about me made him dislike me. I wondered if he knew that I was a Kurd, or were there other reasons? As I lay on the ground shooting, he came from nowhere and hit my back, hard, with the stick he always carried as part of his outfit. Everything about the officers, from their uniforms to the way we had to salute them, was a copy of what the British did during their occupation. I wondered how stupid this officer must be. How could he know that I wouldn't lose my temper and start to shoot at him? Then the lowest ranking officer came over to me, gave me a quick reminder on how to aim, and asked me to try again. This time I was right on and did much better. Apparently, nervousness and my dislike of guns had affected my earlier aim. Also, I did not want to be hit like an animal in front of my service mates anymore.

We were now ready to learn about our main mission—being a tank unit. Machine guns were relatively simple. We wondered how many more long weeks of complicated training would be needed to teach us about tanks.

—

It was now 1977, and many months of service still remained. I was able to continue my visits home. By this time my brother had realized that I was the only one who was writing him back and keeping him informed. I started making audio recordings from all of us to send him. It was so nice when my sisters sang his favorite songs for him. I also started mailing him things that would remind him of home, in spite of the high mailing costs and customs fees. He did not seem to be aware how much of a financial sacrifice it was for me. I did wonder to myself why he never sent us anything from the United States. I just assumed he was going to college and could use every penny. He told us that he was going to "medical school." I was very surprised, since he always had such a tough time with math and science. Of course, then I did not know that things were different in the United States and that there are many colleges and universities that will let anyone who can pay the tuition enroll in any major they like.

At some point, he began asking me to mail him costly items, particularly a certain handmade, one-of-a-kind golden cross necklace from a famous market in Baghdad that dealt only in gold and silver jewelry. Most of the gold items were either eighteen or twenty-one karats. He never said why; he just kept asking me to send them. The cost of the item along with the customs charge usually emptied my entire savings.

CHAPTER SIX
· · · · · · · · · · · · · · · · · · · ·

On and Off the Sandy Hills

M arch 30, 1977, was the beginning of a terrible time for me. My beloved Abdel Halim Hafez passed away in London after a lifelong illness. He was also called El-Andaleeb el-Asmar (the Great Dark Nightingale). I would have done anything to get to Cairo for his funeral, but I could not leave without a passport. I locked myself in my room for days listening to all the Egyptian shortwave stations I could get to hear about reactions to his death. Many of my friends who knew how much I loved Halim were worried about me, especially after hearing about many young girls killing themselves in Cairo when they heard the news. May you rest in peace, beloved Abdel Halim Hafez.

By this time I was desperate to open any conversation with Nadia. One evening I crept quietly to the back corner of the yard where our houses met and climbed our low fence.

Beloved Abdel Halim Hafez

The lights were on in her room, and I actually went over to her window and gently tapped on it. She yanked the curtain open and appeared very shocked. By that time, I had climbed back on the fence in case her father came out. She seemed very angry and also afraid that someone might see me, which I fully understood and respected, but then she waved me up to the rooftop where we both knew we could have a face-to-face meeting. This was the first time she clearly told me that it was over and that she wanted all of the pictures I had taken of her during our relationship.

I was extremely hurt and angrily told her to hold on a second. I went to my room and stuffed an envelope with not only all the photos but also the negatives, which she had not asked for. I stormed angrily back to the roof and threw the whole collection to her. Then I locked myself in my room and cried and listened to sad songs. Giving up the picture negatives was probably one of my worst mistakes, and I am still angry at myself over it. After that, I looked forward to going back to service camp. I had lost my reasons to live, and not just for the loss of Nadia. Why had it happened? Was it something I did, or had she just given up on me and found someone else? Either way, I no longer had her.

Tank training began within days or weeks after my breakup with Nadia. (Like our machine guns, the tanks were Russian-made, mostly T-55s and a few even older T-54s from the '40s and '50s, though still considered reputable. We were told to expect some newer T-62s in the near future.) First we had a lesson about tanks in general and tank formations. The tank had a dome on top (the "hull") and two doors on top called "hatches." Each tank needed four soldiers/officers. First was a driver, who was seated in the front of the tank on the left side. The second person used the right top door and was responsible for radio communication with other tanks and also for loading the tank with ammunition. I was assigned to be that person. The third person entered from the left top door and moved around very little; his main duties involved aiming the tank toward its target. The fourth was seated above the third person and in most cases was a career army officer whose orders were obeyed by the other three. Three tanks made up a unit, and they usually traveled like a triangle; continuous communication was essential. The communications officer (me) also had to operate an antiaircraft machine gun mounted near the right door. I was very happy with my assignment. I had always enjoyed working with radio communications and wanted to be an electrical engineer, so this seemed to be a very logical choice. But the driver's position was the most rewarding, because he was responsible for continuous maintenance and learned a lot of tank mechanics. The only part I did not enjoy in my duties was loading the bullets. They were more than three feet long and very heavy. They were stored in a very narrow area, and so loading them out of this area was a very hard job. Also, the radio work turned out to be quite complicated. If the tank were ever disabled, I would have to remove the radio and take it out in order to make communication with other tanks. I was very busy, and getting deeper into tank duty helped me forget Nadia and my pain. Service had become somewhat more meaningful. Security duty was a different story. I spent the whole time thinking of Nadia. It was a twenty-four-hour assignment rotating three soldiers, two hours on and four hours of rest. Officers would sneak up on us in the dark to test our alertness. Many ended up punished and jailed if they failed to detect these officers. Amazingly, we were not allowed live ammunition at all, even on security duty. But that was no excuse not to take the duties seriously.

I began to reflect deeply on my situation. In many ways, I felt that I would end up ahead of everyone else once given a chance. My pain over Nadia was making me stronger and made it easier for me to deal with my service duties. I often considered my relative educational advantages and my success in the Air Force trials and wondered where I might have ended up if I was not simply a Kurd born in an Arab county. Despite my feelings, I never held anyone accountable for the injustice. I always knew that the politicians, especially the current Ba'ath party, were trying to divide people in order to stay in power.

When I was at home, my sister, Layla, was very sensitive to me, as usual, but had grown even more sympathetic after my loss of Nadia. Nadia no longer communicated with my sisters. I thought that was somewhat strange. Of course, I blamed myself, thinking that I must have hurt Nadia so badly that she did not want to be near anything that was associated with me. Silly, but that is how I felt in those days.

Not having the proof of citizenship had turned our entire family upside down. My sisters had even less of a future than I did. Once they completed high school, they had no place to go. All they could do was stay home and wait for the day they got married. I had another goal—going to the United States—but this goal was not in any shape or form economically driven. We were a relatively well-off family, and we had more than the average income in our area. Our family heritage and history was well known to many, and we were looked upon as very special. Never having cared much for history or learning names of relatives, I couldn't say exactly why, but I knew it was true based on how we were treated. It had always been hinted by many of my relatives that they would be honored if I were to ask for their daughter's hand in marriage. Even without higher education, I could have very easily gone along, picked any of the available girls, and continued my father's business—or any other business, for that matter. It must be highlighted that my goal was formed out of my mother's promise, and I had to honor that. At the same time, my own wish to become part of the American dream was developing.

Back at camp, things had become very routine: morning exercises, announcements, and then learning more about maintaining our tanks. The tanks were never actually operated except when they needed to be moved. After a few months of this, our lives suddenly changed. We were given minutes to assemble and then told to get ready to be shipped to an unspecified mission the next day. A real mission? I could not believe my ears. My mind was bombarded with questions and ideas. *Would I be able to see my family one last time? Would we be sent to fight the Kurds in northern Iraq? How this could happen to me, someone who is not even considered a citizen?* It had never been fair that I was drafted. I did not act on any of the thoughts. I decided to just wait and see.

We were all very confused, worried, and afraid. I don't think any of us slept that night. We collected our few belongings and got ready. It was total chaos as soon as the military trucks arrived. People were jumping onto trucks and then off again. No one seemed to be sure exactly what we were supposed to do. My "favorite" top officer was standing behind me as I tried to board and kicked me in my behind so hard that I thought he was trying to kill me. I had no idea why he did that, but he was an officer with three stars on each shoulder and I was a lonely, drafted solider. I could not question him, and to this day, I vividly remember exactly how he kicked me.

We were packed like sheep into the open trucks, with no idea at all where or how far we were going. We felt disrespected as human beings, and my rear end was still hurting from the kick. After many hours, the trucks finally started moving in a line on the main highway. I looked back and saw that our tanks were coming with us, and each tank was loaded onto a big truck. Our caravan was very long, considering that each tank carrier was at least thirty feet. We drove through the city of Baqubah barely noticed. Based on the highway signs, we were now heading to Baghdad—very slowly. No one knew if we would stop in Baghdad or just pass through. The travel speed was slow at best, and it took us many hours before reaching Baghdad. Huge crowds on both sides of the street were cheering for us in a way beyond imagination.

What is happening? Why are they cheering? Obviously, we had missed a lot of news in our isolated camp. We were simple solders who had not been trained on much of anything. We had not even seen the tanks move from one point to another. What did we know about war? We just kept trying to comfort one another that we could not possibly be going to any war. Slowly we moved through the heart of Baghdad. Where were we going now?

The trucks just kept driving, driving west, without even stopping to allow us to eat, drink, or go to a restroom. Finally, late in the evening, we were ordered out of the trucks at a military camp in the city of Fallujah. We were ordered to assemble in our usual groups to be given assignments for the night. First we had to erect tents, and the cooks prepared us a simple meal. I was assigned security duty for the night, which meant I would get barely any sleep after riding like an animal all day in the wind and hot sun. Early the next morning, we were ordered to collect our belongings, take down the tents, and get back on the trucks. We all were thinking the same thing: Again? Where to? No one could answer.

The roads were now going through desert, and our faces baked in the sun and wind. We knew now that no matter where we were going, it was not going to be good. I had never been outside of Baghdad before other than periodically going to visit my mother in El Najaf, and certainly had never been to this desert. The swirling wind sandblasted us, and we had no escape. Again, we drove all day. But this time, no one was there to cheer for us except the hot wind and the sand. At sundown, it cooled rapidly. We passed through the town of El Ruttbah. From geography class, I knew that it was in western Iraq. Our trucks did not slow down for another hour, when we finally got off the highway and started taking an unpaved road. We got very scared because we had seen signs on the highway telling us how close we were to both Syria and Jordan. On these unpaved roads, the sandblasting got even worse from all the trucks in front of us.

Had we left Iraq? The trucks started to go in many different directions. Ours finally stopped on what appeared to be a hill. We were asked to get off the truck and erect the tent, which was a good thing due to the sudden extreme cold. Soon the truck left, leaving only myself and four others, including a career soldier with a lower ranking than an officer. We got only dry food before having to go on security duty. With only four people, we knew that duty would have to go on almost constantly. What were we protecting in the middle of this desert other than ourselves? Protecting how? Our machine guns did not have any ammunition at all. We could only do what we were asked. It was so cold and dark, with no light other than the stars. We still had no clue as to where we were. What would happen to us? Would we ever see our families again? Should I somehow try to escape? After all, I was in this desert instead of the United States only because I was not an Iraqi citizen. No clear answers existed, so I decided to just keep to myself for the time being.

Only one of us managed to sleep all night; the rest rotated on security every two hours. We knew one thing: in the middle of this desert, no one would come to surprise us, and a car or truck could be seen and heard miles away. I was, however, very afraid of any type of animals that might be found here.

My clothes could not keep out the chill. I found a blanket to cover myself while on duty, and I had to keep moving to keep from shivering uncontrollably. When I finished my two-hour shift, I needed the entire four hours just to get warm and comfortable, and then I had to get up again for two more hours. The morning finally arrived, and we could clearly see where we were—in the middle of nowhere. We stared at each other and wondered about basics like bathroom, shower, washing ... and food. We looked up and saw a cloud of sand swirling our way. It was an open military truck with what was supposed to be breakfast and a container of water. We were told to keep things the way we had them, which was no way at all. The security duty was twenty-four hours, so we did that; on off times, we did whatever we could do in a small tent. One of the crew members had a deck of cards. That was our only entertainment. No radio, definitely no TV. At least we knew we would not have to do exercises or climb walls. By noon, the heat had again become unbearable. I don't think I have ever heard anywhere with such huge daily temperature shifts. As to the basics, we soon realized that was totally up to us to improvise. We were told we had the entire desert to ourselves, so we just each picked our favorite restroom spot. How about showering? We had the whole desert. How and when was up to each man. We spent at least a week like that, never knowing why we were stuck in the middle of a desert. Our midday and evening meals were cooked in huge kettles and brought to us in open military trucks. The motion created swirling sandstorms, and so our food was full of sand. The amount of sand in our food was determined by where we were in relation to where the food was prepared and loaded onto the truck. I can still taste the sandy rice and sandy everything else.

After so many days in the hot sun and sand, we needed to shower. We stacked our belongings to create a makeshift wall, just to block the howling wind. Water was very limited. We took turns in our so-called shower, depending on the water delivery. It was up to us to divide the water as needed for daily washing and restrooms. Ten days had gone by, and we were still unsure if this was to be our permanent place or just some kind of training. Our only contacts were the military truck drivers who delivered the food and water. We didn't even know if we were going to be granted family leave. Finally, at the two-week mark, we were gathered with the rest of the soldiers and taken into a central location to be given some news. Emotions ran high; we were happy, excited, and apprehensive all at once. Finally, the arrogant officer's military Jeep pulled up. When he got out, he was walking like there was nothing on earth as important as he was—a typical attitude, but that day there was a difference, something special, never witnessed before. He was dressed in a field uniform, and the stars on his shoulder, instead of being made of shiny metal, were embroidered. After quite a bit of posturing and showing off, he told us to be proud because we were "going to fight Israel, God willing." The shock was visible on all the faces, and we stood in complete silence. The officer went on to say, "We do not know how long we will be stationed here. As soon as Syria gives us the permission to go through, we will be marching to fight Israel."

I am sure he said some other things, but I was too stunned to comprehend most of them. I did learn that we would be supplied with shoulder-held heat-seeking antiaircraft missiles for defense in case Israel learned about us and attempted to attack us. Fight Israel? Fight Israel with what? We were not equipped with even one bullet. *Is this a joke?* If Israel wanted, all they had to do was send one jet to wipe us all from the face of the earth without one bullet being fired back. All we knew was climbing walls and being humiliated. What did we know about war and fighting? I remember thinking, *Wait, I am not even a citizen and cannot even get into a university or get a passport. How is it I qualify to fight for a country that does not want me?* I actually started to look forward to security duty, because it would give me a full two hours without any interruptions to think and reflect.

When we asked if we were going to get any chances to go home, the answer was, "Not yet, if any." We were told that no one could predict where we would be on any specific day if we were not at war. We were told to accept where we were and not expect much. Everyone's morale was the lowest that I had ever seen it. After the initial shock, however, we all became very happy. Even if we could not go home, even if our living conditions were terrible, it was all okay as long as we were not going to war. We all knew that we were not war material yet, and we assumed that our leaders knew that also. But we still needed to know the real reasons behind all of these "troop movements."

Day after weary day passed for our little group stuck on the sandy hill. One day a couple of shoulder-held antiaircraft heat-seeking missiles were dropped off for us. Of course, they were Russian-made, and I had no idea how old they were. We had no training in how to use them and no detection tools. We pictured what would happen if a jet came over our heads: present ourselves so we can be blown into pieces. None of what was going on made sense to any of us, including the career soldiers. No one believed that we were going to war, but we also knew that if Israel was aware of any troop movements, regardless of whether the troops were trained, Israel had the right to strike first. We were sitting targets with hardly any weapons or ammunition.

Life became even more unbearable in a hurry. On top of having minimal entertainment and sanitary facilities, we were supplied with only a couple of torn and worn blankets and no pillows. We ended up putting our boots under a towel to make a pillow. The first time I woke up after sleeping on my "pillow," I hurriedly went to put on my boots. A big scorpion was inside the first one. I jumped out of the tent to shake it out, and three more fell onto the sand. I checked the other boot and found the same thing. We killed them, but we were all shaken by the knowledge that a deadly desert creature could be that close while we were sleeping. Shaking out boots became part of our morning routine. We learned that scorpions seek a cool place, and the boots must have provided it. I am sure I came very close to being poisoned. I wondered if anyone would have even bothered to send my body home. Considering the way we were treated alive, I think it would have been very easy for the officer to toss my corpse somewhere in the desert.

The only picture was secretly taken in the middle of desert

I suffered greatly from homesickness and concern over how my brothers and sisters and Nadia were doing. Was anyone responding to my brother's letters from the United States? And my skin! The heat and wind during the day and the terrible cold weather at night made it much like what you see on a crocodile. Washing and cleaning in an open desert only made it worse. Sometime after our third week in the desert, the officer ordered the beginning of rotation leaves. When my turn came up, I and a few others had to walk in the sand for a very long time to get to the highway. Private bus drivers were used to this sort of thing, and so we had no problem getting on a bus for Baghdad and to the local bus station, a trip that lasted several hours. Of course, my arrival at home was unexpected, and there was a lot of hugging and crying, especially from Layla. Everyone was shocked to see how rough I looked. I did not waste a minute jumping into a nice hot bath and soaking for a very long time, trying to erase all the sand and the damage to my skin. Only the thought of dinner got me out of the tub—a dinner without sand!

I told them everything I knew about where I was stationed and why I was there. It turned out that they knew at least as much as I did, because they listened to the local, regional, and world news. They were aware of the troop movements, but they had heard that the troops were directed to Syria, not Israel. They also mentioned that Syria was aware of this and was not fooled by talk of "fighting Israel," and thus they blocked the troops from entering Syria. Both Syria and Iraq were supposed to be with the Ba'ath party, but they never saw eye to eye. None of this news made it any easier for me. What would stop Israel from attacking us? How did they know we were not going to fight them? Did they know that we did not even have any ammunition and that they could easily come and destroy us all?

It was nice to sleep in my own bed without any fear of scorpions. Knowing that it was back to the desert the next day did not make for an easy night. I woke up early to make sure that I got back while it was still daylight. I knew that this first long walk from the highway to our tent would be a challenge. The ride on the desolate highway had given me a somewhat more peaceful mind as I thought about what I had heard at home about the purpose of the troop movement. I assumed that if Syria was not going to let us go through, we could not possibly stay there for very long. I was not planning to share any of these things with anyone. I arrived at the tent very tired, with the memory of my short time at home already fading. There was something new—they had brought us our tank and even dug a hole in the sand to hide it and protect it from the wind and the sand. My mates were saying that it appeared we were there to stay and that we would continue our tank maintenance and learning. This was completely opposite to what I had heard at home. But I did not say anything and quickly resumed my duties. Somehow the thought that Nadia was watching from behind the curtains with the lights out was enough to sustain me. When I was off security duty during the day, I started wandering around in the desert thinking of Nadia and singing my favorite Halim songs, just to kill time.

On one of my walks, I saw many holes in the ground and spotted a snake coming out of one them. I stopped about five feet away. The snake did not leave its hole but actually formed itself into a loop around the hole. The snake was no more than three feet long, so the loop was only about six inches across. I was surprised and confused. If it had wanted to find food, it would have kept going, and it definitely did not look like it was sunning. I did not move except to quietly pick up a nearby rock. As soon as I bent over, the head of the snake suddenly lifted off the ground and changed. I had never seen a live cobra, and I did not know that he had assumed a fighting posture. The snake made a huge jump in the air toward me. I had to move fast. The snake was not backing down or running away; in fact, it was after me. I was very stubborn and kept throwing rocks but missed many times. I was getting very tired but was determined to see my fight through. I finally hit it somewhere on its body; it became a bit less mobile but was still in fighting mode. Eventually, I hit its head and declared victory.

I was very hot and thirsty, so I decided to go back to the tent and leave the thinking and singing to another time. When I told my mates about my adventure, our officer's mouth dropped to the ground. I told them it was not really a big snake. He said the size of the snake did not matter. He was pretty sure that snake would have eventually "spit" in my face. That spit would have been enough to blind me and kill me on the spot. He said, "Consider yourself very lucky and never do that again." I started to shake and wondered what would have happened if I had slipped. I still shake when I think about it.

The talk of going to fight Israel became more and more serious. Our daily routine changed to include actual exercises with the tank, and every minute of exercising meant several hours of cleaning and maintenance to the tank. We were even told that we would engage in real, live shooting using the tanks. I was thinking, *You bring us here near the Syrian border, and just because Syria did not let us go through,* then *you decide to train us? How about training us* before *we came this far?* I was not sure what to do. Escape crossed my mind many times, but I also knew that the Ba'ath party would find me, and I would be killed along with my entire family. Not being recognized as a citizen in my own country did not sit very well with me. I was the one who passed the exams to be an elite Air Force pilot but couldn't get in, and I couldn't seek more education because of that, too. I should not die for this country and engage in a war that has not affected me personally! Then I thought of learning to drive the tank. I figured if we ever engaged in a war with Israel, I would need that skill to somehow turn the dome backward to indicate that I would not fight—and try to escape to Israel's side. I did find a way to get my mate to give me a quick lesson on how to drive the T-55. It was not very hard at all. I learned how to maneuver the dome and became very proficient with the tank in a short time.

We were allotted just one actual loading and shooting in each exercise. I had to pull the shell from its compartment and load the tank. The officer cautioned me to stay clear and away from the loading area, as I might break an arm when they fired. The big, used golden shell fell into my area, now red and glowing. The shell made it blazing hot inside the cramped dome. I had to quickly open my door on top of the dome and throw it out. In a real war situation, that shell would have caused a lot of problems. I had heard a promise that the newer T-62s would have an automatic shell ejection, so that would at least make my job a bit easier. Later came the hours of oiling and cleaning the tank, especially the turret. Would we have time for that kind of maintenance during an actual war? Somehow I never did get the logic. Maybe it was just to keep us busy. I was not sure.

After six long months in the desert, near the end of 1977, it was decided to bring us back to our bases without either going to Syria or fighting Israel. Before we could pack for the trip back to our bases, they came and collected *all* ammunition we were carrying. Even our personal machines were emptied. The Ba'ath party and Hussein did not trust its own army to have any ammunition in its possession. The order to bring the tents down was the best news ever, and they came down in minutes. I was happy that we were going back to our base. It did not have many things, but at least we would not have snakes or scorpions to sleep with, sand in our food, or annoying temperature extremes. We were also very appreciative of the fact that we had more than one night to rotate for security. It would be great to get some real sleep. And, of course, we all welcomed the normalizing of our time off.

———

In early 1978, I started to have the sense that I had served enough time and should be let go in the near future if the authorities decided to release some of us. Needless to say, I renewed my quest for the proof of citizenship document when I was home for a day or so every other week. I also kept up the correspondence with my brother in the United States and kept sending him anything he asked for. Of course, I was expecting that someday soon he would be able to return my favors when I got a chance to leave the country. I had never asked my brother for anything. I just assumed that he would gladly do it considering all the time and money I spent keeping him connected with the family.

I knew that Nadia was well aware of me when I was home, though all communication had ceased. I never tried to analyze the reasoning for Nadia's action other than she had either given up on me or had found someone in the university. I still loved Nadia but could do nothing, mostly for the fear of causing her reputation any serious damage.

I had become at ease with the service, because I knew that sooner or later I would be discharged. I looked forward to a new freedom of movement and an opportunity to breathe new life into my quest to leave for the United States. I knew that I had grown because of the service, and I did have a greater sense of appreciation for life. At midyear, another draft amnesty was announced, and rumors were heard that we might be let go to make room for the new draftees.

Soon the rumors became reality for me and many of my teammates. It was great to finally get my *Deftar El Khydma* ("service book" in Arabic). It did not buy me anything special—except the wonderful freedom from fear of checkpoints. And it was nice to start growing my hair again and taking care of it. I did not waste even a day getting back to my impossible citizenship dream. Recalling it now, I realize that it was far more difficult than I had even imagined at the time. But I never thought for a second of giving up and saying, "There is nothing more I can do." I knew that I would have to make my own fortune, considering that all the odds were against me and the amount of time that had gone by since I graduated from high school. My older brother knew everything that was going on, but all he would advise me to do was just make it to a pro-West country somehow and then he would help me. Right, but how could I do that without a passport? I expanded my efforts and started going to the passport offices, too. At that time, money could often accomplish a lot of things if you just knew the right person and had the right timing, so I kept trying. Such bribery was, unfortunately, a very common practice.

My younger brother, Jamel, started to see a beautiful young lady from school. This seemed like a very good match. He invited her to our home several times to visit. Because she was not from our area, there were no issues of people talking or fear for her reputation, unlike my situation. I did wonder how far this relationship might go once she or her family realized that we were Kurds and not Arabs. The situation under the Ba'ath party and Saddam Hussein had become very divisive. I did not offer my brother any opinion and let him enjoy his new love. One must trust and see how things will go. My family, especially Layla, and even my stepmother felt sorry for me because I had no one. I never said anything to anyone, but I knew they felt my pain. I tried to stay focused on citizenship leading to a passport or possibly getting the passport even without the citizenship. I also renewed the idea of finding anyone to take me to either Lebanon or Greece, countries my brother said were open and had a good relationship with the United States. Many people were going back and forth to these countries buying and selling merchandise illegally.

In the evenings I kept myself busy with anything to keep my mind off Nadia. I was now the oldest son at home, and I helped my father both in the garden and the house. I became very enthusiastic about painting the living room and the formal living room. In my heart, I wanted to make our home even more beautiful than it already was in case my brother and his girlfriend became engaged or married. Months and years had gone by in my struggle, but I never succumbed to despair. Regardless of our family's comfort, it never appealed to me to live in a country where I was not recognized as a citizen. I always looked at my situation as being in a large, well-appointed prison with no freedom in sight.

———

In the summer of 1979, I visited one of my wealthy relatives and told him of my citizenship quest and my desire to go to the United States for my education. He liked me a lot and tried to convince me to marry his daughter, settle down, and give up my futile pursuit. He soon realized that there was no giving up on my part, and he respected me for that. He admired me a lot, and he was seeing things in me that I was not seeing. We talked for hours about many things. At some point, he told me to go and visit a friend of his who worked in the passport department and tell him who sent me. Once the friend made the association, I was told to open up to him and see if he could help me. When I left, I was very happy. I was happy without even knowing whether this person could help me. I was happy because this would be the very first time in years that I would be talking about my desires to someone who could possibly help. And if he couldn't help me, maybe he could lead me to someone who could. I am not sure if I slept that night. At the passport department, I asked for the person I had been referred to and was pointed to a window with a long line in front of it. The people around me tried to start conversations about traveling and what my destination was, but I really did not know what to say since I did not know who they were and could not trust them. I felt very awkward. My turn finally came, and I immediately greeted the man with his name. That got his attention, and then he asked how I knew him. I said that my relative had sent me to him to talk to him about something special. I could see he felt a bit awkward, too, and he instructed me to see him at a place and time he wrote on a small piece of paper. I took the paper without even reading it, thanked him, and left. I did not look at the paper until I was on the street. The date was several days later. I went home very happy but kept the news to myself. I was well aware that I could not trust even the walls in our own home. I played my favorite music and sang along in a way that I had not done for a very long time.

I relaxed and waited patiently until the appointed time and place, which was on an evening in a public café. We exchanged basic information: who I was and my exact family relation to my relative who sent me his way. I think he just wanted both of us to be at ease. I explained my situation and the years my father had spent trying to obtain citizenship and my years trying as well. I told him of my ultimate goal and that I had already served my country—or served *a* country anyway. At first, he said that without the citizenship, he could not be of help at all. Deeply disappointed, I stopped even listening to him. Then, at some point, I heard the word "but." That immediately got my attention. He talked about cases of people who were sick and had to travel outside the country to seek immediate medical help. They could get a special passport, which was usually taken away immediately when they returned to the Iraqi airport. It was called a *Laissez Passer*, with a silent *R*. He said that if I was interested in that type of passport, he could help me. In utter surprise, I said, "Really?" Without knowing any more details, I gave him a big yes. He then told me what I needed to bring to him, and how.

I ran to my father's shop to tell him the great news. However, when I got there, it did not seem like the appropriate place to tell him after all, simply because the situation in the entire country had come to the point where no one trusted anyone or anything. I decided to tell him at home. I was full of hope but did not even dare tell my own brothers and sisters before telling our father. I also thought of calling my brother instead of wasting weeks and weeks for letters to go back and forth to help me figure out what I needed to do once I made it out of the country. My father was very happy and did not question the financial cost of the meeting with the official, as he knew more than anyone else how much this meant to me. He totally agreed with the idea of calling my brother, even though he knew exactly how expensive and difficult a call like that would be. It involved calling a live operator, giving them the name and number, and then waiting, sometimes hours, before the connection. The connection often was not the best, but that was all we had available.

It took a few days for my father to collect all the money needed to meet the demands of the man from the passport office. He also gave me enough money to go to the main post office, where there were long distance operators, to make the call to my brother. I was afraid the time differences between Baghdad and the United States might give us problems and also that my brother might say something without realizing that the phone call was being recorded and monitored. After a couple of hours, the operator called my name and directed me to a certain phone booth. At first, I was very cautious, and in many ways I tried to tell my brother to be very careful. He immediately knew what I was trying to say. We seemed to be talking in symbols and code, but we were both on the same page. I mainly wanted to tell my brother that I might finally have found a way to leave. It was not a sure thing, but I might soon. I did not tell him how, and he did not know if this was a legal way through airlines or through illegal cars and trucks. Because of that, he kept telling me that Greece was the ideal place to be. That is what I wanted to know, and I cut the call off, because of the cost.

A couple of weeks later, after satisfying the needs of my new friend, it turned out that he had already started the process, and I only had to run the passport through a few internal signatures. It took several days because of the long lines, but at the end I had in my hands my new paper passport. It clearly stated that it was valid for only one trip and that it would be taken away after returning. That much I had known before applying for it, but seeing entered under "nationality claimed by bearer" that I was "stateless" was something very hard to swallow. Having a state where I was born, went to school, and served several years of my life in its army, only to still to be called "stateless"?

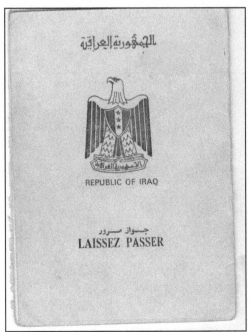

Front picture of my passport (Laissez Passer)

It was September 1979, more than seven years past my high school graduation. I was feeling an urgency not to waste any more time. I started by checking into the Greek Embassy in Baghdad. The embassy officials seemed very surprised to see a passport like mine. They talked and talked among themselves, only to deny me any visa to Greece based on my inadequate passport. I was

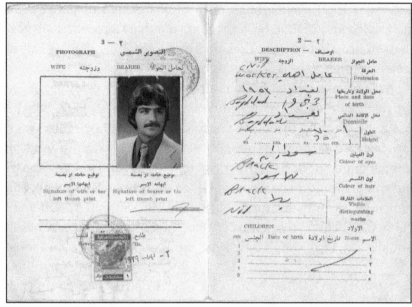

Inside passport (Laissez Passer)

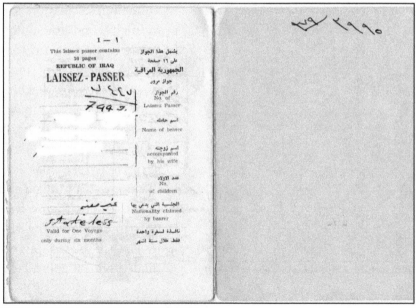

Nationality claimed by bearer STATELESS

I tried very hard to get Nadia's attention but to no avail. I was sensing that my days in Iraq were numbered, and I wanted one more chance to talk to her, even though I could not possibly tell her, or anyone else, that I would be leaving soon. I had to keep the news away from my own relatives for the fear of the news falling into the wrong hands and eventually to the Ba'ath party.

Back at the West German Embassy, the very nice gentleman asked me a few questions about my reasons for wanting to go to Germany. I felt that he knew the real reason, but he never said it to me and was trying to help. How could he *not* know after seeing the handwritten word "stateless"? How could anyone not realize what was going on? After a few more questions, he told me that if I brought in a round-trip ticket returning me to Iraq, he would grant me a visa to visit West Germany. I responded happily, "Of course." I shook his hand and left with a big smile on my face.

My father was very happy for me, too, and immediately handed me some cash. The next day I went to the office of the Lufthansa ticket agent in Baghdad and learned the cost. I also learned that I needed to bring a vaccination certificate before I could buy the tickets. I had the feeling that I still had many obstacles to overcome. But within a few days, I got the health certificate and purchased the tickets. As anxious as I was to leave, I booked them a couple of weeks in advance, as I knew I still had to get the visa from the embassy. It seemed backward to buy the tickets before getting the visa, but I was willing to do what I was told to do. In October of 1979, with the tickets in my hand, I went back to the West German Embassy. I spoke to the same nice gentleman, and I could tell he was pleased for me and was more than happy to stamp my passport with the visa.

I was not sure what to take with me or where I would go when I arrived in West Germany. I just knew that I would connect with my brother, and then we could talk freely about how to go about making it to the United States. I went shopping for some luggage, enough for a few clothes and for the one thing I could not leave behind: my collection of hundreds of cassette tapes of all my favorite songs. They were so heavy! My father asked me to take with me some letters from relatives who had sons in West Germany. I was very stubborn and refused the offer. Maybe I was trying hard to prove to my father that I could take care of myself in West Germany without any help.

I went to bed on my last night in Iraq with very mixed emotions, not knowing what was ahead for me. I was very happy that after more than seven years, I would finally get to leave the country. And I was sad knowing that once I left, I would not be able to come back. I wished I could have had even five minutes with Nadia, but I never did. However, I was very comforted by the idea of keeping in touch with my family and someday reconnecting with Nadia and some of my friends. I made one last try, through my sister, to arrange a visit with Nadia, but she came back very disappointed at Nadia's refusal. I still held a faint hope of connecting with her at some later time with the help of my sisters. I am not sure if I slept at all the night before my father drove me to the airport.

Part 2:

First Taste of Freedom (1979–1980)

CHAPTER SEVEN

Deutschland, My Refuge

I gave all of my brothers and sisters one last hug and jumped into my father's car. I had never been outside the country before, and for some reason I had never even thought about how I would be able to communicate with anyone beyond our borders. I had complete faith in what I was doing and never for a second worried about where I was heading. As we drove closer to the airport, I started to have some anxiety and fear of being discovered and prevented from flying. Soon we arrived, and my father stayed with me as long as he possibly could. I hugged him while thinking that this might be our last time together.

I was very nervous while finding my seat and avoided any conversation with anyone. Soon we started to move on the runway, but for some reason I was still very nervous. Even when the plane was in the air, I was still very nervous. I imagined the plane being returned to the airport just to make me get off. I knew I would not relax until we finally landed. It was hard for me to imagine actually arriving, and so the flight seemed to take forever. I was not even thinking about what I would do when I arrived. I thought only of being free, and I was not going to feel free until I was walking on German land away from the Ba'ath party. A huge wave of relief swept over me as the plane touched the Frankfurt runway. People seated next me must have sensed my relief, because they actually attempted for the first time to open a conversation. I had never carried on a conversation in English before, but it was more natural to me than I had thought it would be. Most of them spoke in English, or at least understood it, though some elected to reply in German.

The passengers began to leave their seats. I had no idea what I was about to face, but I just followed everyone and acted as if I knew exactly what I was doing. Soon we all boarded a transport bus for the main gate. I struggled with my luggage, especially the bag that was full of cassette tapes. At the gate, I assumed that the best way to start would be to find a taxi and go to a hotel to make some phone calls somehow. I hailed a taxi just as a very nice American young lady was getting out, and she handed me a card. I knew at that moment that my mother was watching over me. After the driver finished helping the young lady with her luggage, he asked me, "Where to?" I simply handed him the card, and he knew exactly what to do.

About twenty minutes later, the taxi stopped, and the driver helped me unload my luggage. He pointed at the house that had the address I had given him. I dragged my luggage down the sidewalk toward the front door. Everything was so clean, even better than I had imagined. It turned out to be a family bed-and-breakfast guesthouse. I struggled a little with making conversation, but in the end I decided to stay for the night. I went straight to my room, and even though I was hungry,

I wanted only to lie down and breathe easily after such a long flight full of intense worries. I also wanted to plan for the following day. As I opened my luggage to take out my pajamas, there was an envelope on top of everything. It was from my father. Apparently, he had decided to provide me with the name and phone number of one of our relatives who was living in Germany. I did not know the man, but I trusted that my father knew him and his family. I just sat there crying, realizing how stubborn I had been in my earlier refusal to accept any help when my father was offering it. I quickly understood that I needed any help I could get, as I had no idea how to begin. I had come with only a couple thousand American dollars, and based on the cost of the taxi and the bed-and-breakfast, I knew I would run out of money very soon. I put the name and the phone number aside and decided to try to call the next day. I needed to rest.

After a quick breakfast, I asked for a phone and instructions on how to use it. I was still thinking like I did in Baghdad and did not realize that the German phone system was far superior. I had great difficulty communicating with people who did not know any English. I finally managed to call the number my father had given me, and I was startled when a lady answered. I spoke in English, and much to my pleasant surprise, she was able to speak fluent English also. I told her who I was looking for, and she responded that I had the right number and that the person I was looking for, named Dr. Amir, was her husband. She said her name was Maria and that Dr. Amir had already gone to work. He was a doctor in a children's hospital. She asked me to call again in the evening to connect with Dr. Amir. I was very pleased and thanked her and told her that I would be calling for sure.

The evening couldn't come soon enough. This time Dr. Amir answered, and I immediately switched to Kurdish and explained who I was and how I got his number. Dr. Amir did not question me a lot, as he had been expecting the call. Maybe his father had already called him after he had given the number to my father. He asked me where I was. I responded that I was in Frankfurt. He said he was in Bonn, and I could take the train if I wanted to visit them. I told him that I would for sure plan on that the next day if that was fine by him. He agreed and warned me to be careful when taking the train, as there were many trains every second and I must take the correct one. He took the time to spell out his entire address to me and said he would see me very soon. I was very happy and had a restful evening.

———

The next morning I called a taxi, again struggling with my suitcase full of cassettes. I was shocked to see how big the station was, with many people and trains rushing in every direction. I immediately realized how accurately Dr. Amir had spoken the night before about the train station. As I looked around feeling very confused and unsure, a young lady approached me and asked if I needed help. I am sure that my face lit up with joy when I told her, "Yes!" I showed her the piece of paper with the entire address, as I really could not remember the name "Bonn." She was very kind and gentle and took me where I needed to be. She even helped me purchase the ticket and told me where I needed to get off the train. I realized once again that my mother was not resting behind the veil and was with me.

I did not need to wait long before the right train arrived. I was very thankful to this young lady, my mother, and God for sending me help when I needed it. I got off at the right station, hailed another taxi, and gave him the address to Dr. Amir's house. In only a few minutes, I was dropped off and given directions for walking to the house. I rang the bell. I was greeted by Maria, and she helped me haul my heavy suitcases inside. I was truly blessed that Maria and I could communicate in English without any problems. She made me feel very comfortable. She told me that Amir would arrive in the evening, and we talked about their son and infant daughter. She made some coffee, and we had a great conversation about my goals and my brother in the United States.

Dr. Amir arrived home and welcomed me, and soon we had a nice dinner together. We talked and talked. I told them exactly what my brother had been telling me. I truly did not know the accuracy of it, but I had no reasons to doubt it. I told them that my brother had been in medical school for a few years and that he had a plan in which all I needed to do was make it to a pro-West country. I told them that I did not think that I would be staying very long in West Germany and that I needed to call my brother to see what the next step would be for me. Dr. Amir told me that because I might be leaving soon, he must find out the cost of the call so I could pay him instead of having him wait for the bill. I agreed to that, and he looked up the rate per minute. He told me that it would be very expensive, so I should try to keep it very short. I managed to connect with my brother and told him that I was calling from West Germany. The doctor actually held a timer as we spoke. My brother gave me the phone number of a lady named Mrs. Ruth. He told me to call her and tell her my full story. When I hung up, I immediately paid Dr. Amir.

Apparently Mrs. Ruth was someone who had helped my brother leave Iran, and she was with an American organization called Lutheran Immigration and Refugee Services. The next day, I called her and introduced myself and told her about my goal to make it to the United States. She was very helpful and kind and asked me to come and see her. The problem was that she was in the southern part of Germany, in Stuttgart, and I would have to take a train again. I said I would see her the next day. This time it was a little easier to travel, without having to drag all my suitcases with me. This journey was longer. I was amazed at how beautiful Stuttgart was. To me, it was like heaven on earth. Of course, I hadn't seen many places at that point in my life, but it was the complete opposite of the desert where I had suffered for months.

Mrs. Ruth was very pleasant and inspiring. I told her my story and how I had ended up in Germany. Of course, I told her about my brother and what he had told me regarding the ease of making it to the United States. Mrs. Ruth immediately gave me a reality check. She said that my brother was among a group identified during the Kurdish crisis in Iran and that they had been treated very differently than I would be. He had been taken in a humanitarian crisis. She also said that my brother did not have any idea about the circumstances and the work behind the scenes that had been done to bring him to the United States. She said that it was very clear that I was in a different situation, but one where help would also be required, as she realized the danger to my life if I was forced to return to Iraq. She said that the decision was not hers alone, that she had to consult with others, and that this might take days or weeks. She asked me where I was staying and if I had enough money to last me until they reached the decision. She immediately said that staying with Dr. Amir might be the best solution while I was waiting. She also asked me if I knew of any reasons that they might not agree to that. I responded that I truly did not know of any, but it was up to them, and I would respect their decision. Mrs. Ruth took it upon herself to call Dr. Amir's house with my request and spoke to Maria. Apparently Maria did not have any objections. Ruth concluded by saying that she would be in touch with me as soon as she got an answer from the powers that be. I left the office somewhat puzzled. This was completely different from my expectations, but I really had no choice.

On my return to Bonn, I wondered how it would be staying with Dr. Amir's wife and children all day while he was at the hospital. I was not feeling the greatest about that idea, but there was nothing I could do about it. I was hoping that it was going to be just days before I got to move on to the United States. I told Dr. Amir and his wife about the details that I had learned during my meeting with Mrs. Ruth. They both assured me that it was perfectly alright to stay with them. Dr. Amir jokingly said that once I made it to the United States, I could help him bring his medical practice there. I later learned that he had actually been very serious, as he was not too happy about the many restrictions imposed on the doctors in Germany. I said I would be honored to be able to return the favor and assured him that I would do my best. They gave me a small empty room, the only room they could spare; I believe it was originally their young son's room. There was no bed frame in it, but they provided a mattress and a pillow. I was very happy with the arrangement and fell onto the mattress, very tired. I am not sure that I slept that night, as I had many thoughts going through my mind and went over everything that was said in my meeting with Mrs. Ruth. I began to wonder if I would actually make it to the United States after all. I did not want to be a burden to the family, and I kept trying to think of how I could prevent or at least ease the burden.

I woke early in the morning, but as much as I wanted to leave the small room, I waited until I heard Dr. Amir leaving the house to allow him and his wife to have as normal a morning as they possibly could. Then I opened my door and greeted Maria and their kids. She had prepared a delicious breakfast for me. I asked her about the town and where I could go to kill time without spending much money (one way I had thought of to make myself less of a burden). At that time, when West Germany existed, Bonn was considered its capital. She told me that Bonn's main downtown, or marketplace, was within walking distance. To get there I would need to cross the Rhine River over the Kennedy Bridge. She took me to the balcony and pointed out the bridge and where everything was. I walked slowly to the bridge, making sure that I took mental pictures of my surroundings so I could get back home later. As I crossed, I saw a great deal of activity and shops on the other side. One of the first things that grabbed my attention was an Opel car dealership, which immediately reminded me of my father's first car—an Opel. I spent a lot of time looking in the window and checking out the prices, which were shown in deutsche marks. This was the first time I had ever seen a car dealership. Buying new cars in Iraq was controlled solely by the government, and it was not an easy thing. The next store, which I was very happy to see, was a record shop that sold Arabic vinyl records—everything that I had always wanted when I was back home but couldn't have because they were not available for sale. That is why Iraqi stores that carried cassette copies of all these songs were so popular. Of course, my dilemma now was money and not knowing how much I would need in the unknown time I would be in Germany. I did not buy any records but spent a lot of time looking and dreaming. I soon arrived at the true marketplace where all the bakeries and grocery stores were. The main post office was there, with a large statue of Ludwig van Beethoven in front. I browsed a postcard kiosk and learned that the statue had been dedicated in 1845. I spent all day walking, walking, and walking between stores until it was time to head back home. I had no trouble finding the house, and Dr. Amir was already back at home from his work day. It pleased me to know that I had been away the entire time Dr. Amir was not home. In fact, I resolved to do the same thing every day—leave home early, but preferably before Dr. Amir left, so he would know that I had been away the entire time. I told Dr. Amir and Maria about all the amazing things I had seen, and we had a wonderful dinner together. After dinner, I suggested that I call my brother in the United States to give him an update on everything. Dr. Amir had no objections as long as I was going to pay.

I told my brother everything Mrs. Ruth had told me and that I was waiting to learn what to do next. My brother seemed more interested in knowing about Dr. Amir and his wife, as he had not known them before. He took Dr. Amir's address and phone number and asked me to call him "collect" in the future. I did not even know what collect was, but he explained it to me. I told him that I would keep him updated as soon as I heard anything and ended the call. We all watched a little television and talked before everyone headed to bed. The next morning, as I had planned, I woke up early and left the house before Dr. Amir. That plan made me feel more comfortable, especially since I knew that there was a lot to see and hear at the marketplace anyway. I developed an interest in learning as much German as I could and was always listening to see if I could pick up a German word or two.

In about a week, I received a letter from Mrs. Ruth explaining a logistical problem with my situation that she had learned about after talking to her partners and consulting with the U.S. Embassy. She also said that she would call a few days later and wanted to speak to Maria so I would not misunderstand anything. When she called, she explained to Maria that they would love to help me go to the United States, but I was in West Germany as a visitor who was expected to return to where I came from after a short time. The U.S. Embassy, or any other embassy, could not do anything to take me from Germany to the United States or anywhere else. That would have been a violation of the law. Mrs. Ruth suggested that I visit the U.S. Embassy in Bonn, where they were expecting me and could explain some options. When Maria explained all this to me, I could not contain my tears. I could not believe that all the efforts I had expended all these years might be fruitless after all. Maria did her best to calm me down and kept telling me to be open minded and go to the embassy the next day and see what they had to say. I wanted to know right that minute if there was any hope for me. That night seemed to go on forever.

I arrived at the U.S. Embassy full of hope but also very nervous thinking that there might not be any options. The officer who greeted me appeared to be of a high rank, and he seemed to have done his homework about me and my brother. It did not surprise me to learn that the German government was well aware of how the Kurds in Iraq had been treated. He affirmed that they knew about the killings and that they had no doubt that my life would be in grave danger if I were to return to Iraq. I began to feel comforted knowing they knew that I was not there for economic reasons at all, but rather that it was a life-or-death situation. In the end, he, like Mr. Ruth, told me that for anyone to take me out of West Germany would be entirely illegal. I was listening to this caring officer very closely, and obviously he liked me enough to spend all the time needed to explore my options. However, he actually offered only one real option: to apply for political asylum. I looked at him and told him that I did not know what that was. He told me that I had a good case and that if I eventually did get approved for political asylum, I would be treated like any German and basically could go anywhere I wanted. It would then be legal for the embassy to facilitate taking me to the United States. So I had an option after all. This made me very happy.

The officer was a very realistic person, and he truly wanted to help but needed to give me another reality check before I left his office. He said that the last few years had been a difficult time for all foreign-born in West Germany—Germans were currently under a lot of pressure to reduce that population. Despite my clear case for political asylum, I had to be aware that my application could be refused. He also said the application could take months, even years. He looked at me hard and asked me what would happen to me if the decision was denied, and I was sent back to Iraq. I quickly replied that I would be killed immediately. In fact, I told him that once I was back in Iraq, I might never even make it back to my father's home because the Ba'ath party would be immediately aware that I was up to something. He then took my hands, looked me in the eye as any father would do, and asked, "Are you willing to take that risk?" Without any hesitation, I said yes. I was twenty-four years old, I had no life, and I felt as if I were in prison anyway. Being killed was a far better option than living without freedom, hope, or aspirations. The officer was truly moved by my courage and goals.

The officer sat back and started to plan with me and for me. He told me where to go and gave me detailed instructions on how to start the asylum application process. He said the German government would automatically do the following for all applicants: offer a small monthly living allowance and free schooling in the German language. He explained that applicants were not allowed to work while awaiting the decision. He then told me that when I received these offers, I should refuse them. I did not question the reasoning behind this request, and having full faith that the officer was trying to help me, I agreed. He told me many more things and said he wanted me to stay in touch with the embassy at all times and keep them informed of my progress. He also said that I must keep the contact between us out of German knowledge, as it might unfavorably affect their decision. I promised him that I would do everything he suggested for me, thanked him, and left. I was still hopeful—and also still scared.

On the walk home, I worried about how I would arrange my living situation if the process was truly going to take months or years. I had never planned for something like this. I did not want to burden Dr. Amir and his wife too much, but I knew that I had no choice but to tell them the news, and together we were going to figure out a way to make the asylum happen. I asked Maria for directions to some of the places I needed to go the next day to make the application, and luckily, they were not too far. I was able to relax before Dr. Amir came home, but only a little. Adding weight to my knowledge about the unfortunate position of foreign-born people in Germany, was the situation in Iran. The Iranian revolution had begun several months before my arrival in Germany. The Iranian Shah had been overthrown, and the entire country was in a complete mess. Many Iranians who had escaped were now living in Germany, including Dr. Amir's next-door neighbor. The news reports made it seem as if Iran was making the entire world nervous because of its enormous oil reserves. I was just hoping that Iran's situation would quickly be resolved and would not affect my situation. I began to wonder if I would ever see peace anywhere. It seemed that no matter where I was, there was a situation that made me ill at ease. I was just praying for easier times.

Dr. Amir was eager to hear what I had to say. We lingered over the dinner table talking about everything, especially the unknown length of time for the application and the inability to work or collect any money from the government based on the instructions from the embassy. Dr. Amir declared his support, but I could tell that he definitely had some unspoken reservations. All I could do was thank him and Maria and hope for the best. I called my brother collect and told him everything. He didn't have much to say, and I got the feeling that he was losing interest in me and my well-being after learning that I would have to stay in Germany for an unknown length of time. For the first time, I began to wonder why I even bothered calling him. I had been somewhat expecting that he would ask me how I was planning to pay for everything or at least offer some help, but he avoided the subject completely.

I was purposely avoiding sending any letters to my family in Iraq, as I did not want to bring any attention to them, knowing that all letters were being read and monitored by the Iraqi government. My avoidance was against my desperate desire to communicate with my family to see if anyone had discovered my absence and, of course, to learn anything at all about Nadia. I refrained, assuming that there would be plenty of time for that in the future.

The next day I took the train to Düsseldorf to start my application. It was only about an hour from Bonn. By this time I had become familiar with using the trains in West Germany. They ran like clocks, always on time. The application process was not difficult at all. After I gave them all my vital information and my current address and contacts, they told me I could leave, and they would contact me by phone or mail if they needed any more information. There was nothing more for me to do but go home and start the wait-and-see routine. While doing all of this traveling in Germany, I was feeling a peculiar emotion, in truth, it seemed like almost the same feeling I'd had back in Iraq while trying to avoid being drafted. Although I was not worried in Germany about any checkpoints, I was not sure how long the freedom I was enjoying would last. Because of those feelings I could not truly enjoy the beauty of Germany. But I always hoped the feelings would go away. I went back to my routine of getting up early every day to leave the house before Dr. Amir left and not coming back until I was sure he was home. This was something that I felt good about. Happily, I made a few friends who would meet me at a coffee shop/bar called Aktuell. That helped me to both kill all the hours I needed to be away from home and keep my spending to a minimum.

One day a letter from my brother arrived. I tore it open in excitement, thinking that he had sent me some money to spend and maybe even give to Dr. Amir and his wife for their hospitality. It contained only a short letter and a few pictures of him and his car. He was very proud of it—a 1978 Camaro he had bought brand-new the previous year. The car was very nice, but I was not happy with my brother. What was he thinking? By letting us all know that he was doing fine financially, he might make the doctor and Maria start to wonder why he was not helping me. I just hoped that he would not do anything like that again.

I was still waiting for the results of my asylum application and responding to the official's questions every week. I also responded to all the questions from the U.S. Embassy. However, I was not receiving any clear signs where the application was going exactly. It would soon be 1980, and nothing was clear, except my ongoing struggle.

CHAPTER EIGHT
· ·

The Struggle Goes On

U nfortunately, the news from Iran was now much worse than it had ever been. The world's attention had turned there because many American hostages had just been taken in that country. This news sent a great fear into my being, as I immediately made a negative connection between this world event and my asylum application. I stayed glued to the television for hostage news. I did not understand many German words, but seeing the films was enough to tell me that things were not getting better.

Unfortunately, to add to my total confusion, my brother in the United States kept sending more letters with pictures. Pictures like his large dinner table full of fancy dishes of food when he had some of his friends over. He probably had no ill intentions, wanting only to gain Dr. Amir and his wife as friends, but what he did not realize is that this was making me become even more of a burden, even without any words being said. I could not tell him to stop sending letters and pictures, as I did not want to create any misunderstandings between us before even making it to the United States. Dr. Amir and his wife never said anything, but I could sense their questions about why my brother was not helping me if he could afford such a nice car and home. I started to feel some depression, not from my living conditions, which were great, but from being so much of a burden for such nice people.

I moved into a very sad period where I stayed away from the house as much possible, even allowing Dr. Amir to have an hour or so of peaceful relaxation after he came home from work. I could not stay out too late, of course, because they did expect me to be home for dinner. I also hid in my room whenever I could, just to give Dr. Amir and his wife as much time to themselves as possible. Day after day and night after night, it was the same routine and waiting for good news regarding my asylum application. Every now and then Maria asked me to join her to visit her friends. I truly enjoyed those visits, absorbing many of the traditional German customs and traditions like a sponge. I especially enjoyed the afternoon coffee and *kuchen* (cake). One day I asked Maria why she used certain words with a particular friend of hers. She said that these were formal words, and because her friend was older than she, her friend must initiate the use of informal words before Maria could use them. Maria even made a comment regarding how quickly I picked up on these things and the German language without even having gone to language school. Despite some happy times, I was truly beginning to feel that my being welcome in Dr. Amir's house had long passed. He never said a word, but as they say, actions speak louder than words. His daily interactions with me had changed; I could feel it, but there was nothing I could do. I was very confused and did not know how to behave. I started to go to my room shortly after dinner, complaining that I had a headache. Because of the long evenings in my little room, I started to take sleeping pills to help me sleep. Dr. Amir and Maria did not know that I was not really tired when I headed to my room at six o'clock in the evening. They were not aware that I was taking sleeping pills either.

Soon Christmas of 1979 was upon us, and we celebrated together— just the five of us. I did not see any of their family or friends visiting. I thought it was different, but of course, I was not in a position to even ask why. The same thing happened when we celebrated New Year's Day. It was officially 1980, and I was still waiting for any word regarding my political asylum. One early January evening, I took my usual sleeping pills, but before I had actually gone to my room and closed the door, Dr. Amir made a comment. I don't remember exactly what, but I know it bothered me a lot, and I felt a sudden urge to open up and have an honest conversation with him. I realized that the sleeping pills might take effect soon and wanted to prevent that from happening, so I tried to think of how I could undo them. First I thought of making coffee, but that didn't seem like a good idea. All of sudden I remembered a Christmas gift Dr. Amir had just received, a case of Jim Beam bourbon. I had never drunk whiskey before and thought for sure that if I drank some, it would do the trick. I did not even know how to drink it properly. I took a regular glass, filled it half full, took it to my room, and drank it all. When I was done, I felt ready to talk.

I went back to the living room waiting for the right moment to open the conversation. I sat on the couch as I normally sat and was acting very normal. All of sudden, without warning, I felt my head hit the table in front of me. I remember someone's fingers trying to open my eyes and was aware of some chaos, but I really had no idea what was going on. In the morning, I woke up with a huge headache and was told by Dr. Amir and Maria that I had scared them to the point where they had called an ambulance to take me to the hospital. They had told the rescue person about my situation regarding the wait for political asylum and that I was not a citizen. That person had recommended not taking me to the hospital, because it might hurt my asylum chances. He had determined that I had overdosed on something but that I would be okay. Dr. Amir was very upset with me and he started saying things that were very painful for me to hear. Apparently, I had created a huge scene. I apologized and told them the truth about what I had taken. At that, Dr. Amir became even more upset. He was very late for work, and I was glad when he left and things calmed down.

I walked aimlessly all day wondering what would happen to me. When it was the normal dinnertime, I just kept walking. Finally, when it became dark, I had nowhere to go other than home. I did not have the courage to ring the bell. I did not know what to do. I looked up and saw that it was an easy climb to the balcony. I decided to spend the night there, as I knew they always kept the curtains closed. I sat there for hours in the bitter cold in a state of confusion, not really sleeping, holding my head in my hands. I climbed down in the morning before anyone noticed me and went back to walk the streets. I do not know if Dr. Amir tried to look for me, but that was not on my mind, as I felt I was becoming desperate. I had not even washed my face, and I was very tired.

When evening came, I knew I would have to face reality. Dr. Amir was still very upset with me, and he spared no words. When he finished lecturing me, he told me that they had called a friend, Dr. Adel, who was also a Kurd and who lived in the nearby city of Cologne. Dr. Adel, a single man whom I had met several times, had agreed to let me live with him. I did not know what to say other than thank you. Dr. Amir also told me he had called my brother in the United States. He did not tell me what he had told my brother, only that he had let him know I was moving. I did not ask for the reasons for all this, as I knew the doctor had been looking for an excuse to get rid of me. I think he had given up on me getting my asylum and had assumed that I would be sent back to Iraq. Dr. Adel was already on his way to pick me up. I went to my room and stayed there until I heard him at the door.

Dr. Adel was not very nice to me right from the beginning. I wondered what Dr. Amir had really told him. I kept my silence the entire drive to his house. He showed me where I would sleep and gave me a list of rules that I must not break. He stated emphatically, several times, that I must not use his phone to call my brother—ever. I think he was afraid I would run up a very large phone bill and be sent back to Iraq before he knew what the bill would be. I assured him that I would not call my brother at his house, only at the post office. After all that, he gave me a little money to shop for groceries for dinner the next day. He also gave me a copy of his door key. All of sudden I felt like a maid or a slave, but my response was only, "Thank you." He appeared uninterested in any further conversation and went on about his business. I went to my sleeping place and fell into a dead slumber.

The next day I needed, first of all, to locate the food market. I was very careful not to get lost and traced all my steps. I did not know how to cook, and I was not familiar with anything, so my only option was to get frozen food that required only heating. Once dinner was ready, I went back out to find the post office so I could call my brother and tell him what had happened. I did have enough money with me, and the postman tried the call, but there was no answer. I did not know my brother's schedule or the time difference between Germany and the United States, so I left to try again another day and time.

I started to walk the streets of Cologne. One of the main attractions was a very large cathedral that I was told had survived the war. I walked by it every day, constantly amazed by how tall it was. I definitely had my walking exercise covered. In the evenings, Dr. Adel was the complete opposite of Dr. Amir. He did not want to have any conversations with me other than reminding me not to use his phone. He obviously did not trust me, for whatever reasons. He also voiced his displeasure with my dinner selections, but I never said anything in reply, not wanting to start any arguments.

I finally managed one day to reach my brother on the phone. I was afraid that what Dr. Amir had told him before he made me leave his house might have made my brother worried about me and that he might try to come to Germany to see me. I had been afraid that the reason I hadn't been able to connect with him was that he was on his way. Much to my surprise, he was angry with me. I asked him why. He simply said, "Dr. Amir told me what you did." When I told him the story about the whiskey, he said, "What whiskey?" The doctor had apparently made up a story for him. My brother did not want to disclose exactly what Dr. Amir had told him, but I certainly knew that he was upset.

I was very sad after that conversation and realized why Dr. Adel was treating me as he did. I tried to imagine what story Dr. Amir had told Dr. Adel and my brother to justify kicking me out. But I could not bring myself to blame or be angry at Dr. Amir, as he had hosted me for months. I was very disappointed with my brother and began to wonder if all this effort to join him in America was worth it. I started to think about all I had done for him when I was in Iraq and the little, if anything, he had done for me. All the golden crosses, all the tapes and letters, and now my own brother was giving up on me. I was heartbroken. I went back to my daily routine and made several calls to Dr. Amir and his wife, Maria—just simple calls to say hello and thank them for everything they had done. I wanted them to know that I had no hard feelings at all. I never attempted to visit, and they never extended an invitation. Dr. Adel never offered to go with me anywhere or visit anyone. I was there as a servant to him, no more than that.

Near the end of January 1980, I finally received the letter I had been waiting for. My political asylum, against all odds, had been approved! The government agency instructed me to take several steps toward getting my permanent residency in Germany, a status as close as any foreign-born could come to being a citizen. I immediately called the American Embassy with the great news. They advised me to finish up everything the German government wanted me to do until I received the final document. I promised them I would do that and keep them posted. I also called Maria and Dr. Amir to tell them. I knew that they had given up on me when Dr. Amir had pushed me out of his home, but I fully understood their entire situation. Dr. Adel did not express much of any reaction. I think he was just happy that I was going to leave his house very soon.

―――

By early February, I had completed all required paperwork and received my permanent German residency. The American Embassy, along with Lutheran Services, started the work to get me ready to leave for the United States. Lutheran Services took complete charge of all expenses and airline tickets. I did not even have to think about those things. One of the first questions I was asked was where I would like to go in the United States. The irony was that, though I had spent so many years trying to go to the United States, I had never once thought about where exactly. I was familiar with the names of some states, such as California, Florida, and Texas. As I tried to think of an answer, one of the ladies at Lutheran Services asked me, "Would you like to join your brother in North Dakota?" After the recent events, I was truly not sure if I should, but I did not want to disclose any of that dirty laundry and responded with a yes.

After a couple more days, while the American Embassy was still working on my papers, Lutheran Services gave me the airline schedule from Germany to North Dakota. They also gave me a button to wear during my flights, as there would be people waiting for me from Lutheran Services at every airport stop I would make. It was very comforting to know that I would be taken care of throughout my entire journey. The first flight was from the Cologne/Bonn Airport, located halfway between those two cities, to John F. Kennedy International Airport in New York City.

I called Dr. Amir and Maria to let them know that I would be actually leaving in a matter of days. Maria offered to pick me up and take me to the airport when I knew the exact day. I told her that she did not need to worry and that I would be practicing every day to ride the train from where I lived to the airport to get used to the route and get an exact sense of what time I must board. She wished me well, and I again thanked her and Dr. Amir. I also called my brother to let him know that I would see him in a few weeks.

Within days, I received all final papers from the American Embassy, and I was ready to depart whenever the final arrangements were made by Lutheran Services. They gave me a sheaf of airline tickets with the first one dated February 24, 1980, and going all the way from Germany to North Dakota. They instructed me where on my clothes to wear my button, to identify me to the people who would be waiting for me at each stop along the way to North Dakota. On top of all that help, they gave me several hundred dollars in spending money.

Dr. Adel never offered any advice or a ride to the airport, and I was fine with that. On the twenty-fourth of February, I woke up early, even though I did not need to leave until the afternoon. I dressed and zipped up my luggage, which was already packed and ready to go. As the time came closer, I took all of my luggage to the sidewalk and locked Dr. Adel's house for the last time. I dropped the key into his secure mailbox, and that was the end of my stay with Dr. Adel. I got to the bus station a few minutes before the bus to the airport was scheduled to arrive. I had learned that the buses were very dependable. At the airport, I called Maria one last time from a phone booth just to say goodbye. I cried for a long time. I was truly sorry that after all they had done for me it had to end the way it did simply because they grew tired of my long visit. I knew deep down if they had known that I was leaving soon, none of that would have happened.

When I arrived at the airport, I went to the correct gate wearing my button and was greeted by a very nice lady who told me that someone else would be waiting for me at the designated time in New York. She gave me a few more last-minute instructions while making sure I boarded the plane. Then she wished me good luck.

Part 3:

Realizing Mother's Dream (1980–1985)

CHAPTER NINE
· ·

The Beginning of the Dream

I t was a long flight, but it did not seem long. My mind was very busy processing everything I had gone through, including the lack of support from my own brother. When I thought about joining him, my emotions were all over the map, but I decided to open a new page. That new page would begin by going beyond the moment I caught on to the fact that he had been ignoring me until he realized that I was the only one sending him gifts and letters from Iraq.

Most of my fellow passengers were asleep, but my mind would not stop turning. Finally, we touched down at Kennedy. I made sure before I left the airplane that my button was displayed in the proper location.

As soon as I walked into the waiting area, a lady introduced herself to me as being from Lutheran Services. She welcomed me to the United States and told me that she would take me to a nearby hotel. She also told me to expect someone in the morning to pick me up from the hotel and take me to another airport where I would board a plane to a state called Minnesota. I was very tired. I faintly remember stopping for a bite to eat before falling into a very deep sleep.

In the morning, the second Lutheran Services lady made sure I was boarding the airplane to Minnesota before she left. I felt completely taken care of thanks to that organization. I have no idea how I would have managed without them. I am forever grateful. The lady told me that someone else would be waiting for me in Minnesota, so I did not need to worry at all, and I never did. The flight was very uneventful. The third Lutheran Services lady, in Minneapolis, told me that there was a two-hour layover before my final flight to Minot, North Dakota. We spent the two hours talking, and she asked me about my journey. She also told me that there would not be anyone from Lutheran Services waiting for me in Minot, because my brother had been informed of my arrival and would be waiting for me. I was feeling eager to see him again and eager to see how it was going to go.

Again, the kind Lutheran Services lady made sure I boarded the right plane. In no time at all, we were descending to the Minot airport. I could not help but look down. All I saw was the whiteness of snow. The houses seemed miles apart. Where, exactly, was I going? This picture was so different from the busy streets of Germany. I reminded myself to reserve judgment until I got to see my brother and where he lived. Only a few other people got off with me. It was a very small airport, and I spotted my brother right away. He was with a few of his friends, and they were all waving at me. I greeted them. They were all Kurdish people who had arrived in Minot around the same time as my brother. He immediately suggested that we all go to Country Kitchen for coffee and lunch. It turned out that Country Kitchen was their daily hangout place.

The airport was north of Minot, but the whole city was no more than five or six miles wide. My brother led me to his 1978 Camaro, and all of his friends headed to their own cars. At Country Kitchen, we all gathered around a big table. Everyone was very friendly, and they all wanted to hear about my experiences in Germany. I found out that my brother was, unfortunately, the only one among his entire group of friends who was going to college. The others were all just working to provide for their families. I say "unfortunately" because I had wanted to be among people that I could use as role models. But I immediately told myself that I had enough drive on my own, and nothing would stop me from achieving my goals. Only one out of the entire group of friends used to live in Baghdad like we had. The rest had always lived in northern Iraq and had lived through the war between the Kurds and Arabs.

We spent almost two hours at Country Kitchen. My brother then said he had to go home, as he had to go to work. "Work?" I asked. He replied yes, that he worked from evening until morning at the Air Force hospital, and that is how he got to go to college in the morning. I was very surprised but agreed, and off to his home we went. His apartment was only a couple of miles away. He helped me unload my suitcases. I was shocked speechless to see how small it was—only two small rooms. One was the entry/living room/kitchen combined, and the other was his small bedroom with a tiny bathroom inside. He said I should take his bedroom, and I responded, "No way." I was not there to inconvenience anyone. I had learned my lessons from my experience in Germany. He agreed and explained that the couch in his living room was a sofa sleeper, and I could open it up after he left. I said that would be fine for me for now. After the quick tour of the apartment, it was time for him to go to work. I did not ask him, but I did wonder why he could not even take a night off from work to spend with his own brother. This bothered me a great deal. Once I opened the sleeper sofa, there was no room to move around. Those nice pictures he had sent did not reflect the reality he was living at all. Oh, how I wished he had not sent them. I am sure they confused Dr. Amir and his wife.

Within an hour or so the phone rang, and at first I thought it must have been my brother checking on my well-being. But it was a cousin of ours who I had not seen or talked to in years. His name was Tony. He said he was calling at that time because he knew my brother was at work. I asked him why he had waited for my brother to leave. He said it was a long story and soon I would understand for myself. I said, "Okay. Well, where are you?"

He said he was in a city called Minnetonka, Minnesota. Minnesota was the next state over, and Minnetonka was five hundred miles away from Minot. Tony said he had lived in Minot for a little bit and had finally had it with my brother. After he moved away, he was much happier. Apparently, Tony had learned from the other Kurdish friends about my arrival. He also said that he would have come to welcome me, but he did not want to be near my brother. He promised to stay in touch and would come and visit me when I had my own apartment.

The phone call disturbed me a little, but because I had no reason to stay up and was very tired also, I attempted to sleep. That was difficult, as the couch was very old and I felt like I was sleeping on bare springs. I must have finally fallen asleep, because I woke with a start in the early morning when my brother opened the door, and it hit the couch. That alone describes how small his place was.

Of course, I immediately got up and folded the couch up so my brother could come in. He took his shower, made a quick breakfast for both of us, and immediately left to go to college. Here I was in this tiny room by myself again with nothing to do and nowhere to go. I looked out of the only window and saw the snow on the ground. I wondered how people managed to go about their business. I had never had to deal with snow before. My brother had an old console TV that got a few channels, but it did not interest me at all. He did not have a cassette player, so I could not play any of my music that I was longing to hear. I spent the day just looking at my many cassettes and imagining actually getting to play, listen and enjoy them again.

The morning dragged by, and I was beginning to wonder when I would get a chance to sit down and talk with my brother and make plans for what to do next with my life. I was very anxious and did not want to waste any time. Shortly after noon, my brother came home and said he was tired, which I could imagine he was. He told me that he had to get some sleep before going to work. His bedroom was divided from the living room by just a curtain. As soon as he went to sleep, I could not even move around, because I did not want to wake him up. I was very disappointed but did not have anyone to voice that to. I sat quietly until about four in the afternoon when he woke to get ready to go to work. As before, he took his shower and then made something for us to eat. I was very hungry, as I had not eaten since the morning. During the meal, I asked him when he would finish his medical school. He was very evasive in his reply and just said he had many years to go. I was wondering how many years it took to graduate from medical school. At least I thought that was what he had told me he was doing when I was still in Iraq. He then rushed off to work. I spent the evening wondering if I had made a major mistake when I decided to come to Minot instead of a bigger city in some other state. I had nothing to do other than look out the window and every now and then watch a car going by. I opened up the old sleeper sofa and tried to sleep. The next morning started early with the same door slam on the couch announcing my brother's arrival. I quickly got up and wanted to put the couch away so he could make the breakfast and go to college. I was pleasantly surprised when he told me that he was going to sleep, and I could go back to sleep too if I wanted, as it was the weekend and he did not have college. I was not tired, but I knew I had to be very quiet, so I went back to bed. Just before noon, I heard him waking up, so I did the same. After his shower, he made breakfast for both of us, and for the first time, we had a chance to talk. I asked him many questions that apparently were not good questions to ask, and I felt that I must have touched on some painful issues. One of those questions was, "Do you have a girlfriend?" I assumed everyone had a girlfriend or a boyfriend based on what I had learned.

"Girlfriend?" he replied. *"Oh, you are going to find out how easy that is."* Based on the tone of his voice, I took that as a "no." I also took it that he must have stories to tell but was electing to wait for another time to tell them.

The other difficult question was, "What do I need to do to start college?" After all, I was eight years behind, and I did not want to waste any more time.

My brother's response was very surprising: "You need to wait at least a year before you think of college."

My jaw dropped to the floor. "A year? Why do you say that?"

He replied, "You need to get your English speaking much better than what it is now."

"Well, I can start by taking mathematics and physics classes until my English gets better," I replied. Normally, those classes do not require full fluency in English, and I was very strong in mathematics and physics. My brother was not convinced and kept telling me that he had a lot of trouble with math classes. I did not want to remind him that he had always been weak in math and science. I decided to table that subject for a while and asked him what I needed to do to look for work.

His response was somewhat strange. He said, "Well, you need to get a Social Security card first. And not having a car will make it difficult." I responded by saying that I expected him to help by taking me places until I got a car. He did not seem very interested, as though he truly did not want me to get started with my life.

My brother said that normally, and especially on weekends, he got together with his friends at Country Kitchen. I was happy about that and responded that it would be great to see them again. Then he told me how he truly felt about these friends and went into some negative detail about each one. His comments were not very flattering. I think he was expecting me to follow along with what he was doing or feeling toward each one. I simply responded that I would do my best just to avoid irritating him. Because he wasn't planning to leave for a few hours, I told him that I would like to use the time to write to a few friends back in Germany. I also wanted to write to our family to tell them that we were together in the United States and to ask Layla if she had heard or seen anything of Nadia. I had been thinking about Nadia a lot and was hoping that someday soon I could have more independent and open communication with her. I asked my brother for some paper and a couple of envelopes. He found them and angrily handed them to me, but I could immediately feel that he was not very happy.

The Germans were the friends I used to see every now and then at the Aktuell cafe, and I wrote something quickly. I just wanted to stay in touch. With the second letter, I wanted to take my time and include a special message to each brother and sister. While I was writing, my brother was doing his daily routine, and at some point he started to make remarks. It seemed like they were addressed to me, but he was not talking to me directly. He went outside and came back in several times. I asked him if there was anything wrong. He angrily replied that his apartment was rented from an elderly couple who lived next door, and he normally liked to shovel the snow out of the entire driveway. I said, "Well, that is very nice of you, but what is the problem then?"

He said something about how he expected me to help him by doing that shoveling. I was taken aback and replied, "Brother, I just arrived, and I have no idea what you do or what anyone else does. I do not even have the right clothes or shoes for this weather like you do. I just came from Germany, and I am dressed as I was in the streets of Germany." He switched the topic quickly by saying that he needed to buy me some proper clothes. I did not expect that kind of reaction from my brother that soon and wondered what the real issue with him was. After he finished shoveling the driveway, he came inside and reminded me to get ready to go meet his friends. I put the letters to the side and took my shower. As we drove, I noticed how careful he was with his car. He did not want me to touch anything. He gave me a long lesson about his great cassette deck and how much he had paid for it. To me, it was just a car; of course, I did not dare tell him that.

Being at Country Kitchen with my brother's friends was more relaxing that day than the first time, and we all had a chance to get to know each other better. They all appeared to be very genuine and nice. My brother was acting like they were his friends, but I knew that behind their backs he had said very bad things about them. I started to wonder what exactly his problem was. Because I did not have a job, car, or my own place, I kept my opinion to myself, not wishing to start any arguments. One of the friends was going to high school. He claimed that he had graduated from high school in Iraq, but because he did not have a copy of his diploma, he could not get into any college, although he was allowed to attend high school as a senior. His name was Ram, and he was married to a nice lady who had escaped from Iraq with him. I particularly liked Ram, a lot. He had many hobbies and loved playing guitar. That was something I had always wanted to learn but never had the chance. Ram was also into cars and fixing them. He was a truly well-rounded person, and I wanted to get to know him better. For some reason, my brother particularly did *not* like Ram, and that was my main source of confusion.

As we all talked, I noticed that when the friends asked me about Germany and my life there, my brother was eager to show that he knew more of the German language than I did. I had never even mentioned my German-speaking abilities, but my brother seemed to find it important to make it clear to everyone that he knew more. Of course, I knew that was not the case at all, but I let him take the subject as far as he wanted to. I immediately sensed that my brother had a need to present himself as the best in everything. I was not interested in competing about something that was of no value to me. Deep down, I cared only about starting college. I was more than ready to make up for lost time. Soon everyone was ready to go home. As we drove away, my brother again started putting down everyone we had been sitting with, especially Ram. I sensed some jealousy against Ram from my brother.

At that moment, I realized that I had a big problem at hand. I had never known my brother to be so critical of everyone and use the mechanism of lowering everyone as a way of lifting himself. I did not like that type of attitude and wondered what he might be saying about me to others. Back at the tiny apartment, I realized that this was all the excitement we were going to have that weekend. And soon, I would be jailed there again while my brother went to college and work. I had only one thing I needed to do—finish writing my letter to my brothers and sisters. I did not want to do that while my brother was home. We spent the rest of the weekend at the laundromat and, of course, at the car wash with his blue Camaro.

The following week was no different than the first week. He came home early from work, made a quick breakfast, and left me alone all day with nothing to do. On Monday, I finished writing my letters. Now all I needed to do was to ask him to take me to the post office to mail them, but I knew he wouldn't have time for that until the following weekend, so I didn't even ask. The thing I remember most vividly about that week, is the most overwhelming feeling of being trapped. I was trapped in the land of the free, a land which I had tried so hard to come to.

My brother was not in any hurry to help me break free. He was treating me like a young boy who did not know anything. I had no one to talk to or discuss any options with. Deep down, I knew at the right moment I would open up to tell him how I felt. On Saturday he took me to the post office, but I could tell by the way he talked and acted that he was upset. I was not sure why he was so upset, other than our having to be there before 10 a.m., as it closed early on Saturdays. He had a post office box and had to go there sometimes anyway. He picked up his mail and walked with me to the postman's window but stayed behind me. I felt very awkward, as I had been expecting him to pay for the nominal postage. Instead, I was forced to tap into some of the money I had left over from my time in Germany. I had to give the postman a hundred-dollar bill for less than a dollar of postage. I think I even made the postman upset, based on how he gave me the change. I put the money in my pocket and silently went to the car, where my brother was already waiting for me. I thanked him, but all I was really thinking was how much I had done for him when I was back in Iraq. It was clear that he had no appreciation for that, and I felt truly unwelcome.

———

During the weekend, the Kurdish group got together as usual at Country Kitchen. It was becoming obvious that the excitement around my brother and his friends did not go beyond sitting together at Country Kitchen drinking coffee. Every now and then they would make a comment or two about other customers. When my brother went to the restroom, I took the opportunity to ask Ram to call me sometime at my brother's place. Ram immediately knew that there was something wrong, and he promised to call me. My brother and his friends were not the only ones who sat around like that at Country Kitchen. I began to see that many of the faces were pretty much the same faces, no matter what day it was. Country Kitchen did not seem to mind at all.

I clearly saw another week coming with nothing to do, but I was determined to change my situation very quickly. Ram called me at home the following week at a time he knew my brother would not be home. I explained that without a car or a job, I was feeling like I was in prison and that my brother had not made any effort to help me. I told him I needed to start getting out and getting acclimated to people and living in this place in order to go to college. He understood my frustrations, and apparently he knew a thing or two about my brother's attitude. He promised that he would talk to the principal of his high school to see if I could be allowed to accompany him to class. I asked

Ram how I would get there. He said that if the principal was okay with the idea, he would pick me up in the morning and bring me back home after school. I very much liked this plan, but we were both worried about how my brother would react. We decided not to say anything until we learned the principal's decision.

A week later, Ram called me to give me the good news that the principal had no objections or reservations. Not only could I go with him to high school, but I could attend his classes and be anywhere the students were. I liked that a lot, but now I needed to get my brother's agreement. I could not think of any reasons why he would dislike the idea, but based on what I had seen, there were no guarantees. His general negative demeanor and comments about getting our two daily meals had all led me to believe that he was not happy to have me with him. Out of respect for his schedule, I elected to wait for the weekend to tell him. Rather than agreeing or disagreeing, he asked whose idea it was. I said that the topic had just come up casually, and it was not anyone's idea in particular. Of course, I could not tell him that I had asked Ram to help me. I was not sure if he was satisfied with my answers, but in the end, I could see he felt like he had no choice but to say yes. I could tell that he was trying to hide his anger, but he was very unsuccessful.

I waited for the Country Kitchen get-together to tell Ram that my brother had agreed. Everyone was very excited about the news except my brother. Ram and I decided that he would pick me up on Monday morning and that I would be prompt. The rest of the weekend did not go very smoothly. His actions proved that my brother was still upset, but with no car, job, or place of my own, I was forced to accept the situation. I did feel a strong urge to remind him of everything I had done for him back in Iraq but kept silent. I figured that if he, an adult, could show no appreciation, talking to him would not make any difference and might open us up for an argument.

On Monday morning I awakened full of energy. I had a couple of hours to spare, so I gave my brother all the room he needed to take his shower and make breakfast. He did not say even a word about my upcoming day. No words of advice, not even a "have fun."

I eagerly watched out the window for Ram's arrival. He was on time, and I climbed into his cute little BMW. He was very pleasant, as always, and asked me if I was having any problems with my brother. I told him no but also explained that I did know my brother was not happy. A few minutes later, we arrived at the front gate of the "Magic City Senior High School." Ram took me to the principal just to say hello. The principal was very charming and respectful as he welcomed me to his campus. I stayed with Ram the entire day. I attended each and every class and shadowed him during all breaks and the lunch period. Many of the students were very curious about me, and a lot of young girls wanted to join us for lunch. I was overjoyed to have a chance to meet and communicate with people instead of being locked in a small room with nothing to do. I had a great day. Shortly after I got back to my brother's place, he returned from class and, as expected, did not bother to ask me about how my day had gone. He just went to his room to get a few hours of sleep. He had brought me a postcard from my friends at the Aktuell. I was happy to read it and planned to respond in the next day or two. I knew that I had to be very quiet and not do anything that might wake him up.

After he left for work, my mind began to turn to getting a job and a car to gain my freedom. I did not know how to go about any of that, but at least I had started the thought process. I went to bed knowing that I'd had a great day and that I was capable of getting along with the students in the high school, despite being several years older. Realizing that age was not going to be an issue was very comforting. Ram picked me up each day that week. He was very accommodating and always on time, and he never made me feel he was doing me a big favor, even though he truly was. How different Ram, a total stranger, was from my own brother, whom I had done so much for. What if I had not even done those things? How would he have treated me then?

CHAPTER TEN
. . . .

Commitment without Commitment

Time was moving somewhat slowly for me, but March 1980 eventually arrived. I knew my brother was against my trying to enroll in college that September, but I felt that the conversation was not over. I was tired of waiting for my brother's approval and disapproval.

My brother surprised me by telling me we were moving to a bigger apartment. He told me that he expected me to pay half the rent, as he knew I had about $1,500 left in my pocket. Of course, I agreed because it was the fair thing to do, but I asked him to help me find a job to make money and maybe also get a car. He had made the decision to move without any input from me. I had no choice but to go along. The apartment was closer to his college and work. He did not have many possessions, so the move was very smooth. The new place was nice. It had a small living room, separate kitchen, and two bedrooms. One was very small, and the other was regular sized. Of course, I do not have to say which room became mine. But I did not have many things besides my cassettes, so it was fine. Many young ladies at the high school had started to pay attention to me. I just assumed it was because I was different looking and they were curious. I was not thinking about finding a girlfriend, as I still had my heart with Nadia back in Iraq. My full intention was to keep trying to open communication with her and look for chances to bring her to the United States, though I had still heard nothing. One day, an attractive girl surprised me by asking me what I was going to do for Easter. I had no idea if my brother was planning anything, so I said, "I am not sure, but probably nothing. Why do you ask?"

She said that her father was going to take her and her brother to a nice restaurant, and she would love to have me join them. I told her that I would let her know by the next day. When I asked my brother if he had any plans for Easter, he became very defensive. "What do you expect?" he shouted angrily. He said that he was busy with work and college, not to mention taking care of me, so he had no time or plans for anything else. I calmly told him that I was not expecting anything, and it was nothing more than a question. I then told him about my invitation. Rather than being happy for me, he warned me to be careful. I guessed that he had stories involving his relationships with girls that he had never told me. I hoped that someday, once I had a job and some freedom, he would open up to me. I simply responded that I would be very careful and that he had nothing to worry about.

The next day, the blonde, beautiful young lady, Cheryl, was waiting for me. I told her that we could get together, which made her happy. Then I told her that there was a problem—I did not have a car and did not know the city at all to walk anywhere. Cheryl was very supportive and told me not to worry, because they would pick me up. I did not know the exact address of our apartment but was able to give her directions relative to the college nearby. We agreed on a time for Easter Sunday, April 6, 1980.

On the Thursday before, my brother announced that he was inviting a few of his friends over for lunch on Easter. I was very surprised and confused, as he had just told me that he had no plans. What changed his mind? I did not dare to ask, but I reminded him that I had been invited elsewhere. He pretended to not know about my date and was very upset. I told him I was sure that Cheryl would bring me back home right afterward. He angrily stormed out of the room. I felt trapped. I had not come all this way and made all those sacrifices only to be treated like a child.

On Easter Sunday morning I was ready and stayed out of the living room to avoid any problems. When the doorbell rang, my brother answered it. He yelled some very unkind words to me in Kurdish as to what to do with the person at the door. I froze in anger for a moment but soon collected myself and went to the door to greet Cheryl, and we went to the car. Her father was driving. I said hello to him and her brother and sat quietly until we arrived at a fancy, crowded restaurant. Cheryl's father treated me very warmly and asked me a lot of questions. We all came to know one another, and I felt very fortunate to be liked so quickly by Cheryl and her family. After lunch, they asked me if I wanted to go with them to their home. I truly wanted to but remembered how upset my brother had been. I apologized and told them maybe next time. They understood and kindly took me back home. A few familiar friends were there, as well as another lady whom I had not met before. She was a nice lady and was apparently an officer at the Air Force hospital where my brother worked in the housekeeping department. Everyone was having a great time, and I apologized for not joining them for the meal.

After a few hours, they all left, and I asked my brother about the lady. I knew he was not telling me the whole story, so I kept on asking.

He finally admitted that he liked her but did not know how to tell her his feelings. I simply said, "If you like her, why don't you just tell her how you feel?"

He dismissed me with a wave of his arm and said, "You don't know anything about these things; you just came to this country."

I simply said, "If that is what you think, then you are right." I knew that these types of things were universal, and I thought I knew a thing or two about that, but whatever. I knew my brother was still thinking as we did back in Iraq, and apparently living in the United States for so many years had not changed him much.

He ended the conversation by saying, "I think I will just send her a letter." I could not believe my ears but kept my feelings to myself.

In the following days, I talked to Cheryl many times at school. It was clear to me that she was very interested in a relationship, but I explained to her that I had a girlfriend back home in Iraq and that I had only one hope: doing everything in my power to reconnect with her. I felt very bad for rejecting Cheryl, as she was very attractive, but I kept true to myself. Despite the thousands of miles, I was not going to entertain the idea of having a relationship with anyone else unless Nadia married someone else. Nadia and I had never had any commitment to each other, not even verbally, but my commitment did not require any promises or papers. I constantly blamed myself for not having kept even a few pictures of Nadia. I wrote another letter to my family, as I was beginning to worry for the lack of any response from them.

During the remaining high school days, I attended all of Ram's classes with him in a high-energy mode. I was asked many times in various classes to talk about Iraqi culture. I found out that I had no problem standing up in the classroom and talking about whatever was asked. Lacking full command of the English language was never a reason to be shy or nervous. The way I looked at the situation, right from the beginning, was that I knew and could communicate in many languages. I was always proud of who I was and was not about to let anyone ignorant of that make me feel bad about my accent.

Another young lady who was in many of my classes grabbed my attention. I knew I could not have a relationship with her because of Nadia, but that did not mean I could not like this young lady. Her name was Laura, and she was from a very small town about thirty miles south of Minot called Max. I did not understand, and still don't to this day, why I did not give Cheryl a chance, in spite of her interest in me, but I did begin to pay attention to Laura. I tried hard to be around Laura, and I asked her if we could have lunch together someday.

Laura was caught between a rock and a hard place. She didn't say no but never said yes either. One day near the end of the school year, she finally admitted that she had a boyfriend but added that the relationship had ended. She then agreed to meet me for lunch. The year was ending, so I did not have a lot of room to maneuver. A day before our date, Laura came to sit with me while I was in the cafeteria alone. She told me that she was sorry, but she could not keep the date after all because her boyfriend was back in her life. I did not move from my chair for hours. I just sat there looking down and feeling very sad.

Soon the high school year ended, and I was determined not to go back to just sitting at home and waiting for my brother to come home or wake up. I knew I had a purpose, and I needed to begin realizing it. I had overcome too many impossible obstacles to just settle for what my brother decided for me. I started making demands on my brother to help me find a job. I only asked him to drive me to different places so I could fill out applications. He finally started to look in the newspapers for me and agreed to take me around. I had a job at last, in a big dry cleaning shop in Minot. The hours were very early in the morning until the afternoon. At first, my brother agreed to drive me to and from work, but after a few days, his acquiescence started to fade.

The distance to work was not too far at all by car, but it was a bit harder on foot, as I had to walk on the highway and cross a small bridge. It was very clear that my brother had a problem with me, and apparently, he had become very accustomed to being alone. I did not make a big deal out of it when he told me that he could not take me to work; I just left early and walked instead.

I must mention and honor the role Mr. Charles Hoffman played at this time. Mr. Hoffman had taught science at Minot State University and retired a few years before my arrival. He was still full of energy and was always willing to help others. He had helped my brother and all his Kurdish friends when they arrived in Minot a few years earlier, especially by sitting down with them for hours in order to teach them the proper use of the English language. He did all of that without expecting to get paid for his services, and he was not. I found him very inspiring. I never saw him using a car for transportation. He preferred to walk, no matter how far he needed to go and what time of year it was. He was the one who came to welcome me to Minot when he heard about my arrival. He also offered to help me with my English.

I am sad that I did not spend as much time as I should have with him. Mr. Hoffman was married to an Englishwoman named Ruth, and they had several children. I found her to be the complete opposite of her husband, but this was a very superficial impression, as I did not really know her. Maybe she was just irritated by all the time he spent away from home helping others. In June 1994, after I had moved out to Minnesota, Mr. Hoffman passed away, and I am sorry to say I could not attend his funeral. Minot State University named an auditorium after him, which was more than fitting.

In the beginning of this book, I promised that I would talk more about my last name, Haaland, at the appropriate time. I knew that in the United States people had last names and it was a common thing, but in Iraq, we did not use last names. People were called by their first name followed by their father's first name. If more identification was required, then they used the grandfather's first name. The idea of adopting a last name was born for me while I was in Germany. I had my mind set on Janssen because of my love for David Janssen from *The Fugitive* television series, of which I never had a chance to see the ending because of the 1967 Israeli-Arab war.

When I arrived in Minot, I realized that my brother had already thought of the same thing and had adopted the name Haaland many years earlier. When I asked him about its origin, he introduced me to Mr. Olaf Haaland, his wife, and one of his daughters named Joan. My brother and Joan were very good friends. Joan Haaland played music like no one I knew and was looking to perform at a professional level.

Mr. Haaland had been the sheriff of Ward County for many years, 1957 through 1979, retiring just before my arrival in 1980. He had extended a helping hand to my brother and all of his Kurdish friends. In appreciation to Mr. Haaland and to honor everything he had done, my brother asked Mr. Haaland if he could possibly adopt his last name. Mr. Haaland was flattered, and so he agreed. My brother went to court for the legal name adoption. I was still thinking of Janssen, but after my brother explained what he had done, I did not think it was a good idea to adopt anything other than Haaland. I then asked my brother to get Mr. Haaland's permission for me to adopt his last name too, which he granted. My brother helped me with the application, and I paid the fees and started the process. Several months later, I went to the hearing, was told of my responsibilities, and was issued the legal certificate. I kept my father's name as my middle name. I was not trying at all to lose my identity and was still proud of my heritage and ancestors. I knew only that having a last name would make it easier for me and my children if I decided to get married.

Because the circumstances of my arrival in the United States were much different from those of my brother, I did not have the pleasure of being with Mr. Haaland as much I might have wished. However, I always had high regard for him and gratitude for everything he did for my brother and all of his friends. I did meet with Joan Haaland many times. Mr. Haaland and his wife, Doroles, moved to Oregon shortly after I adopted his last name in 1981.

Mr. Haaland, like many people in the area, liked ice fishing during the long winter months. Most lakes in that area freeze over to the point where trucks, snowmobiles, or all-terrain vehicles (ATVs) can be driven onto them pulling ice houses, which are no more than trailers that are completely enclosed. Holes for fishing are drilled through the ice inside these houses, and the houses are left there until the ice is no longer safe. Some have everything a man needs, like television, satellite hookup, and a heater.

Mr. Haaland's story does not have a happy ending. In January 1992, he came back to Minot, as he had done many times since he moved to Oregon, to be with friends and family, especially to celebrate Christmas and his birthday on January 3. His love for ice fishing was still alive, and he and his younger brother, Martin, went out on Garrison Lake in a celebratory mood. A few days later, on Tuesday, January 7, Olaf and Martin decided to go out again. When neither one of them returned home as expected that evening, their families reported them missing to the authorities at 7:15 the next morning. The authorities immediately conducted massive ground and aerial searches. At 1:45 that afternoon, their truck was spotted submerged in the icy waters. Apparently, as Olaf and Martin were driving around on the ice looking for a good fishing spot, they had encountered a weak area that could not handle the weight of the truck. They found Olaf first, and Martin soon after. Mr. Haaland was seventy-five and Martin was only seventy. May you rest in peace, Olaf and Martin. Many years later, Doroles Haaland moved back to Minot to be among friends and family. Joan also moved to Oregon after graduating, and she is still living there with her husband and their beautiful children. I am grateful to say that I am still in touch with both of them.

Mr. Olaf Haaland

In June 1980, I was working at the dry cleaner's and starting to earn some money. Minimum wage was fine with me, as I did not have many expenses besides my half of the rent. Cars parked on the street with for sale signs started to get my attention, and I asked my brother to help me negotiate a purchase. Again, and for whatever reasons, he was not very cooperative. I then decided to ask our friend, Ram, for help, as he knew a lot more about cars than my brother. Of course, I also had to apply for a driver's license. Ram assisted me with my application. The written portion of the test was a little challenging, but I passed. Next would be the real test—behind the wheel. Ram and I found a nice car at a reasonable price, but my brother was not in agreement. I decided to ignore his negativity and took out a bank loan and bought the car anyway, even before passing the behind-the-wheel exam. It was a gray, mid-seventies Pontiac Firebird with manual transmission.

My brother did agree to pick me up from work and take me to the test site using his car. I thought the test would be easier because his car had an automatic transmission. The morning of the exam, I reminded him that he needed to pick me up after I got off work. He somehow found a way to turn my friendly reminder into a huge argument and shouting match. I stormed out, telling him angrily to just forget about helping me. Because I was now late for work, I had no choice but to take my own car to work so I would have it later for the test. Of course, I still could not drive it legally without the company of another driver. I decided to break the rules, and while I was driving, I tried to think of how I could avoid the problems that might arise when I arrived alone for the test. At the test center, I saw many other test-takers arriving, each accompanied by a person who then left the car and left them alone. Soon my passenger door was opened and an officer sat down and asked me to drive away. I felt better when I realized he had not even noticed whether I had company. I performed all turns and parking flawlessly. At the words, "Congratulations, you passed," I finally relaxed. I finished up the paperwork, paid the fees, and drove myself home—legally!

At home, I wanted my brother to wake up so I could tell him the great news in a positive way. I did not want to revisit anything about our morning, figuring I needed to spend my energy wisely. But instead of waiting for him, I decided to break my normal routine of sitting around the apartment and drove to Country Kitchen to see if any of our friends were there. As expected, some of them were.

I truly felt a sense of freedom for the first time. With my new mobility, I started actively looking for a different job. The dry cleaning job was very dirty work. I also needed more money to maintain the car and wanted a part-time night job so I could attend college during the day in the fall, just a few months away. Soon I was hired as a cook trainee at a restaurant in the North Hill Bowl, located just a few miles north of our apartment. The job was challenging and fun at the same time as I learned to cook things in sequence in order to finish each part of the order at the same time. My coworkers and I had great times laughing and joking in the kitchen. This was definitely different from dry cleaning.

The crew included a senior cook, a couple of waitresses, and another fine lady, the baker, whom I truly enjoyed. She was like a mother to all of us and was there only a few nights a week. Denise, one of the waitresses, was only about sixteen or seventeen. She would laugh and enjoy listening to me talk and make comments about my accent. Sometimes the baker would say to me when she saw Denise, "Dave, your girlfriend is here." This really surprised me, and it also made me very embarrassed. The fact was, I did like Denise a lot, but I had the same issues as before. I still had not heard anything from my family about Nadia. Denise was also a lot younger than me, and I was not sure if that was even acceptable. So, though I kept my feelings about Denise to myself, apparently the baker was wise enough to see right through all that.

During this time, and against my brother's objections, I was checking out Minot State University and speaking with advisers and counselors. I collected stacks of information about the entire process, especially financial aid and how to apply. I took care to keep all talk of college away from my brother. Most of my free time was spent reading about all my options and filling out forms and financial aid applications. This was not easy, because I did not have full command of English or know the proper way of doing things. But I was determined, and speed was not my concern as long as I was moving forward.

After comparing the numbers for college expenses and what I was going to receive in financial aid and student loans, I knew that working two or three nights a week for a few hours was not going to be enough. I needed to either supplement my current job or find a full-time job. I was not competing for high-paying jobs. In fact, most of the jobs I was applying for paid around three dollars per hour. My main concern was the work hours, as college was going to be my number-one priority. After a few weeks, I found a job that was exactly what I was looking for, at the large, multistory Medical Arts Clinic in Minot. It was five nights a week starting at five o'clock and going until ten or later, depending on what I had to do. There was some Saturday morning work, too, which was great. After the clinic closed for the day, I was required to clean, collect the garbage, and mop and occasionally wax the floors. Of course, I had to leave the North Hill Bowl, which also meant no longer seeing Denise at work. I was definitely starting to see a pattern with girls or women that I liked—I always had to move away before anything could even get started. I loved working at the clinic. The hours were great, and there was a group of six or seven of us to take care of everything. Everyone's job was clearly prescribed and did not change from night to night. Though most of the clinic staff were leaving when we started at five in the evening, many nurses and doctors were still there finishing up their duties, and we had to work around them. But that was fine with me, and I hoped to keep the job through college.

During this time, my brother decided to buy a used mobile home in a nearby mobile home court. He wanted me to be a co-owner. He said it would be more private, with no people coming and going as in the apartment building, and he could have his own garden, which was also nice. Aside from how I felt about his treatment, he was still my brother, and I was gaining more freedom, so I agreed. As usual, I received the very small room, despite the even split in cost.

In September 1980, and against my brother's wishes, I started attending Minot State, registering for mostly math and science classes. I relied on my strong abilities in these areas and did not think my slow reading and limited comprehension of rapidly delivered lectures would present many problems. Initially, I did not know how the college system worked and did not know the difference between quarters and semesters. I felt like a sponge, absorbing anything and everything, and wanted to be part of this college community. I had no plans other than completing college as quickly as I could to make up for all the lost years.

I was keeping in touch with my cousin Tony, who had moved from Minot to Minneapolis. He had married someone from North Dakota and they had a son. Tony did not have anything nice to say about my brother. He told me how my brother had tried to control him when he lived with him. He didn't have to tell me a whole lot about the control issue, as I had figured that out very well for myself. I truly wanted to see my cousin and his family, but he refused to visit while I was living with my brother. I promised him that if I ever had a chance, I would drive out of North Dakota for the first time to see him. Five hundred miles was a long distance for a car that had not been tested yet.

College was consuming most of my time. I had to look up almost every word in the dictionary. Understanding a paragraph took me more than half an hour as compared to a second or two for anyone else.

But I was never discouraged, as I knew that in time things would get easier. I always had my eyes on the final prize—a degree in electrical engineering. Minot State did not offer that degree, but I could finish their two-year pre-engineering program and after that transfer to either Fargo or Grand Forks, both about two hundred miles away in two different directions. I did not like the idea of having to transfer but would do anything for my engineering degree.

CHAPTER ELEVEN
· ·

Another Holocaust?

My cousin called me unexpectedly one day to tell me the most horrific news about both my parents and his parents. Unlike me, he had good communications with his relatives in Iraq. He said they had been collected and deported to Iran without any warning, although some of his and my brothers had been detained and sent to jail and were still in the country. My father's big house had been taken over by the Ba'ath party, most Kurds had been deported to Iran, and the future of our families was very much unknown. It brought me to my knees. How was this possible? How would I ever learn more about my family? The only bridge to my family and my homeland had been destroyed, and I did not know anyone whom I could trust to try to connect with. This was something I had never expected to happen. All of a sudden, I was someone with no past and a very undetermined future. I asked myself, *Who am I? How can I ever connect and learn about my heritage and proud ancestors?*

I realized that as a young male, I probably would have been sent to jail instead of being deported, but despite that, I was feeling very guilty for not being with my family in these terrible times. I cried for my parents when I was home alone but tried to keep my emotions inside when I was at college or work. And I could not stop thinking about what might have happened to Nadia and her family. I knew that there would not be any way to find out about them either. I began to question my life in general. I did not feel that I deserved to be spared any of these tragedies and atrocities. I was feeling very sick, guilty, and sad.

The living situation with my brother did not improve at all. Despite the fact that I had my own bedroom and car, he was making an issue about almost everything. His relationship with the next-door neighbors was deteriorating very fast also. He made an issue of it any time any of them parked their cars past the line he had drawn to indicate the border between each mobile home. Yes, my brother drew an actual line on the pavement. I could not believe that he was acting in such controlling ways. The final blow came one day when he took the few food items I had bought, like chicken, out of the refrigerator and placed them on the counter. The refrigerator had plenty of room, but that was his way of enforcing his superiority. I asked him why he did that, especially when we were splitting the cost of everything. His response was that everything in the mobile home, even the old television and beds, was his. That shocked me. I told him that I would begin to look for my own place. I think he felt that I was joking, because I did not have anything in the line of furniture or dishes.

My evening work at the clinic fit very well with my college hours, and it was providing me with a sense of belonging. Most of the clinic employees—the nurses, customer service representatives, and billing staff—were female. I found it easier to connect with women than men at that time. I thought they were more compassionate and able to open up than males. This was something very important at that time in my life, as my brother was no company at all. I felt I was all alone in this world. A kind word from any of them meant a lot to me, and I appreciated all of them.

It hadn't taken me very long to understand what I needed to know about college credits and courses required for graduation. I was able to plan a road map and schedule for myself. I have always been able to put together and manage what I need, and I truly feel this ability is a gift from God. Attending the same college as my brother and learning more and more about college ways, I realized something that quite astonished me. Of course, I was a freshman in college. I understood that, but I learned that my brother was no more than a sophomore in biology. Sophomore? What had he been doing all these years? Why was he telling me he was attending medical school? Of course, I had to ask him why. His answer was that working and going to college was not that easy, and he was taking only one class at a time. I could not believe he had wasted so much valuable time and was not making the progress I thought he was making. I started to think that the reason he had been against my desire to attend college as early as I wanted was that he did not want me to have a chance to find out about the lies he had been telling me for years.

I ended the quarter with a B in one class and a C in the other. But with what I was going through, working, and the language barrier, even a C was more than satisfying for me at the time.

That fall, Iraq started a war against Iran. This added to my sadness in a way that I did not know how to deal with. First, Saddam Hussein deported thousands of Kurdish families to Iran and then began invading Iran. Iraq invading Iran? Where was my family? Why are the United States and all other "civilized" countries keeping silent about these atrocities? I was feeling guiltier by the day. Before this new war, Iran had gone through its own problems against the Shah, on top of the American hostage issue. Hussein had many goals when he started this war. His top goal was to take back what he had given up a few years earlier to the Shah when he wanted the Shah to close the border against the Kurds. Hussein was also trying to take a place on the Arab world stage like the one held by the Shah of Iran and Nasser of Egypt. His ego was big enough that he would do anything to establish himself as the leader of the Arab world and beyond.

The war between Iraq and Iran kept getting worse, and I still had no way to get any updates on my family or my brothers in jail. I was emotionally torn. While keeping up with college and work, I was hopelessly following these sad events that were completely out of my control. However, I managed to keep a smile on my face and kept my sadness to myself. I had managed to survive my first quarter despite the language difficulties and everything else. I had purposely made it easy on myself by starting out with only introduction to algebra and beginning German. I did not want to try to conquer heavy topics until I was used to how everything worked.

I had also managed to rent an efficiency room for myself. My brother did not take the news of my moving out very well. He was not worried about me or my well-being, only about what all our Kurdish friends would say about him. I told him that I had not gone through all the troubles of coming to the United States just to be controlled by him. Now, I was truly alone in this world with no shoulders to lean on.

The cold weather and driving in the snow and ice did prove to be a huge new challenge for me. I had to let the engine run for many minutes just to melt the ice from the windshield. Starting the car was an issue, as the cold often made the battery weak. North Dakotans did not plow the snow from their highways until it stopped coming down, because the wind would work against their efforts. This made it very difficult to get around, especially for a newcomer like myself.

I am proud to say I never starved, though I was not able to afford much more than a dozen eggs and a loaf of bread at each store visit. My wages at the clinic had started at less than three dollars per hour. After college, car, gas, rent and utilities, food was almost the last thing on my budget. But I never felt sorry for myself or doubted that I was doing the right thing. I kept reminding myself to keep my eyes on the prize.

My cousin and I started to communicate a lot more, because he knew that I was living alone and no longer had to worry about any possibility of my brother answering the phone. He started to open up and tell me how my brother had treated him when he was living with him, even telling him what roads to take or not to take when he lent him his bicycle. That did not surprise me at all. He said my brother always tried very hard to get a girlfriend but was never successful. My brother's pride had prevented him from speaking to me about this topic, but I had come to the same conclusions. I did not know exactly what his issues were. He was handsome, had a nice car, and spoke superb English. I thought it must be his attitude and his negative outlook.

My cousin was, like me, worried about our families, and he became my only source of information through his Iraqi connections. He offered me some small hope when he mentioned a friend of his whom he was trying to get in touch with, and he said he'd try to connect me with that friend. He had known this man in Iraq and they had remained friends after they both came to the United States. His friend was trying to go back to visit Iraq, and that is why my cousin wanted him to connect with me.

I made many friendships with girls, both at the clinic and in college, but they were limited to just saying hello and general conversation. I did not take these friendships any further than that, because I still had not heard anything about Nadia. I had vowed to myself that I would not consider dating until I knew something about Nadia and her well-being. My biggest fear in regard to her was that I had tarnished her reputation by simply being her friend. God knew that I never touched

Nadia or looked at her in other than noble and honorable ways, but I was afraid that others had not seen it that way. I knew that if she had been labeled less than honorable, even erroneously, her life would be over, as no man would ever consider her for marriage. Those were the truly sad traditions and customs of that time and they were not fair at all toward women. Because of that, I was not going to date until I knew she was safe.

Ever since my arrival in my new homeland, I had been keeping in touch with Dr. Amir and Maria in Germany. I was very proud and happy that I had stayed true to myself in this way. I was grateful to them for everything that they did for me and the comfortable living situation they provided. I realized my life would not have been the same without them. I never once blamed them for the misunderstanding that led to my leaving their house.

Winter quarter began, and I kept it very light again, simply because of lack of money, the language barrier, and my full-time night work. I kept on track with math, specifically trigonometry, which was my favorite topic even back in Iraq, and some sports credits. I knew I could understand trig even without fully understanding English. I had made myself a detailed plan and was not worried—I would increase my credit load once I was fully acclimated. I was truly having a great time with my lean college schedule. I was not having any issues and wished I had taken one more class, but in many ways it worked out for the best because I was learning everything I needed to learn about my job. It became a very natural thing, and I felt very capable at it. At mid-quarter, I noted that I was nearing my first anniversary in my new homeland. I reflected on all that had happened, starting with being left in that small apartment all alone with nothing to do, to where I was now—living on my own, driving my own car, working full time, and, most of all, going to college and being well along on my path to my degree. I was very proud of myself and my accomplishments. I knew I had a long road ahead of me but was confident I would get there.

Winter quarter ended, and it turned out that I was accurate in my prediction about trigonometry—I had my first A. I am not sure if I saw another A after that, but to me that was not the most important thing. I knew I was not at the same level as most of the other students, but I realized that I did not have the right environment to earn A after A. Passing with a C was more than enough for me, and I was not wasting any time. I heard from my cousin, and he connected me with his friend who was going to Iraq in the next weeks. I asked the friend to go by our home to see if it was still standing. Of course, I also wanted him to check on Nadia's house to see if they were still there and, if they were, to try to learn about Nadia's fate somehow. I drew a map showing both houses and how to get there and quickly mailed it to him. Now it was just a matter of time. I was afraid for him, as that crazy war between Iraq and Iran was becoming more involved, and both sides were reporting many casualties. I did not see an end in sight.

I stayed focused, despite all the emotional roller coasters, continuing in spring quarter with my strong suit—math and calculus. I also took chemistry, which was not at all a favorite topic, sports, and music. As an engineering major, I had many required math, calculus, and physics classes. I handled it all like a game. I played to my strengths while I was getting stronger in my communication and reading abilities.

A communication came from Dr. Amir and Maria that they were visiting Canada and would like to come and visit me. I was very excited and shared the news with my brother. Although I had moved away from him, I still kept in close contact out of respect. In many ways, I had forgiven him for his disrespect and ill treatment of me. I had long since processed the experience as something I had to go through to help me grow and learn. Of course, I did not have any room to host Dr. Amir and his family, so I suggested to my brother that I would have them stay in a nice hotel with all the amenities, such as the Ramada Inn. My brother, with his controlling nature, objected immediately and said that they could stay with him in his bedroom in his mobile home, and he would take the small bedroom that used to be mine. I did not like the idea, because I knew how Dr. Amir and his family lived in Germany. Living in a mobile home was just not suitable. My brother did not see it that way, because to him the mobile home was a big upgrade compared to how he used to live. Although I considered Dr. Amir and his family to be my guests, which would give me the final decision, I gave in to my brother out of respect, despite what I thought to be his poor judgment.

Dr. Amir had rented a van in Canada, and they were sightseeing as well as visiting. Because he had mentioned it to me in Germany, I knew he was also looking for a new home. I think they had already checked out Canada, and now they were checking out the United States. In many ways, I felt sorry that their impression of the United States was going to be limited to Minot, North Dakota. When they arrived, my brother took over as if they were his guests and as if they knew him and not me. He was acting very strange, trying very hard to push me to the side and never taking me into account in anything he planned to do. One of the first places my brother took Dr. Amir and his family to eat was none other than Country Kitchen. I was very irritated and would have preferred to take them to a more selective and private place. Maria made a comment about people drinking coffee from mugs. I knew exactly what she meant, as I had become very familiar with the customs and traditions in West Germany when serving coffee or wine. They were at that time very strict in regard to what type of cups to use, depending on the time of the day or occasion. Drinking from mugs or drinking in the car was unheard of then.

I stayed with Dr. Amir and his family at my brother's mobile home until it was time to go home and returned in the morning to be with them. I realized how much more convenient and comfortable it would have been if I had insisted on hosting them in one of the hotels, reserving a room for myself and my brother if he had wanted. I knew my idea had been the best. My brother was definitely trying to make them his friends by pushing me out. He had started this effort when he sent all those pictures to us in Germany. I am sure Dr. Amir was under the same impression I had been—that my brother was attending medical school and would be able to help him with ideas about what any doctor would need to practice medicine in the United States. I am sure Dr. Amir was disappointed that my brother had no idea how to answer any of his questions. They stayed for only a few days. I was very happy to see their visit come to an end, as my brother had showed yet another side of his immaturity. I had tried very hard not to argue or show my brother any disrespect while Dr. Amir and his family were visiting. I had taken a few days off work and was happy to get back.

Spring quarter ended, and I got the B that I had been expecting in calculus. However, I'd had a rough time with chemistry (a subject I had never liked) and also struggled to get past the professor's southern accent. He was a very nice and likeable person, but I could only understand about half of what he said. My dislike for chemistry was the primary reason that I never pursued medical studies. But as always, that C was as good as an A.

When I collected my thoughts about my first year of college, I felt great about my accomplishments. I remembered how much my brother had resisted. He had made up so many worthless reasons for wanting me to wait at least a year to start. I had already earned twenty-six credit hours, and I realized that this was only the beginning. There was so much more to come. I treated those credits as a gift, because if I had listened to my brother, I would not have had them. More importantly, I was getting used to college life, even while working full time. I learned that the college offered courses during summer break, but when I saw what was being offered, I decided to just take one credit in required physical education—just enough to stay connected.

I wanted to recharge my battery, and I did not have enough money anyway.

I received a call around that time from my cousin's friend, who had returned from Iraq and had seen our home. He said it looked as if the Ba'ath party had made it into their local office. He was very sorry and told me how sad it was to see such a beautiful home go, just like that. I told him how much that home meant to me. Then I asked him if he had made it to Nadia's house. He stopped for a few seconds and then actually started getting angry at me for "doing what I did." I asked him to tell me what he meant exactly. I begged him, but he would not answer. Then he told me that she was married and had moved to another area with her husband. The news made me both very sad and very happy—happy that she had a new life ahead of her and comforted that no rumors had destroyed her marriage prospects. Again, I asked him several times to tell me what terrible thing I had done, but he still refused to say, so I thanked him and ended the call. I could not think of anything, except maybe that I might have broken Nadia's heart. I often prayed that I had not done anything to hurt or offend her, recalling all the times I had tried to say goodbye but could not. I decided to put all these issues behind me and just be happy she was married. It was time for me to move on with my life.

Now I could open myself to the possibility of finding someone to date and love. I did not have any criteria for this woman; I would just use my intuition to recognize "the one." There were two at the clinic whom I would have considered, but they were both in relationships. I always kept a good relationship with those two and always wished them well. I never confessed to either one that I liked them, but I still wondered if they somehow felt my brief interest in them.

At quarter break, I decided to visit my cousin in Minnesota, because he had not come to see me. I had never driven outside of Minot, not even to the surrounding areas. How difficult would a five hundred-plus mile drive be? What cities would I see? Would I like it? The biggest question was what if I had any car trouble? What should I do? These were not unusual issues, but I had never encountered any of them. I planned my route, took a couple of vacation days plus the weekend, and off I went. In the beginning, the drive was somewhat exciting, as everything was new to me. The highway itself was somewhat boring, as there was nothing to see. My cousin had given me a list of all the cities I would see along the way. After about a hundred miles of nothing except some tiny nondescript towns, I reached the city of Bismarck, North Dakota. Bismarck was nice, and definitely bigger than Minot. Later I learned that it was the state capital.

After a short stop in Bismarck, I hit the interstate, knowing that I had at least four hundred miles to go to Minnetonka. The drive became a bit more enjoyable, as there were many more cars and trucks and the speed limit was a bit higher. I drove through many more little towns, and then I reached my next planned stop at Fargo, my halfway point. This city was even bigger than Bismarck, and there were many places to eat and shop. I stopped only long enough to eat and check on my car. The interstate was becoming more interesting and enjoyable, with more green grass and trees. I was officially in Minnesota as soon as I left Fargo. After about two hundred miles, I came into an area where I had to pay more attention, as I was now near what I had learned was called the Twin Cities. I followed my cousin's directions all the way to a gas station near his house in Minnetonka, where I called him. He soon arrived, and I followed him to his apartment.

I was happy to catch up with him and meet his wife and little son. We really had not had a lot in common back in Iraq. He did not care for school, and I was the complete opposite. He told me the full story of how he had made it to United States through Greece. He was working in a factory and seemed very happy. He showed me around, and I realized how much bigger Minnetonka was than Minot. There were so many things to do. I really liked it in Minnesota. The one thing that surprised me about my cousin, and that I disliked, was his excessive alcohol drinking. It seemed as though he could not sit anywhere without a can of beer in his hand. I never really cared for drinking beer, even when I was in Germany. I liked an occasional glass of wine, but I did not need to have it day and night like my cousin did.

———

I sensed a lot of friction between my cousin and his wife, which made me very uncomfortable. I elected to stay clear of all their arguments, most of which seemed to be about money, or the lack of it. I wondered why he was spending all that money on beer if they were having financial difficulties. It seemed that misplaced priorities were the real reason for their troubles. My visit was very short because I had to leave early on Sunday for a full day of driving. The gas expense and restaurant stops had put me into a little difficulty financially, but I was happy that I had managed to see my cousin and his family.

The rest of the summer went very fast, and soon it was time to register for the 1981 fall term. I took more calculus, engineering graphics, and my worst enemy, chemistry. I just wanted to get that hated requirement out of the way so I could see the road map to graduation more clearly. I took only thirteen credit hours, which seemed to fit my time and budget very well and also allowed me extra chemistry study time. College had many attractive women, but unfortunately, none of them seemed to be in my classes. They all seemed to be in accounting or other majors, such as child psychology. I had no free time for other college activities where I might meet them. All I had time for was going to class, studying, eating, and working. I was missing out on many college activities and socializing opportunities, but I had my eyes on my classes first and foremost. I always trusted in the divine and knew that if it was meant to be, it would happen. I was having a painful struggle with my chemistry class, and it was affecting my other classes. But I was determined to pass it, even at the cost of my health or my very limited social activities.

I also started to keep my eyes open for another place to live. My room was barely sufficient, and not having any windows to the outside was a big issue. I also could not imagine inviting any of my friends over for any reason, because it was just pretty small. The landlords were truly nice people, but I had to look out for myself and my comfort. My dedication to college paid off at the end of that quarter. I passed all three classes, but I did not score higher than a C in any of them. I knew that if I hadn't taken the chemistry class, I would have done better in the others, but I was happy that I passed chemistry. Of course, my short celebration was spoiled by the knowledge that this was only Chemistry I, and I still had to take Chemistry II.

The quarter break was not long enough to do anything special. I had my master plan to follow, and I revisited it constantly to see if I needed to make any positive changes. There were a few high-demand required classes that were hard to get a seat in, such as English 101. By the time my turn came up to register, that class was already filled. I kept changing my plans because of classes like that. I ended up enrolling in more math and calculus, engineering graphics, and Chemistry II. I knew Chemistry I would have given me some helpful preparation to help me pass Chemistry II.

I called or visited with my brother at least once a week, if not more. Of course, I ran into him many times between classes, but we never really sat down for a break together. He was always trying to tell me what I should do or not do, even in topics that he did not have enough knowledge in. By that time, I knew that this was just his way, and I did not take his so-called suggestions to heart. I always knew that I was on the right path, and there was no reason to change. Life in general was very busy for me during those years. I had to work very hard and for many hours for less than four dollars per hour, and I had taken a Saturday morning job to supplement my income at the clinic. The only free time I had was literally Saturday evening and Sundays. I used Saturdays to catch up on sleep. My Sunday schedule rarely varied. I slept in until noon and then went to the laundromat and the supermarket. I would then cook enough food to last me for the upcoming week. If I had any extra time, I would meet up with my brother and all the Kurdish friends at Country Kitchen. That was how I spent my days week after week.

My Sunday visits to the laundromat were actually amazing. It was a combination laundromat/car wash located near my old workplace, the North Hill Bowl. I was meeting and having conversations with many different people, but it seemed the theme was always the same. Most of them were elderly women, and I think they wanted to talk to me simply because I looked different from everyone else. The conversations usually started with questions about where I was from. That was a great icebreaker for talking and talking. And just before I had to leave, the person I was talking to would say the same thing: "Oh, my Lord, you really should write a book. Someday, you will get married, and your children will want to know all these stories." I heard it so many times, but I never thought twice about it at the time. It was always a mystery to me, and I often thought, *Who am I to write a book?* It seems as I have always been guided to write a book, but I was not listening and dismissed the calls. I had only one thing on my mind—getting my college degree.

The Iran-Iraq war continued to escalate, and the news about thousands of casualties from both sides was filling the news media. But I knew no one who had ventured to either country to ask for any news. Had my family made it to Iran safely? And if they had, how had the Iranian government treated them? My roots had been cut off by Hussein and his actions toward my family and his war on the country to which they had been deported. My anger toward Hussein made me shy away from making contacts with any Arab students. This was just a natural feeling. I never even tried to rationalize it. I did not hate anyone; I just did not sit with anyone who was Arab. The amazing thing is that I still always listened to my Arabic music by Abdel Halim Hafez, Nagat, and others. This was the only thing that was connecting me to my roots, and I knew no one could ever take it away from me. In no time, winter quarter 1982 was over, and I was still doing okay in general. I got Cs in everything except engineering, where I scored a B. But my C in Chemistry II was more important to me than anything else.

I finally moved out of my basement room into a new place. I rented an entire attic that had been modified by the owners of the house to make it into a living space. It had a small, separate bedroom, a living room area, and a very small kitchen and bathroom. I even had my own entrance, steps up the outside wall. It was a great improvement. At least I was able to look outside if I left the door open. The family was very kind and nice, and they had an attractive daughter, whom I, unfortunately, never had a chance to meet.

I again missed out on English 101 for spring quarter. I began to wonder what it would take for me to enroll in the class. I quickly switched to other classes instead. I took more engineering and math and other less favored, but required, classes. By this time, I was becoming a familiar face around campus and was able to get dinner dates with a few of the girls, or at least as many as I could spare the time and money for. I was also worried that getting into a relationship might distract my focus away from my number one goal, even though I desperately desired the closeness. It was not a very easy feeling.

CHAPTER TWELVE
· ·

When a Dream Weaves into a Nightmare

In 1982, I started doing something that has since become a semi-tradition—going to church every Sunday. At first, I only went to churches where someone I knew had invited me. Both my brother and I received many such invitations. I did not even care which church it was—Lutheran, Catholic, Assembly of God, Baptist, or any other. I had been exposed to Judaism, Christianity, and Islam. I learned very early that at the end of the day, we are all talking about the same God and that we are all one. Regardless of our faith, skin color, or language, we all belong to Adam and Eve. Having this kind of background and faith made me very strong, and I was not afraid or reluctant to visit any place to worship God.

I began to ask friends at the clinic about the churches they attended, paying special attention to anyone whom I liked and wished to know as a potential girlfriend. Though I had never developed the courage to ask any of them out, I was assuming that if they saw me attending their churches, it would give us more topics to talk about when we met at work. Looking back, I realize that I would have attended any church at all, depending on which girl I was interested in. I ended up at some point having attended all the churches in Minot. Regardless of the intentions, I am truly glad I did. I believe that it made me a wiser person with a deeper faith in God. Although no relationships ever developed from this practice, I did not stop. I truly believe that I was guided to attend these various churches for a higher purpose without realizing it at that time.

As the weeks went by, I realized that I had completed nearly two years of college. My grades were still mostly Cs and Bs, and I was still happy with them. I registered for two summer school classes in 1982 to speed things along. One was a required elective, and the other was the long-awaited English 101. There was a minor problem, but I did not care. I would have to commute to the Air Force base fifteen miles north of Minot for the English class. The distance was not the problem. The problem was that it was held for five hours, one evening a week. Fortunately, the clinic approved my request to take one evening off for each of the next seven or eight weeks. I was very happy that I could at last stop having to juggle my schedule and move on to English 102. I also knew that it would cost me about sixteen hours on each paycheck for the next several pay dates on top of the extra driving expenses. But I was determined, and I considered all of that to be a small, temporary problem. As you will soon learn, this class had a permanent impact on my life, in ways words cannot possibly describe.

By this time, I had made good friendships with many of my clinic coworkers. They took time from their busy schedules to care about me.

Some could see that I was not just another maintenance person. They saw in me a hard worker who was not ashamed of doing anything to provide for himself and put himself through college. Of course, there were also some who did not see any of that, and to them, I was just another janitor. There were many in between also. I never judged anyone or tried to force anyone to give me any more respect than what they already gave me. I never considered educating anyone as part of my mission at that time. I assumed that if I could not teach them by example, then I could not teach them in any other way. One of the few nurses who truly cared for me was Linda. She was always pleasant with me and many times stopped to ask how I was doing. She also invited me to her lovely home. I enjoyed Linda and her husband, Ken, a lot and shared many things with them. They became like family to me.

Soon summer classes started. My on-campus class had only a few students due to summer break, and I was looking forward to going off-campus for English 101. I soon realized that many of my fellow students in the English 101 class were not attending Minot State; they were in the class only because they needed this class. There were only ten of us. The instructor told us that we would get a ten-minute break every hour, and that each night would be broken up to simulate five different classes. We would get five different homework assignments, one for each "day." Everything sounded great to me. I was eager to finally get through the class. The students were mostly men, and so I started paying attention to two ladies sitting next to each other several rows in front of me. I had not seen either one before, so I assumed that they were not from Minot State. They were always together, even during the breaks. They looked like they might be sisters. I tried to summon up the courage to talk to them. I did not succeed that first night but figured I still had about six more chances if it were meant to be. I was not overly stressed out when I got home. The nice thing was that I only had one class during the day, and it did not start until late morning. I stayed up to go over the class assignments and even watched a little TV. I enjoyed every chance I had to watch *The Tonight Show* starring Johnny Carson, followed by *The Late Show* starring David Letterman at the beginning of his career.

Summer school was pretty much to the point. I tried to arrive at class right on time and did not go to the student union cafeteria. I found myself with a lot of time to study before going to work. Most of my Kurdish friends were at work during the day, so I was alone with no choice other than staying in my apartment to study, which was great for my studies. But living alone was not very easy, especially knowing that my family was going through tough times and I was not sure if they were even alive. I had to adapt very quickly to keep my focus on finishing college.

At work, I tried to help my budget by staying a little longer each of the other four nights by doing extra projects, like removing the wax from the floor and rewaxing it or spot-shampooing the carpet. This was a very detailed type of work, and it usually took several hours, depending on the area. Although we were all one team, we were also very independent, and each one of us did what was needed to do to get a job done. We ran into very few problems with one another. Despite the low pay, that was a job sent from heaven. It allowed me to take care of my college expenses, and it never caused me to take any worries home with me. I was very blessed.

I was very ready for the second week of English 101. I had completed all my reading and writing assignments and was ready to keep going. I was hoping to get a chance to speak with one of the ladies by herself, as I knew that I would not have enough courage to say anything if they were together. At the end of the class, I had only one chance, in a group setting, to get to know everyone. I paid extra attention to the two ladies, who did, in fact, turn out to be sisters. Karen and Cindy were from a small town about fifty-five miles south of Minot called Underwood.

They were both attending a nursing program, and English 101 was a required class. That small talk was our only connection.

I was not sure which one I liked more. Of course, I knew that if I had the chance to speak to one of them, regardless of her answer, I could not possibly ask the other one out. So which one should I choose to pursue over the next five weeks? I was not particularly attracted to either one in the way that I had been attracted to others in the past, and it was nothing like love at first sight. I was mostly very curious about them. They were definitely very quiet and certainly not what one could call wild women. Five weeks later, the class came to an end without my getting a chance to speak to either one. I was not happy about that, though I was happy to complete the course. I was able to put my curiosity behind me and looked forward to the next few weeks without any classes. I checked my road map to graduation and was happy to see that I was still on track. I received a B in English 101 and a C in the other class. And of course I had added another nine credit hours to my total earned credits.

I kept in touch with my brother and our friends as much as I could, mostly on weekends. No one had any good news about what was going on between Iraq and Iran. Many on both sides were being killed for no good reason. I wondered if I had known how deeply I would be disconnected from my roots if I would have ever left. I had always counted on being able to talk to at least Layla to help me make plans for the future. I loved it that I was fulfilling my mother's dreams, but I needed my family, too. There was enough sadness, guilt, and self-blame to last me several lifetimes. But I knew that I could not change what had happened and that I had only one choice—completing my degree.

Wanting to have some family connection, I paid another visit to my cousin in Minnetonka before the end of summer break. I could afford to take off only on weekends plus an additional day, starting the drive at midnight and driving all night. Though concerned about the reliability of my car, I loaded it up with cassette tapes and went anyway.

It was now almost time to move to either Fargo or Grand Forks for the last two years of my engineering degree work. I had been well aware of this from the beginning but had never been exactly sure how to go about it. I knew I had to have a job similar to my current job. I was not familiar with either city and did not know which one I should target. I knew I had to make my decision during fall quarter 1982. I took on a full credit load of four classes. The interesting thing is that by this time, I was already ahead of my brother in college credits. I avoided talking about it whenever he was around. I knew it was not a pleasant topic for him.

I was very busy, always either coming or going from one class to another, but I was not having any problems in keeping up. In many ways, I found this busyness a great escape from my own reality and sadness about my family. I had not learned this coping mechanism from anyone; it just evolved naturally from my earlier life. I guess I am a survivor in every aspect of the word, without ever looking at myself as one. I just thought I was doing what anyone would do if they were in the same situation.

One of the most pleasant surprises that fall was running into Denise, who had worked with me two years earlier at the North Hill Bowl. I had liked her then but had never asked her out, because I had not learned the fate of Nadia at that time and could not think of anyone else, regardless of the miles between us. I was very surprised to find Denise so pleasant and cheerful. She was very happy to see me, maybe even happier than I was. We talked for a while, and I learned that she had started college that year. She was thinking of accounting as a major, so I knew I probably would not have any classes with her in the short time I had left on campus. I told her that I looked forward to seeing her at the student union someday to have some coffee and talk. She thought that was a great idea. I left with a great sense of connection to her. A mystery was now at hand. I wondered, why was I attracted to

Denise more than anyone else I had met in North Dakota. Her outer beauty was at best average, so I knew that was not the reason. Did she possibly remind me of someone I knew? I could not think of anyone. I ended up giving up on the reasons and just trusted my heart and soul. I was determined to keep my eyes open for her around the campus in the days ahead.

Medical Arts Clinic was having their annual Christmas party, and they wanted to get an advance head count. Would I be bringing anyone? I recalled the previous year's party and how awkward I felt being by myself. I'd had to sit with other groups or couples and act happy while feeling very awkward inside. I was hoping that it could be different this year. Maybe Denise? One can only wish and dream. In the next days and weeks, I did see Denise around the campus, but it seemed that each time she was with one or another long-haired man in torn jeans. I developed the impression that she liked hippy-looking men. I always dressed like a clean-cut businessman and immediately assumed that she probably didn't like that. But I still liked her and wanted to get to know her better. My wishes about Denise came true several times that fall. We sat together in the student union for as long as either of us could, once for more than an hour. During our first visit, we talked mostly about my days at the North Hill Bowl. She was laughing about all the trouble I'd had pronouncing some of the food names and ingredients. It was all very innocent, and we were having a great time. I had just started getting comfortable enough with her to ask her to accompany me to the upcoming Christmas party when suddenly the images of all the long-haired men came to mind, and I became discouraged and afraid. As time went by, this kept happening. We would sit together a lot, and Denise always seemed even happier than I was. We shared a lot of stories and laughter, but I never ever had enough courage to ask her out. I blamed myself and called myself a coward. I remembered having the same problem back home with Sabah. I did not know what to do then either and never had the courage to ask any friends for advice.

I kept my feelings to myself. I often wondered if Denise knew how I felt about her and questioned how a young man like me could do all the terrifying things I had done without any fear but still feared rejection from one gentle, harmless person so badly. I was the one who had left my home and parents to be in a foreign country. Yes, that was me, so why was I so scared of a simple no?

Another quarter ended with mostly grades of C. Again, I was fine with that. The only sad thing was that I was completing the quarter knowing that I had never asked Denise out and would have to move to Fargo or Grand Forks. This scenario was becoming too familiar, and I was at peace with what was going to happen. But which city? The general opinion was that Fargo was a much better and bigger city than Grand Forks. Despite this consensus, I wanted to see both for myself. I never accepted other people's judgments at face value. I had seen Fargo briefly but not Grand Forks. Grand Forks was about 250 miles away, so I needed to plan my trip carefully and allow time to possibly look for a night job if I liked it there. I had planned to leave early Saturday and be in Grand Forks before noon. I knew that I would have a lot of time to look around. I would stay the night if I ran out of time and return to Minot early Sunday. On Friday evening before going to work, I packed my car for the trip, checked the engine, and changed the oil. At that time, my car was burning oil, and I had to keep a close eye on the oil level at all times. I thought it would be a very good idea to have several quarts of oil with me on this trip, just as a precaution. There was a Kmart very close to the clinic, so I checked with my coworkers and got their okay to take my fifteen-minute break to go buy the oil. At eight o'clock I ran to my car, drove to Kmart, grabbed the oil, checked out, and ran toward the door to get back to the clinic on time.

The next few minutes by the front door of Kmart were life changing. I heard my name being called several times. I stopped and saw a young lady running toward me, still calling my name. When she got closer, I recognized her. It was Cindy from English 101. I was very surprised that she even remembered my name. After a quick hello and how are you, Cindy said, "Karen is here, too," and began calling for her. I was very confused about all of this, but everything was telling me that Cindy somehow wanted to connect me with Karen. Why? I had no idea.

Soon Karen joined us, and I realized that my fifteen-minute break was over. I did not know how to get away other than saying that I had to run back to work. I also said, "If you like, my work has a Christmas party coming up. Can we exchange phone numbers?" Karen was open to the idea. We handed each other little slips of paper, and I made it back to work only a few minutes late. No one said anything, and it was fine. When I got home, the incident at Kmart and the way Cindy had called out to me was on my mind all night. Why had it happened? We really had not talked all that much during class. And what made Cindy think that I was interested in Karen? Yes, I had wanted to talk and get to know them both, but we had not really connected and I thought I had moved on.

Early Saturday morning, because I was awake, I decided to leave even earlier than I had planned. I always looked forward to this type of trip in the car, because I had a chance to listen to my music as loud as I liked and sing along without anyone hearing me. This was my very first time taking these roads and highways. Despite that, I arrived in Grand Forks around ten o'clock in the morning. I stopped at an Arby's for an early lunch and to allow the car to cool down so I could check on the oil level. I was hoping to have a chance to talk to some locals, but at that hour the restaurant was not very busy. I added the oil the car needed and decided to first of all get some kind of gut feeling for the city.

I figured there was no sense in looking for jobs if I did not like it there. I drove around aimlessly for a while and then asked for directions to the University of North Dakota (UND), also to get a gut feeling. I truly did not like Grand Forks as compared to Fargo. I just did not get a good feeling for it. That was truly sad, because UND did have a great academic reputation. Despite the initial impression, I decided to drive around a little more to see if I could find any reasons to change my mind. I drove and drove for two additional hours and finally decided to find the highway that would lead me back home. I had concluded that Grand Forks was not going to be my choice. I also realized that I would have to make a similar trip to Fargo to confirm my decision and that I would have to find a job with similar hours in Fargo. I had no time to waste.

I crawled into bed very late, thinking of my Sunday chore routine and also of the Christmas party that was coming up. I had promised Karen I would call her about going with me. I wondered how soon I should call. I did not want to appear anxious, even if I really was. This was all new to me, and I truly did not know the right thing to do. I just did what seemed right and decided to wait a week before calling.

I woke up late on Sunday and went to church, as I often did. I had my chore routine down to a science. Immediately after church, I would change clothes and take my laundry to the laundromat. I would leave it there while I went across the street to do my grocery shopping, unless I had gotten into a conversation with someone at the laundromat. I always did whatever I needed to do to save my time. I knew I still had to go home and start cooking, cleaning, and ironing, while allowing enough time for me to go to Country Kitchen in the evening to catch up with my brother and all our Kurdish friends. I can truly say in those days Sunday was the only day I had a decent meal, simply because I usually cooked for the entire week. After cooking, I usually ate as though there was no tomorrow and put the rest in the fridge. I did not have any extra money to eat out or any luxury like that. My diet was very boring and seldom included any fruits or snacks. It was the bare minimum to survive, but I made it through. Our friends and I were meeting at Country Kitchen merely to connect and we often were having only coffee. Occasionally, we had a dessert with our coffee, but hardly any meals.

I told everyone at Country Kitchen about my trip to Grand Forks and my decision not to go there. I think they were all happy with that, but they were also hoping that I would not go to Fargo either. To me, not going was out of the question, because that was the only way to get my degree in engineering. I had heard many good things about the university in Fargo—North Dakota State University (NDSU).

I was still working on a few more credits while trying to find a job in Fargo, 250 miles away. This proved to be very challenging while also trying to keep my full-time job in Minot. Travel plans to Fargo were always contingent on the weather and road conditions. Traveling in winter in that flat country could become impossible when visibility was impaired by as little as one inch of snow being blown around by the wind.

I was never discouraged; I just considered it another challenge like the many I had met thus far. I tried to connect with Karen several times about the Christmas party. It took me several calls. We didn't talk long, simply arranged the pickup time, and she gave me directions. This call left me with many questions but no answers. I had not sensed any positive feeling at all from Karen that she was excited or looking forward to this party. She was not warm at all like Denise or other girls around the campus. I decided not to make too much of it, until we actually met in person.

My stress and emotional tension was mounting, even though I had fewer credits than usual. I was very torn. I badly needed emotional support from my family, and oh, how I wished I did not have to work. I think it was all because of trying to find a job in a town where I was not living. I wondered if anyone would even hire a nonresident.

CHAPTER THIRTEEN

· ·

An American Is Born

Finally, the evening of the Christmas party arrived, and I was anxious to see how my experience with Karen would be. I washed and vacuumed my car, showered, and gave myself extra time for the drive. Underwood was exactly at the halfway point on the way to Bismarck. It was a very small town. I did not have any trouble finding the address and rang the doorbell. Karen answered the door, all ready to leave. Where was her family? Was this normal? I could have asked her, but what did I know? Karen and I exchanged very few words on the drive back to Minot. I found her to be very quiet. Was she always this quiet, or was she just not interested?

I acted as much a true gentleman as one can be. I introduced Karen to everyone we encountered at the party. We mostly stayed with my coworkers but occasionally moved to say hello to others. The party was mostly a holiday dinner; there was no music, dancing, or anything else. But we had a great time talking to all the nurses, and of course, it was nice to be seen dressed up instead of wearing my work clothes. I avoided drinking because I was driving, and I did not see Karen drinking either. When we saw a few others leaving, we decided to leave as well. I knew that I still had a more than one-hundred-mile drive round-trip.

I offered Karen the opportunity to stop somewhere for coffee, but she declined. I had hoped we could get to know each other better. I understood her request to drive home, so I did. In the car we made only small talk about some of the people at the party. There was never a moment when we talked like two people on a date. I was well aware of the tension, and I did not know how to react to it. I wished we could just fly to Underwood, as I was uncomfortable and was not having fun. At her house, Karen opened her door before I had a chance to get out and open it for her. She jumped out, said a quick thank you, closed the door, and quickly walked to her house. I watched her and was frozen for a few minutes before I was able to back up and drive home.

The entire time while driving home I was trying to understand what had just happened. Karen had not invited me to go inside; I hadn't even received a small goodnight kiss. I was very tired and was questioning if it had all been worth it. I was wondering how often I could do things like this with an old car that was burning oil like mine was. That date made me drive more than two hundred miles for four hours. I knew I had to rest and think more about my so-called date. I was the subject of many questions the following week at work. Who exactly was Karen? How had we met? Most of the comments were very reserved, but many times I heard people say, "She is different." How different? I never asked, but maybe if I had asked, I wouldn't have received any honest answers anyway. I told everyone the truth: "Karen and I just met, and we are just friends."

Despite the snow, over the next six weeks I continued the job search in Fargo. I was even willing to drop my Minot classes if I found a job in Fargo and they wanted me to start right away. At each visit, I drove around and stopped by every business where I saw a potential for hiring. I bought all the local newspapers so I could go over the want ads at home. I had no luck—not even an interview. I wondered if my Minot address was a red flag. After three wasted weekends, I knew that financially I could not keep this up. I lost hope and did not know what to do next.

I asked some of my college professors for advice, and they all told me to talk to the counselor. The counselor gave me only one option: change my major to any major where I could get a four-year degree from Minot. I agreed that it did seem to be the only option for now. The trouble was I had been dreaming of being an electrical engineer. What could possibly come in as a close second to that? I also reminded the counselor that I wanted to utilize most, if not all, of my math credits. The counselor promised me that he would review all my classes and credits and come up with my best scenario. When I checked with him a day later, he told me that I should switch to computer science. That major required a great amount of math, and I already had that and more—all of my courses and credits would transfer. I took him seriously and immediately revised my master plan. I saw that I could still graduate on time, so I switched. No more trips to Fargo, unless it was for pleasure.

Winter quarter 1982 ended with some of my worst grades ever, despite the light schedule. I think it must have been all the activities and trips. I knew that I needed to put that quarter behind me and look ahead to my new major. During the last weeks, I made several calls to Karen to plan another date, but she always said that she was busy. She never said that she had no interest in dating me, but by the same token, she did not really show any. I was confused. Should I just give up on her or be patient?

I tried to make up for the previous quarter by taking on more than the usual courses and credit hours in the spring. I was very happy to be able to keep my job at the clinic and be around the people whom I enjoyed. I met a nice lady who was originally from Korea and was attending college majoring in nursing. She had a little boy and was divorced. Her ex-husband was stationed at the nearby Air Force base. Week after week, our friendship became stronger and stronger, and we went out for dinner or coffee occasionally. I did like her company, but I never looked at her as someone who could be a long-term girlfriend. I did enjoy being with someone other than my brother and my regular friends.

As always, I had little time for much beyond work and study other than the occasional dinner date, which had to be well planned into my busy schedule. In spite of that, I kept trying to contact Karen. I finally succeeded, and we planned a date several weeks later. I was able to focus on my college classes, and I was doing very well. I could finally clearly see the day when I would graduate. I also knew that I was a few years older than most college students, and for some reason, I was starting to feel an urgency to have a real relationship that would lead to marriage. That was how I was brought up, and to me, it was the right thing to do. I neither had nor wanted to have many girlfriends at the same time to choose from.

I worked for a few hours on the Saturday of my date with Karen before driving the fifty-five miles to Underwood. This time I was given the chance for a short visit with her mother. The drive to Minot was just as before—no small talk, no questions about me, my family, or my studies. We went to a movie and had dinner. Afterward, we stopped at Country Kitchen so I could introduce Karen to my friends and have some coffee. The conversation was still reserved and formal. Karen was unlike anyone I had ever met. There was no ease in being with her. As we were leaving Country Kitchen, she asked me to take her home.

Just as before, she opened the car door, said goodbye, and went inside before I had a chance to get out of the car. This time, I hadn't expected anything, so I just backed out of the driveway and drove home. I again had the same mixed emotions about the amount of time and effort I had spent on what seemed to be an ungrateful person. I didn't try to figure it out. I just wanted to go to bed.

The next day, it seemed as if everyone at Country Kitchen wanted to talk about my date from the night before. Once all the jokes and comments were over, they asked me how serious I was in my relationship with Karen. I said there was nothing between us yet and that I was still working on it. They were all of the opinion that she did not show any interest in me at all. As much as I had to agree with them, I denied their appraisal and began to defend her, saying things like, *"She is shy,"* or *"She is very reserved."* None of them believed me and still thought I was very wrong. We ended the evening by agreeing to disagree. I was not sure if my relationship with Karen would ever materialize into anything, but for some reason I could not give up completely. I was open to other relationships, but my schedule made it very hard to meet anyone new. I kept my friendship with my Korean friend, but that was a friendship only, with no expectations.

That spring quarter ended with great grades—Bs and a few As. The war between Iraq and Iran was still ongoing and still no news from my family or anyone else. At times, the only way I could deal with it all was to go to my apartment and cry myself to sleep. Sometimes, I would drive aimlessly for hours playing my cassettes of sad music until the sadness and anger released.

Something happened in the spring of 1983 that at the time was not any event to think or dwell on it, but for some reasons only recently, it kept coming to my mind very often and I become very angry at myself for not acting differently when it happened back in 1983.

A few days before the break, a friend of mine whom we had many classes together approached me and kindly asked me if I liked to go with him to visit his parents in Williston, North Dakota? His name was Matt Stone and he lived at the college dorm because he was from Williston, North Dakota which is a city west of Minot and it is about 120 miles away. I had a great respect for Matt because he was very smart and helpful to me. I was very thankful, but I hadn't ever been to anyone's house and I was afraid that I might not be well accustomed to traditions yet. I sadly refused the invitation and made up a silly excuse. Matt understood and he went farther by giving me his house telephone numbers and said *"Just call and let me know if you changed your mind."* I took the phone number and told him to count on me doing just that.

When the college break was upon us, I met all my Kurdish friends including Ram and my brother at our usual place Country Kitchen. During that outing, I mentioned the story of the invitation from my friend Matt. It seemed as everybody was against my refusal and they all encouraged me to call him and just go. I pondered on my friend's suggestion all night and on Saturday morning, I decided to call Matt and tell him that I changed my mind and asked for direction. I started driving my little old car toward Williston. After about three hours, I arrived at Matt's parents' house. No one else was there besides Matt and his parents. Matt's dad was a very famous and successful medical doctor in Williston and apparently they were very well off financially. Their house was very average home and did not show their wealth.

We spent a beautiful time the day and evening and finally it was time to go to bed. In the morning we all were awake and had a very nice breakfast. No one asked or invited to church as I was expecting which was fine by me. Shortly after breakfast, I asked for permission to take a shower as I normally do every day in my place. The small bathroom was across the living room and it was used by all that morning. Instead of getting the permission, I was told to wait a bit to *"get it ready"*. I said okay but I was wondering to get it ready for what. I didn't ask, but that is what I had on my mind.

A few minutes later I was given the green light to take the shower. I grabbed my bag with my clean essentials and closed the bathroom behind. As I was getting ready, I noticed a big role of money rolled and had an elastic band around. It was placed right on the vanity and meant to be noticed. I did not touch it, but looked closely and I think they were all of $ 100.00 denominations. I went on to take my quick shower and left the bathroom in a big hurry. I definitely knew why that money was placed where it was placed, but my shock prevented me from saying anything or act any differently. Shortly after lunch, I got ready to leave and thanked everyone for being a good host. Unfortunately there was a heavy snow storm which made the drive nearly ten hours' drive. The severe driving condition did not allow me to think about the money in the bathroom.

———

For some weird reasons I never said anything to Matt about the money and eventually moved on from it until just recently. This story for whatever reasons kept resurfacing in my memory. I get angry every time I recall it. I picture myself facing the same situation, but this time I act much differently as if I wish I could turn the clock backward. I picture coming out of the bathroom after seeing the money and grabbing a pen and a paper. Go back to the bathroom and turn the water on as if I was showering, but instead write a note. The note simply says *"I might have no money now and work as a janitor for living, but I am very rich inside. No amount of your money will be able to lower me to the point of stealing from someone who invited me to their home or from anyone from that matter. Why did you invite me if you did not trust me? Was it my skin color that made you to test me? What was it exactly?"* After writing the note, I would leave it next to the money. Leave the bathroom as I had showered. Act as if I needed to buy something from a store near buy. Take my few belonging to the car and drive home. By the time they realized I was not coming back, they first rush to find the money before calling the police. Once they realize that I did not touch their money and read my note, I wonder if they realize what a mistake the have made. I wonder if they would have drove to apologize or just let go. You just never know because I acted so cowardly at that time. I keep reliving this incident after all those years.

I had definitely made up for my mediocre winter quarter and decided to take a few courses on campus in the summer of 1983—English 102 and another one. This would both keep me busy and hasten my graduation. I also made a couple of short visits to my cousin in Minnetonka, which required grueling all-night drives in my not-very-reliable car. I enjoyed these visits, regardless of my disapproval of his lifestyle. It seemed as if my cousin was living for beer drinking only.

I did not overburden myself in the fall of 1983 with classes, as I was actually ahead on my master plan. Though I was still trying very hard to connect with Karen, I had made a few more friends, going out for simple lunch or dinner dates. I went out several times with a pharmacist from the clinic. I did not find the chemistry I was looking for in her, but having a friend was what I needed. I ended it after she asked me not to reveal our friendship to anyone at work. I asked her, "Why not? What do you see wrong in anyone knowing about our friendship?" She did not answer me directly, but I sensed that she did not want anyone to see her, a pharmacist, being friends with a maintenance person. I mentioned my feeling to her and explained that, yes, I was a maintenance person and very proud of it. I was doing whatever I had to do to provide for myself while getting my education. I told her I was only about a year from being someone with a degree in computer science. I was very angry and told her not to worry about anyone knowing we were friends, because we were not anymore.

This incident had a major impact on me. It made me more determined than ever to reach my goals. I saw that even though the pharmacist enjoyed my company, she could not see me for who I was—a proud and driven man. I had known from the beginning that I was doing great. Yes, I did not have a lot of money, but I never needed to ask anyone for help either. I had nothing to be ashamed of. I thought it might be awkward seeing her at work after that, but that did not happen. I went about doing what I needed to do around her without ever needing to dwell on anything. There had been no attraction on my part to start with, so it was a done deal, at least at the time. It turned out that it was not completely done. Even now, when I am giving someone advice on various topics, I bring up the story of how I ended my friendship with Mary Beth, a story that will forever remind me how proud I have always been of myself, regardless of the circumstances.

I did see Denise many times during that quarter. As usual, we sat for hours together in the student union talking and laughed together like no one else, but for some weird reason, I never asked her out, even though I kept seeking her out. The meetings looked and appeared to be accidental, but they were not. I always put myself anywhere I thought she might be. I was tremendously afraid that if she said no, I might never get a chance to sit with her again.

Fall quarter ended with Cs, but I knew I was very close to my goal nevertheless. I shied away from carrying a full winter schedule because of my dislike of driving in the snow. I had a few more dates with Karen. She never had any input on what she might like to do. We always did the same things—movie, dinner, or drive around. I still did not feel comfortable enough with Karen to take her to my apartment or become romantically involved.

I continued my usual connections with my brother and cousin, but my connection with Dr. Amir and Maria had stopped for no apparent reason at some point after they moved to a new address in West Germany. I thought perhaps his family in Iraq had been affected by Saddam Hussein's mass deportation of Kurds. It is very sad to know that these atrocities against innocent people, and all prior deportations by Saddam, never received any protest or acknowledgement from the international community.

Winter quarter ended, and I realized I was only one year from graduation. I was anxious, because I knew I would probably have to move away to find a job utilizing my degree, but I was also excited and ready for a new start. Where would I be going? I had taken enough math classes and had begun taking mostly computer classes.

During all those years of working at the clinic, I had received only a few tiny pay raises, no more than twenty-five cents an hour. I was still making no more than four dollars an hour. However, budgeting was never an issue, as I had mastered my finances. I was also keeping my student loans to a minimum. I was still very close to Linda and Ken, and I had been able to create strong relationships with a few other employees as well. I attended many of their weddings and other happy occasions. I was very relaxed working there and felt appreciated.

Spring quarter ended well, with Bs. I registered for two heavy classes for my last summer session, challenging myself to work harder than usual. I also continued my attempts to date Karen, though it took me several months of trying to connect between each date. I don't know why I didn't give up. I had given up much more easily with many others.

My thoughts were focused on Minnesota as the place I would go after graduation. My cousin and I planned to check the newspapers for computer jobs and information about Minnesota companies during my next visit. That definitely seemed like my best option. As usual, I left for Minnetonka on a Friday night to be there early Saturday morning. Though very tired, I was still very eager to go out with my cousin to look at companies. I was hoping to see if I could get any gut feelings about them and my potential for being hired at any of them. When I was only an hour away, in St. Cloud, I began speeding. That resulted in my first speeding citation, and I knew it would have a major impact on my budget. I took the citation as a bad sign, while hoping that I would be proven wrong.

When I arrived, I saw something very unusual. My cousin was lying on the couch, and he was not in the mood for any company, not even me. "What? Are you sick?" I asked. He said he wasn't. I did not know what to think, so I just took it easy and didn't mention our deal to drive around. Something was not right. Had the citation really been a bad sign? I told my cousin and his wife about it, trying to ignore his attitude. Even though it was clear to me that I wasn't welcomed, I was too tired to even think of turning around and heading home. A few hours later, when it was lunch time, my cousin and his wife did not scramble around as they usually did to put food on the table. They asked me if I was okay with that, and I said that I was not a stranger and would eat almost anything. I was very curious but did not know what to ask. Later, when my cousin was in the mood to talk and we were alone, I asked him to tell me what was going on. At first, he did not want to tell me anything. I had to threaten to leave and never speak to him again if he did not tell me what was going on. Only then did he confess to me that in the past he'd had to borrow money before my arrival to show me that he was doing well financially and was able to spend as much as he liked. This time, no one would lend him anything. He was basically broke.

<hr>

I was shocked and asked him why he felt he had needed to do that. He said he had been trying to prove to me that he was doing well in spite of his lack of education. He said that back in Baghdad he and his family always looked up to our family and how well my father was able to provide for us. For the first time, I sensed anger from him toward my father for not helping them more. I defended my father and said that taking care of us and our education was all he could do. My cousin did not like my insinuation that he and his brothers were not interested in education. The talk became very hurtful and frank. I told him he did not need to feel bad about not taking me around to places as we had planned; I had come to see them, and that was more than enough. The next day, I returned to Minot very disappointed. In addition to spending money I did not have on the trip, I had also been ticketed for speeding. I had not accomplished anything I was hoping for and just caused myself a lot of headache. But as always, I was able to put it all behind me.

In the fall I eagerly registered for my last college year. It was time to realize a dream for which I had waited years, going past many obstacles and leaving my family and loved ones behind. I was determined to finish according to my schedule. With all the coming life changes, my sense of urgency to find my soul mate, life partner, or whatever I was thinking of those days was getting stronger. I have no way of knowing why I created that sense of urgency, but I did.

I continued trying to run into Denise based on my detective work about her schedule. Sharing a table at the student union was nothing but pure joy for both of us, laughing and telling jokes. To this day, I don't know why I never asked her out. At the same time, I kept calling Karen. I was becoming accustomed to not getting a date until about the third call. She never said "no," but she always had an excuse. I never sensed that she was truly avoiding me. Otherwise, I know I wouldn't have kept trying. It was just a different way of not saying yes. Dating her was very expensive. I don't know why I didn't just ask her to drive to Minot instead of having me make the trip four times in one night. Nobody else at work or school was in my sights as a future friend or mate.

Though my degree was still the most important thing, fall quarter ended with all Cs. My attention was becoming scattered, and I was beginning to lose my focus. I knew that I would have to plan carefully to graduate in May 1985. I was feeling disappointed in myself, even feeling like a failure, because I realized that I would be moving out of Minot without finding my partner or soul mate. I made up my mind to not give up and to keep looking in the short time I had left. What a silly way of looking at the situation! Not even once did the idea occur to me that moving to a bigger state would present more opportunities to meet friends.

Hope and gratitude came rolling back on New Year's Day 1985 for everything that I had seen and done, after all I had been through and sacrificed. I had no doubt that all was in divine order, and it was going to be worth it. What's more, in a few weeks, I would be eligible to apply for U.S. citizenship. Actually, this would be my first and only citizenship, as I was never a citizen in Iraq. The word *stateless* on my so-called passport was and still is imprinted in my mind and memories.

In February 1985, I contacted the authorities regarding my citizenship and was told that there would be an opportunity to meet with the review board in May at the federal courthouse in Minot. They conducted these review board meetings only twice a year. I did not want to wait that long. They had no objection to meeting earlier if I was that anxious, but I would have to drive to a town called Portal, North Dakota, near the Canadian border. They explained that this was only the approval process and I would still have to wait until May for the formal ceremony. I did not waste any time thinking about my options and drove to Portal on March 15. That was truly a day that I will never forget. I was so honored to be keeping my mother's promise. I knew that she was looking down from heaven and was very happy for me. So was everyone at work and all my college friends. I knew that this was just the beginning, and in a few months, I would attain another longtime dream and graduate from college.

I continued to see and enjoy Denise's company, but never on a real date. The irony is that though I had never felt anything like that same ease or enjoyment with Karen, Karen was the one with whom I kept trying, and trying, and trying to connect with—as if she were my only chance.

CHAPTER FOURTEEN
· ·

Realizing Two Dreams in a Week

One February day while I was at the student union having lunch with some friends, a student I had met briefly named Patty Francis came over and said she wanted to talk to me in private. I immediately went to her table. She said that she had enjoyed talking to me in the past and hearing my stories, that her major was journalism, and that she was one of the main contributors to the college newspaper, *Red & Green*. I thanked her for the compliment and wondered where she was going with this. She said she would love to do a story about me. "Me?" I asked. "Do you think my story will be of interest to anyone?" She nodded enthusiastically, saying she had no doubts. I then replied,

"If that is what you think, then I have no problem telling you whatever you need for your story." We scheduled a meeting for a few days later when we would talk, and she would take a few pictures.

Patty came prepared with a camera and a tape recorder. She was delighted to hear that I had jumped at my first opportunity to get my citizenship by driving up north to Portal and not waiting three months. I explained that it had been my mother's dream for me, and I had to fulfill it as soon as I could. We spent a couple of hours talking about how I came to leave Iraq and about my time in West Germany. She took a few pictures of me and told me the story would appear in a few weeks. I said I would look forward to that, thanked her, and went on my way. After a few weeks, the article had not yet appeared. I forgot about it and continued my studies and work.

When winter quarter was finally over, I found I had not scored very well at all. I think I must have been distracted by all the excitement around getting my citizenship. I did not waste a whole lot of time pondering it; instead, I looked forward to spring 1985—my graduation quarter. I needed only five more courses. All five were difficult and required my full attention, unlike the prior quarter. I was very happy and thrilled to be so close to my goal but also sad to leave all my friends behind, especially Denise. I was wondering if I would be able to stay in touch with her somehow. I told her that I would be moving to Minnesota, but I never told her anything else. I knew that Denise was two years away from graduating.

I started the last quarter full of hope and excitement, very determined to do much better, and after a month, everything was going according to plan. One morning as I was running to class, a friend excitedly called my name, so I stopped. He was holding up a copy of *Red & Green*—with me on the front page! After class, I eagerly read the article and thought it was quite good. It described how I had left Iraq and talked about my plans to move to Minnesota to seek employment in the field of computer science. I picked up a stack of copies to share with friends. In a few days the story had taken over the college,

House defeats MSC library appropriation

Quam

by Michael Vann

The message for students hoping to enter a brand new library at Minot State College sometime soon is: More waiting ahead.

The defeat of Senate Bill (SB) 2048 early last week brings to an end the hope for a new library for MSC, at least for this session. The bill was killed by a vote of 48-56 with two representatives of the House being absent.

Oscar Quam, director of business affairs, said the bill had been divided into two major parts. The first dealt with the idea of leasing equipment by the state institutions.

The second dealt with the concept of a bond issue held by the state to build a number of buildings at state institutions. The projects under consideration besides the new library at MSC were: a new computer center at North Dakota State University-Fargo, an agriculture mechanic building at the North Dakota State School of Science-Wahpeton, a new chemistry building and the purchase of North Hospital at the University of North Dakota-Grand Forks, renovations at the state penitentiary in Bismarck, renovations at the Grafton State School and a new storage building and renovations to eating, dining and clinical areas at the state hospital at Jamestown.

According to Quam, the bonds would have been paid for from state appropriations over the biennium. Of the total bond issue, MSC would have been granted $6 million for the new library. The college would then have been allowed to raise up to $1.2 million from contributions and federal funds that may have come available for the project.

Quam said there was a lot of confusion concerning SB2048 in the House last week. He said the House voted 55-51 in favor of considering the concept of bonding. It was thought that a "constitutional majority" was a minimum of 54 to be in favor, but the eventual ruling was that it only needed a majority of the house to be considered as a concept.

Quam said the house then decided to take a look at each of the bond requests separately, but then it discovered that the bill had to be accepted or rejected as a whole and passing the separate parts would make no difference. There was considerable debate over the bill, but the final outcome was a defeat.

MSC's proposed library is a three-story structure to be located on

North Dakota Legislature

1985-87 Biennium

Allen Field and is designed to be a regional facility.

Long-range plan geared for completion. Page 4.

RED&GREEN

The courtship of racquetball. Page 6.

Vol. 66 No. 25 April 10, 1985 Minot (N.D.) State College

An American

To David Haaland, freedom isn't just a word anymore, it's a new sensation.

by Patty Francis

"If you have a goal and an aim, you can get anything here," said David Haaland about his new home—the United States of America.

Haaland, a defector from the country of Iraq, recently became an American citizen after five years of impatient waiting. During that time, he has attended Minot State College studying computer science and mathematics and is expecting to graduate this spring.

Haaland said he sent his citizenship application forms to a review board in Minnesota after a five-year naturalization process was completed Feb. 26, 1985. "The next week, I went to Minnesota and called them up. I couldn't wait for them to call me," said Haaland. They told him they had sent his papers to Portal, N.D.

When he returned to Minot, he called the Portal review board and was told he would have to wait until May, since the board only conducted the interviews twice a year in Minot. With "freedom" so close at hand, Haaland asked if he could go to Portal rather than waiting until May. "They were nice and told me if I wanted to take the time to drive up there, I could." So he did.

After quite a few questions, form signatures and paying his fees, Haaland became an American citizen March 15, 1985. This five-year journey was the easy part, however, compared to what he initially went through to leave his native country.

The most difficult part of his quest for citizenship, he said, was obtaining a passport to leave his native country. "They (the Iraqi government) knew I was pro-Western countries, and because of that, I was not entitled to do anything," explained Haaland. "Actually, I was in a big jail....There was a big danger on my life."

Haaland's brother Robert, also an MSC senior majoring in biology, defected five years before David from their native city of Baghdad. Haaland said his brother told him his best chance of getting to America was via some western country that had "good relations" with America.

"It took me a couple of years, but with the help of some of my friends, I obtained a fake visa to West Germany," Haaland explained that at this time, he couldn't come directly to America, because there wasn't an American embassy in Iraq due to poor international relations.

"When I landed in Germany, I still couldn't believe I was there. All the time I was on the plane, I was thinking, 'What if the Arab plane turns back for some reason, and they discover my fake passport?'"

Haaland left his parents and 10 brothers and sisters behind when he came to America. He said it was "too dangerous," and they decided to not "take the chance at the time."

Citizen page 8

In his pursuit of American citizenship, David Haaland's first and most difficult task involved finding the means to escape his native country of Iraq.

R&G Inwords

In the outdoor season premiere, the Minot State College women tracksters finished third at the Wildcat Invitational meet in Wahpeton last Wednesday, while the MSC men's team crossed the finish line in fifth place. The University of North Dakota-Grand Forks claimed the titles in both divisions. Page 6.

Another one joins the rest as Red & Green sports editor Bryan Obenchain joins the ranks of broadcasters and writers who have named their own version of an All-American team. In this week's Sports Table, Obenchain's Outstanding 5 plus 1 team has a definite eastern flavor. Page 7.

Front page of Red & Green

8 April 10, 1985 Red & Green

Freedom new sensation to Minot State student

Citizen page 1

He said his family wasn't even allowed to see him off, because Arabic airports and airplanes were often subject to terrorist attacks. "Everyone was afraid they'd set off (officials) would discover my fake passport" while the officials were ensuring that he was not a terrorist.

When he reached West Germany, he said he had to first become a permanent resident before he could obtain a passport to America. "After I became a permanent citizen of West Germany, I was sure that I didn't have to go back to my country...I had my fake passport for a month and within that time, I was in touch with the American embassy."

With the help of his brother in

deported his family to Iran. "They (the Iraqi government) took over everything - belongings, furniture, my father's business - everything."

He said it was some time before the Iranian government allowed them to enter the country. "They lived in the border until the government approved that they were safe." According to Haaland, the Iraqi government often deports Kurdish people to Iran and plants Arab spies among them.

He said his family is still "starting from scratch" after five years in a foreign country, and is still trying to overcome the language barrier. He said, "It's impossible for me to visit them" because of the unstable atmosphere between Iran and Iraq.

"Everybody down there is in danger, whether you're active or

Despite his difficulty, Haaland began working at a local health clinic in November, 1980, where he works now. He said he has been sending resumes "all over," and if he doesn't receive any response by June, he will probably move to Minnesota. "The sad thing is there is nothing here for a computer science major."

Haaland said his stay in West Germany before coming to North Dakota helped him to adjust to the different climate. "It's a little weird, but I'm getting used to it. I had to get used to it in Germany before coming to America, so it wasn't so bad."

Although his diet has changed somewhat, he said he manages to work homemade cooking into his schedule now and then. "The main dishes in Iraq include soups and

❝ ...I was thinking, 'What if the Arab plane turns back for some reason and they discover my fake passport?'. **❞**

—David Haaland

Minot and the sponsorship of the Christ Lutheran Church of Minot, Haaland reached Minot Feb. 26, 1980, and eventually, Minot State College.

Haaland said much of his reason for leaving stemmed not only from his beliefs, but also from the fact that he is of the Kurdish nationality. The majority of Iraq is Arabic, and this majority dominates the government.

"They (the Arabs) don't want the Kurds to get their education, because they might try to overthrow the government." He explained that the Kurdish people once resided in their own country of Kurdistan and have since been "split into five pieces" by war. Kurdish people are now situated in Russia, Syria, Turkey, Iran and Iraq, and are frequently at war with each of their respective governments to gain independence.

One month after Haaland came to Minot, the Iraqi government

not," said Haaland. "You get shot if you have a different belief.

"I was lucky and actually, it was my last chance to leave. There was no hope for me there, and I knew my life was in danger...The war really got started after I left and who knows where I'd be now if I'd stayed any longer."

He said the war between Iraq and Iran has left the Iraqi government so low on resources and people, they are shooting anyone who refuses to fight. "They're desperate to take anybody now, because Iraq is not a big country and they are running out of people."

Haaland said although he learned some English by listening to the International radio program, The Voice of America, he still encountered much difficulty with the language when he came to Minot. "I still had language difficulties...no friends and no one to lean on. My brother couldn't help that much."

rices...so I can find all the ingredients around here if I miss the food."

He said he also frequents many of the area's fast food joints. "I like to eat a lot of hamburgers, french fries, pizza...just like any other American.

"To me, within five years of being here and facing all these problems, supporting myself 100 percent and going to school, that proves that anyone can do anything if they put their mind to it.

"There's no reason anyone should say 'I can't do it,' no matter who he or she is....It was difficult for me, but I'm becoming more comfortable every day."

Haaland said he probably couldn't have done it with less difficulty if he had started out in a larger city. "Minot was a good start for me. The people are so nice....No matter where I end up, I'll never forget I made it in Minot."

Deadline

The deadline for all advertising, Classifieds, Campus Notes, Letters and Clippings is noon Friday prior to the publication date

Inside page of Red & Green

Citizenship

Pictures taken by my friend, Linda of citizenshp

Party planned and pictures taken by my friend, Linda

My Citizenship

and everyone wanted to talk to me, whether I knew them or not. I felt like a campus celebrity, but I did not quite understand why they were all so interested in me.

In the following weeks, I was being greeted by people outside the college. No matter where I was, people would come up to me with smiles and congratulations. I learned that the issue had been reprinted several times because of the demand. Apparently, people were taking the article home and sharing it with their families. I finally understood the appeal one day when my friends and I went to a restaurant other than Country

Kitchen for dinner. An older lady came up to me and wanted to shake my hand. I stood up and gave her a hug. She said many flattering and encouraging things to me, such as, "My son, you opened up our eyes to how good we have it and how much we don't appreciate what we have." She warmly welcomed me to my new home and new country.

I continued to study hard despite my exciting "brush with fame" episode. My cousin in Minnetonka said I could move into an extra room he had in his apartment for a few months until I found a job and could be on my own. It was his idea, and he was very excited about it. At first, I was not as eager, but after several phone calls, I agreed. I boxed some of my belongings and shipped them to my cousin just to make it easier on myself when I was ready to move.

One day I was amazed to get a call from Karen, for the first time, telling me that she was coming to visit me. I welcomed this but didn't know what to make of it. Why now? Why the sudden change of heart after all the effort on my part? The following weekend Karen surprised me again by driving to Minot and driving herself home, and this continued to happen. Soon she not only came to visit but decided to stay and spend Saturday nights with me and leave on Sundays. I was completely over-whelmed by this sudden change of heart but did not waste a lot of time in trying to figure it out. I was just happy about it and only looked ahead. The quarter ended, and I had passed all five courses and was eligible to graduate. The big day was Friday, May 24, 1985, scheduled only one week after another major event—the citizenship ceremonies on May 17 at the U.S. District Court of North Dakota. It was truly difficult to say which one was more important. I told everyone I knew, including my friends at work. I was very excited and had not even thought about who would be at these events other than myself, but it was not going to be that simple. My friend from work, Linda, asked me if anyone was going with me. I answered, "No, why?"

"I am coming with you, David," she replied. Linda actually took some time off from her nursing schedule to come to the courthouse to see me and some other people from all over the world going through the ceremony to become citizens of the United States. I was so very proud to finally be a citizen of a country, no longer stateless. Linda took many memorable pictures, and we went back to work a few hours later. She had arranged a big celebration party in the break room with cake and a lot of cards. Most of the doctors and nurses and all the other employees came to wish me luck. Linda truly made the day even more memorable than it already was. I did not have the means for such a celebration, and having her take it upon herself meant a lot to me. I have stayed in touch with Linda and her husband Ken, no matter where they are living. For some reason, Karen did not attend the big event. I am not sure if I had even invited her.

I was still flying above the clouds the following week as my graduation day neared. My cousin and his family were coming to town to help me celebrate. I planned to let them use my bedroom, and I would sleep on the couch. Then I learned that Karen was also planning to come to my graduation and would also be staying at my apartment. I did not worry, as I knew we could manage for one night. I thought that we would all be so busy visiting that no one would be able to sleep anyway.

They all arrived on Thursday, May 23. I had invited my brother to come and stay too, but for some reason, he had made himself unavailable. I was not sure if it was because of my cousin, but in any case, I didn't think that was a good reason. He did say he would attend the ceremony the next day. My cousin took us all out to dinner, and we did lots of talking. His wife then went off with some of her old North Dakota friends, and we were all sleeping when she finally came back.

I went to campus a few hours before my guests to take part in the graduation rehearsal. I eagerly scanned the audience as the ceremony was about to begin and finally spotted Karen, my cousin and his family, and my friend, Ram, and his wife. I did not see my brother and hoped to find out what had happened to him after it was over.

Graduation

Cheers and camera flashes were all over. I was hoping that either Karen or my cousin had brought a camera to capture the moment. The governor of North Dakota was the keynote speaker. I was hoping to have my picture taken with him when he handed me my diploma, and I did. When my name was called, I was very surprised to hear many cheers for me from all corners. I had not known that all these people knew me. After the ceremony, I found Karen, Ram, and my cousin, and my brother was standing with them. I asked him why he hadn't sat with the others, and he gave me some kind of excuse. I said nothing, knowing that he was probably hurt that I had graduated before him, despite his early start.

We decided to go out for lunch, but once again, my brother did not join us because of yet another excuse. Though upset with his childish behavior, I did not want to show my displeasure on such a day, and we went on without him. After lunch, my cousin and his family went to visit friends, and I went to work. We planned to spend the next day making plans to finalize my move. I hoped it would go well, because my cousin and his wife seemed to be at odds all the time, and his wife seemed a little domineering. I made every effort to stay out of their constant arguments.

The next day my cousin and I finalized all the arrangements. He promised me his son's room, which had a mattress but no bed. I told him that would be fine and that I could wait to buy a bed until I was on my own. He also promised to take me with him to the factory where he worked to inquire about a job with him until I was able to find a job in the computer field. I was happy about that, as I needed some income so I would not feel like a burden on him and his family. I would give notice to my work and landlord, and be in Minnesota by the end of June 1985. My cousin and his family left the next day, and I did my cleaning and laundry, sorting all my remaining belongings to decide what I could carry with me in the car and what I could donate or toss. I was happy that I had no furniture to worry about.

Karen was aware of my upcoming move to Minnesota, and she came to Minot to be with me every chance she had. I started to think seriously of what to do about our relationship. I still did not know the reasons behind the sudden change in her behavior. I did know that in spite of the change, I still did not relate to her as I had to Denise or Nadia. However, I often questioned my own judgment and assumed it was just my imagination. At that point, I was not able to see my move to Minnesota as a new opportunity in a much bigger state. I was seeing everything only as the end of my days in North Dakota—a very strange feeling, but that is how I was looking at it. And feeling that way, I started to think of maybe becoming engaged to Karen before I moved to Minnesota. Why? I have no idea. To this day, I have no answer to that question.

I did not discuss the idea of getting engaged to Karen with anyone; I just tried to think of a way to make it happen. First, I had to find a place to buy the engagement ring. My criteria were that the store would let me return the ring in case she said no and that they would let me buy it on credit, as I was quite short on cash. After some searching, I found JC Penney met my criteria; I could even exchange the ring later for something bigger or better if we chose to. That was an easy solution, and the engagement ring was bought. I made sure I saved the receipt as a backup plan. I still have that receipt.

Next, I needed a special restaurant for the proposal. I looked very hard and finally found the Field & Stream, located a bit north of the city out by the airport. It was quiet and romantic, a rare thing for Minot at that time. I was very nervous. I had called the restaurant ahead of time and asked for a private seating area. I waited for the right moment and proposed. She accepted without hesitation. All that was left was to pick the date, sometime in mid-June 1985, and hope for the best.

In the weeks before I left, I painted the small kitchen as a thank you gesture to my nice landlord. There had been no lease or deposit, but I wanted to spare him the expense of getting the apartment ready for the next tenant. I said goodbye to many close friends at the clinic with a promise to stay in touch. Denise had not attended my graduation, and I did not see her afterward. I wondered if I would ever run into her again. I was sad to leave all my Kurdish friends behind, especially Ram and his wife, and I promised to stay in touch with them, too.

My brother was not happy that I was going to live with my cousin, but I had realized that he was not going to be happy no matter what I did. I loaded all my remaining possessions into my car, ready to drive off to begin a new chapter of my life. It had been only five years and a few months since I had arrived from West Germany. I knew that I had done well, and I was ready for whatever challenges I might find in Minnesota. I also had several thousand dollars worth of student loans, but I planned to repay them at the earliest opportunity.

Just then, some very ill-timed problems came up with my car. I had been driving the older four-door Audi for the past several years. I was totally in love with it, but I always had issues repairing it. The nearest dealer for Audi was located in a town called Mandan just outside of Bismarck, so any time I needed service, it was a two-hour drive, a wait for the service, and a two-hour drive back. It became very costly, but I just could not see myself without this fine car. On the way to Bismarck (which, fortunately, was on the way to Minnesota), I had to trust the first mechanic I found just to stay on the road. This was a big mistake, as I ended up spending a lot of money without resolving the issue. When I finally made it to the Audi dealer, they immediately knew what the problem was and replaced a computer box. But the damage had already been done by the other mechanics—they had forever ruined some of the wiring.

After a very long drive worrying about whether my car was going to make it, I arrived at my cousin's. He had already talked to the manager about my living arrangement, and she was fine with it. We unloaded my car in a couple of trips to my bedroom, where I found all of my boxes that I had shipped earlier. I washed up and relaxed, ready for dinner. My internal alarms started to go off, as I noticed that my cousin's wife did not seem to be happy at all. I was not sure if it was because of me or because they'd had an argument before my arrival. I did not say anything but took a mental note and hoped that I was wrong.

On Monday, my cousin did not go to work. He must have called in sick, but he was not sick at all. He just wanted to spend the day lying around by the nice pool that was available for all the tenants. Though I was eager to begin my job search, I just spent that first day at the pool too, because I wanted to get along with my cousin. And I did not have a typewriter, which I would need to work on a résumé and cover letters.

The next day, my cousin did not go to work again, and again he was not sick at all. Their finances were already tight, and I wondered how much worse it would be if he lost his job. I reminded him how he had said he would take me to his place of employment so I could look for a job, but he had better things to do than listen to me. I decided to go and explore the area on my own, even though my car was giving me a lot of trouble. Without a reliable car, it would be nearly impossible to do anything. The highways were more extensive and complicated in Minnesota, unlike Minot, where a stalled car did not create a major issue.

When my cousin had spent a full week without going to work or giving a good excuse, I started to worry a lot, as their financial situation was becoming very serious and their relationship was becoming more and more explosive. I was caught in the middle many times. The refrigerator was empty and there was no money to buy any food, but my cousin was enjoying the poolside as if there were no issues at all. I did not have any money to fix my car or buy a different one, I was new to the state, and I had not established any credit history to rely on.

In the midst of all this chaos, my cousin's wife started to blame me for her husband's behavior and his not going to work. I tried to tell her that I wanted him to go to work and take me with him to look for a job, but she did not want any part of my answer. I don't think she had ever liked me, even before I moved in with them, but now she had a "reason" to blame me. My cousin never could reason with his wife and always avoided her, which made her even more explosive. When he stormed out of the apartment after one of their arguments, she took it out on me, calling me every name in the book, and ordered me to leave their apartment right away. So I went out, telling her that I was going to look for a place, but I did not even know how to do that. I just wanted her to calm down.

I went over to join the crowds of people by the pool and wait for my cousin to come back. When he did, I immediately told him everything his wife had said and that I needed his help in finding a place of my own. I was not sure how I was going to pay for it; I just needed it. My cousin did not know what to do either, but then he said, "Let me talk to the manager to see if she can somehow help." He had always had a good relationship with Linda and her husband, the co-manager. I told him not to forget to mention that I currently did not have any money. We went back to the apartment to try to have a peaceful evening. I went to my room to ponder my dilemma.

The next morning, my cousin did not go to work once again. Before noon, his work called him to tell him that he was fired and needed to go and pick up his belongings. He did not appear upset, as he had wanted to be fired and was expecting it. He said he would talk to Linda when he saw her at the pool. I actually never wanted to use the pool, because I was only a guest and did not feel I had that privilege. Besides, I was a terrible swimmer (or a good sinker).

That afternoon, my cousin gave me some good news. Linda and her husband had agreed to lease me a two-bedroom apartment. I could move in immediately and did not even have to pay the balance of the July rent. My rent would begin in August. I was very happy about the deal. I signed the lease and received the keys. My apartment was in a different building, which was nice, as I no longer wanted to come face-to-face with my cousin's wife.

The apartment was clean and ready to be occupied. I moved all my belongings in, happy to be done listening to arguments and accusations. I immediately had a reality check. I had nothing to sit on. I did not have anything to sleep on either—no mattress or pillow, no television, nothing to eat with, and nothing to even eat. Nevertheless, I was grateful for the opening of this door after a door had been closed in my face the day before. Not having a chair to sit on was the least of my worries, and I immediately told myself, *If you managed to sleep in the desert with snakes and scorpions sharing your self-made pillow, you can manage here.* I remembered seeing a gas station called Food & Fuel within walking distance, so I went there and bought a bottle of soda and a snack. I walked back to the empty apartment where I sat on the carpet in the corner and ate my snack. I was happy how things had turned out. There was nothing for me to do except unpack all my boxes. I stacked all my cassette tapes into neat piles but had no cassette player. However, my car did. I truly enjoyed myself for the first time in several days. After listening to my favorite tape while sitting in my car, I decided to go back to the empty apartment and find a way to sleep. I piled up some items of clothing on the carpet and made a pillow of others, though I had nothing with which to cover myself. What I had was a lot of time to reflect on recent events and what I should do from that point on. I always trusted that everything would work out. I went to sleep very peacefully.

I woke up in the morning, realizing again that I did not have anything to eat or eat with. Money and credit was very tight, but food was a necessity. After finishing my shower, I decided to drive to a Kmart about four miles away in Minnetonka. I was very careful and stayed in the right lane to be close to the shoulder in case I sensed any potential trouble with my car. I made it there fine, and the first thing I bought was an air mattress and a pump. I also bought a toaster, bread, a dozen eggs, a couple of plates, forks, a cup, a coffee maker, and coffee—and I was ready to celebrate my abundance.

Back at my apartment, I made coffee, boiled eggs, made toast, and had the best meal I'd eaten in several days. I pumped up the mattress so it would be ready to go that evening. The next priority was finding a job, as I was going to need to pay rent in a couple of weeks and get a reliable car as soon as possible. I checked with stores and gas stations nearby in Excelsior and Minnetonka. A gas station near the Kmart, called Jet, had an opening, and I filled out the application. The next day they called to offer me a cashier's job. I jumped for joy and affirmation. There were papers to sign and a brief training period. The pay was minimum wage, but that was not the important part for me. I just wanted to feel better about myself and know that I was making some money to keep myself focused on finding a job in my computer field. I started working the next day. I was not worried too much about my car troubles, as the job was a little more than four miles away, and I knew I could walk it if I had to. During that time, whenever I saw an application for a credit card, I took one and applied, regardless of what the credit card was for. I wanted to have cards for all the gas companies, retail stores, or any other. This was my way of trying to overcome my lack of money and to also build a credit rating. Within weeks, I was proudly adding credit card after credit card to my wallet. No matter where I needed gas, I could stop to fill up because I had the appropriate credit card.

I talked to Karen periodically and gave her updates on what was going on with me, and she gave me updates on herself. The reality was that even though we were engaged, we did not have those long romantic phone talks like you would expect. I can honestly say my emotions and feelings were not any different while talking to Karen than when I was talking to my own brother. It is strange but totally true. I also kept in contact with my brother, despite his cold reception to my phone calls. I never knew his exact issues, but his behavior never stopped me from reaching out to him.

My car was becoming a mystery, as I did not know when it would work and when it would not. I did not have enough cash for a mechanic who specialized in German cars. My job search was truly stuck because of that. The living arrangement was getting very old also, as the air mattress was really uncomfortable. It seemed as though I was getting up more tired than I was before I went to bed. Lack of any tables or chairs was not helping matters either. My diet was mostly eggs and toast because of the price and the ease of preparation.

I encountered several days when my car did not start, and I had to walk to work. That was easy during daylight, but more difficult going home at night. Once in a while I could get a ride with a customer if they were headed west. If I couldn't get a ride from the gas station, I just walked; I never tried to hitchhike. My cousin never offered to help, and it seemed as if he and his wife had completely forgotten me.

I learned from my brother that Ram had been instructing him in how to buy cars at auction and sell them for profit. I told him I thought it might not be so easy for him, as he did not have the knowledge about cars that Ram had. Of course, my brother never liked anything I had to tell him. I also learned that he was trying to sell his Camaro, and I told him that I would like to buy it. The price sounded very reasonable. He asked me where I would get the money, and I told him that I had a good relationship with a banker in Minot and was sure I could get a loan. We made an agreement, and all I had to do was let him know when I could fly to Minot to close the sale. I said I would check on the ticket prices and let him know.

Part 4:

The Dream Turns into a Nightmare (1985–2012)

CHAPTER FIFTEEN
· ·

The Unity Candle

One-way tickets to Minot were much more expensive than I expected. I was told it was because Minot was a small airport with very limited flights. As soon as I had enough money from my job, I purchased the ticket. I was counting on my gas credit cards for the five-hundred-mile drive home. My brother was waiting for me at the airport. I somehow expected he would give me the car keys, but that was not the case. He drove us to Northwest Bank but didn't seem very happy to see me, even after months of being away from each other. I was very quiet and did not act like a buyer acts before buying anything. Nothing like, "Let me see under the hood."

We greeted the banker and told him what we were there for. He pulled records about me and checked to see if there was any information that had changed. Everything seemed fine until he asked me the killing question, "Do you still work at Medical Arts Clinic?" I responded that I worked at the Jet gas station in Minnesota. The banker closed his eyes and said, "I am sorry, David, I really cannot approve of a loan if you moved to another state." I was totally crushed and tried everything to change his mind, but to no avail.

I was feeling stuck, as I did not have enough money to even think about flying back to Minnesota. In the midst of my dilemma, I came up with the idea of calling Karen and telling her about my issues. I did not feel right or comfortable asking Karen to lend me money for the airline ticket, but I wanted to see what other opportunities might present themselves. A couple of hours later, Karen called and said she would come to get me and take me to their house. On the way, she offered her little car for me to use. She said she could easily walk to work and had no real need for it; she could always use one of the many cars her family owned. I liked the idea a lot but wanted to make sure that she was telling me the truth. I never liked to impose myself on anyone, even my fiancée. She insisted it would be fine, and I accepted. I told Karen's parents the entire story about how much I needed a car, both to look for a job and to get to my gas station job. After dinner, I excused myself, because I still had about a nine-hour drive to Minnesota.

I was still furious with my brother about his lack of generosity and also very grateful to Karen, wondering how I would have been able to return to Minnesota without her help. I was starting to think about setting a wedding date, in spite of what various people had been saying to me. The general comments were that I did not seem madly in love with my fiancée and maybe I should wait a bit longer to see whom I might meet in Minnesota. I was somewhat in agreement with them, but I also somehow felt obligated to move forward to what I saw as my inevitable next step—marriage. I could not imagine breaking my engagement. This feeling was strictly based on my moral values and not how I really felt. The car incident and Karen's gesture had helped strengthen my resolve. With my new mobility, I put my job search into high gear. I talked to everyone I encountered about my degree in computer science. To get as much of a head start as I could, I pored over the *Minneapolis Star & Tribune* Sunday paper. I revised my résumé and cover letter many times, writing it down on paper every time I thought of something that I should have included. I was hoping to soon have enough money to buy a typewriter. At the Jet gas station, I was doing a great job. I was attending to customers, emptying garbage, sweeping, doing everything that needed to be done without ever thinking or saying that any job was beneath me. I always did everything as I would expect it to be done if it were my own business. Karen and I set our wedding date: October 19, 1985, at, of course, the Catholic Church in Underwood, North Dakota. The biggest worry was the weather. In North Dakota, one must take the weather very seriously any time after September 1. We just had to hope for the best. I did not have anyone who could participate, so all of the planning was handled by Karen and her family and friends. The only decision I had to make was choosing the best man and the groomsman. With great hesitation, I picked my brother for best man, just for being my brother. I asked my friend, Ram, to be my groomsman.

In August I started a temporary data entry position at Share Development Corporation, a healthcare insurance provider in Bloomington, Minnesota. I was told that the position might be extended, depending on my attitude and work ethic and, of course, the company's need. The location was not too far from where I lived. The pay was only a bit better than minimum wage but still more than what I was making at the gas station. Though it had nothing to do with computer programming, I immediately saw the opportunity and gave the gas station the required two weeks notice. As long as I was working and looking to move ahead, I did not care what anyone said.

It felt great, and I much preferred dressing in business attire for work, something I never had the chance to experience at the clinic or Jet. I loved everything about the job. I had a nice cubicle and was able to meet many nice people with different backgrounds and job titles. I worked primarily for one manager, updating data sheets and producing reports. Though it was very interesting compared to anything I had done before, it was still well below the capabilities I had developed in college. But I always wore a big smile, telling myself I had the best job in the world. I never wanted anyone to know that I was feeling underutilized, but at the same time, I was always on the lookout for opportunities to talk about my qualifications when I felt it was appropriate and the person I was speaking with was capable of helping me.

―――――

I continued to work on my résumé and pore over the newspaper ads. I also made myself a small database of all companies with programming vacancies. Once I could afford a chair and bed, a typewriter to send out cover letters was definitely next on my priority list. My manager really liked my work ethic and wanted to help, but he had no influence over hiring for programming positions. However, he kept encouraging me, and I appreciated that.

My wedding date, October 19, was fast approaching. I still had to go to Underwood to apply for the marriage license and meet with the priest at the Catholic Church. I was able to get ten days off from my job. I was truly out of my comfort zone during the entire week before the wedding. I met many people whom I did not know. I was uneasy about their possible reaction when they saw me for the first time. I knew that minorities were not commonly seen in even the bigger cities in North Dakota at that time, and in a small town like Underwood, they were even more of a rarity. And even more rare than that was a minority person marrying a local girl like Karen.

For many, I was the first minority they had ever seen. I could read many people's minds, but I never said anything. I was very thankful that I had become a citizen before getting married. I had never thought about it until I saw some of the reactions during that week. I knew some people might have grouped me with other immigrants who get married solely to become a citizen. It was strange that anyone would feel that way on what is supposed to be the happiest day of a couple's life.

The hardest part was meeting the Catholic priest to get his blessing and approval. He was very old and had a heavy accent. He was very hard to understand, even for the people who listened to his sermons week after week. I had a very tough time answering his questions, and the meeting seemed to take forever. It was a great relief to leave his office. I had my fingers crossed that it would go better on the wedding day.

The rest of the evening was very hectic for everyone, especially Karen's parents. They were trying to make sure everything was going to be ready and that their house was ready to be seen by their relatives and friends. It seemed as though no one was resting. Everyone had a job to do to make sure that Saturday would go very smoothly. I was very restless, as I was a stranger among them all. On the big day, everyone got up very early. The wedding time was set for midafternoon to allow travel time for all of Karen's relatives. I was all dressed up several hours before the wedding, and was relieved and surprised to see my brother arriving early, without any complications. That was so unlike him; I had been expecting the worst. Of course, not to disappoint me with too much unusual behavior, he started to talk badly about our friend Ram, my groomsman. He said that Ram would for sure be late because he had seen him in Minot running around doing this and doing that. I knew there was plenty of time, so I excused myself in order to not have to listen to my brother's negative thoughts and complaints. Somehow, my brother was always able to find me and feed me more of his unnecessary fears. I was very happy to see Ram and his wife arrive in plenty of time to go over last-minute details.

As the wedding time arrived, I was happy to be done with a very uncomfortable situation among so many people whom I did not know.

I was also nervous about making any mistakes as I had witnessed very few weddings. Everything began according to plan. Karen's family lit both of the wedding tapers, a ceremony that is usually done by the mothers of the bride and the groom. The tapers represent two individual hearts aflame. The bride and groom take the tapers over to a decorated white unity candle and light it. The two flames then burn as one, the two families become one family, and the two lights become one light. The priest exclaims with great hope and enthusiasm, "Let this light shine for all the world to see!"

After Karen and I exchanged our formal vows, we lit the unity candle together, still according to plan. It was supposed to stay lit until the very end of the wedding, after everyone had left for the reception and just before cleaning and closing the church. Only one mistake in the plan was made during our wedding, but it was a very big one, made by my best friend and groomsman, Ram. He was supposed to put out the two taper candles, which he did. But then he followed that by extinguishing the unity candle, right in front of all the wedding attendees. I was not watching when he did it, but the gasp sound by everyone was enough to make Karen and me turn around and see what had happened. I did not want to ask what his mistake might mean. I pretended that it never happened and went outside the church to greet everyone and accept their well wishes.

At the reception hall, our wedding cake was waiting for us. We began the celebration by cutting pieces of cake and feeding them to each other. We also opened some of our gifts. The reception lasted several hours. Once the last guest had left, my new in-laws helped us load the gifts into our car.

Karen and I had reserved a room in a nice hotel in Bismarck. We thanked everyone and drove off. We were both very tired and looking forward to a quiet and peaceful night, knowing that the next morning we had to tackle the eight-hour drive to Minnesota. It was a very ordinary night, as if we had been together for years. I truly cannot say that the night was romantic and full of passion. For some reason, I had been hoping for some passion and romance from Karen. Maybe I was still trying to figure out her sudden change of heart after all of my one-sided attempts to get closer to her. I was always thinking that maybe in the days and years ahead, Karen would somehow warm up to me. That drive to Minneapolis was not any different from two brothers driving. No passion, no holding hands or leaning against each other. I was not even sure if she liked the music I was listening to on the radio.

As we passed through North Dakota towns and cities like Jamestown and Valley City, Karen told me that she had relatives living in many of them. We did not stop at any, as we had planned to keep going until Fargo, the midway point. I could not get my mind off something strange, something that bothered me a lot, but I could not talk to Karen about it. I had met most of Karen's family, but I never saw her older brother, Ron, any time during the entire wedding day. No one even mentioned his absence. I was not sure if Ron disapproved of the marriage, or if he had a conflict with his sister. I suspected it was the former. Not only was Ron absent, but so were his wife and children. I wondered what kind of family discussion had taken place when they learned about our wedding, but I just kept driving.

Just outside Excelsior, I remembered that there was only an air mattress waiting for us. I told this to Karen, but at that point, she did not appear to care. We both just wanted to relax. I stopped at a McDonald's drive-through in Excelsior, as I knew I did not have anything to cook with. We unloaded all the gifts, because I did not want to leave them in the car all night. My cousin came to greet us. When he learned about the air mattress, he mentioned that his next-door neighbor was moving out and selling a water bed very cheap. I said we would go look at it.

〜

The next day we bought a few essential cooking and food items at Kmart and then went to see the water bed. The price was very reasonable, and we decided to buy it. We somehow managed to cook and eat dinner without a dining table or chairs. We did not have a television, so we just kept busy on our job searches and went to bed, hoping the next day would be more productive.

I had a few free days left before having to go back to work, so I decided to use the time to continue going over the wanted ads. Karen had worked in a nursing home in Underwood as an LPN after completing a two-year program. She looked in the paper for nursing home jobs and found one advertised that was within walking distance.

A day or so before I had to go back to my temp job, I got a call from CC Systems in Eagan, where I had applied some weeks earlier for a job, not as a computer programmer but a computer operator. Fully aware of my lack of real-world experience, I would have done almost anything to work my way into a computer programmer job. The company was located about fifteen miles farther than my current place of employment, but I assumed that the wages would be higher and worth the extra drive. The amazing thing was that Karen also got a call from the nursing home about a job only a few hours later. Could our financial hardship finally be coming to an end? Karen came back even happier; she had been offered the job and would start on the same day I had to go back to the insurance company. We planned an exciting weekend of clothes shopping and comparison shopping for furniture. We lived within a few miles of several big shopping malls and decided on Ridgedale and Knollwood. Karen bought some nice new clothes, and we went home, ready to start an exciting new week.

Back at work, I told my manager that I might be back from lunch a little late, because I had to do something with my car. In reality, I made the short drive to CC Systems for my interview. I met with the head of computer operations. He had no questions regarding my qualifications but did wonder why I would apply for a computer operator position instead of computer programmer. I had to be careful on how I responded, as I did not want it to appear that I was having a hard time finding a programmer job. The interview went very well, and he went over the wages and benefits. The wage was not near what I had expected, but it was a little more than my temp job, and most importantly, I would be working with many computer programmers.

I left with a good feeling and was offered the position the next day. We immediately went to Montgomery Ward and ordered a couch with matching love seat, a big console television, and a dining table with six chairs. I charged everything on my Montgomery Ward card. We left the mall very happy and excited that we could finally invite some of Karen's relatives over.

All of a sudden, we had a home where we could actually sit, eat, and watch television. For the first time, we felt like we were living a normal life. That same day, Karen called one of her uncles who lived in the northern suburbs about thirty miles away. They would come to visit us in a few weeks.

CHAPTER SIXTEEN
. . . .

The American Dream Begins (Sort Of)

I was very excited and full of hope about my new job at CC Systems. It seemed very simple, requiring only detailed attention to monitoring computer jobs and being ready to mount proper data tapes onto the computer when needed. Much to my pleasant surprise, there would be a lot of interaction between me and the computer programmers. Even though the shop was disappointingly small, fewer than ten programmers, I was ready to seize any opportunities for a programming position. I was well aware of my lack of real experience. I knew that I needed to be patient and perform very well as an operator in order to get the support I would need when the opportunity for promotion presented itself.

I worked hard and made friends with most of the programmers, joining them for an occasional lunch or other opportunities to socialize. Most were upset to see the company let me work as an operator with my college degree in programming. One of them shared with me stories about how they were treated by the manager and confided that she was also looking for a different job elsewhere. She promised to try to help me whenever I needed help. Her name was Karen. I was very grateful for the people I was working with.

Karen was also starting to show some dissatisfaction with her job at the nursing home. She told me stories about how the facility did not care for the elderly residents. I listened but could not make any judgments, as I was not sure if Karen had any personal issues or if she was telling me the truth. I left it up to her on what she wanted to do with her concerns.

Karen's uncle and his wife came to visit; it was the first time I had met them. I cooked some of the dishes I had learned from watching my mother years ago, such as sautéed and spiced mushrooms, zucchini, and tomatoes with rice. I had become almost professional in cooking some things due to having to cook for myself every Sunday when I was in college. The visit went very well. The entire conversation was about their grown children and relatives whom I did not know much about, but I listened anyway. I did find it very strange that they did not show any interest in me, my background, my family, or anything else related to me. I just listened and made a great attempt to be part of the conversation, as any good host would do, despite the frustration of being ignored as though I were not even there. I did not question them, only wondered if this is how people acted in this country. I did not think it was appropriate to see this kind of treatment so soon. After all, I had thought I was now part of the family.

My job at CC Systems was going well, but I continued to get a bad impression about the way the manager was treating the programmers.

They were all looking for jobs elsewhere, but the job market was not very good, even for experienced programmers.

One day my coworker, Karen, told me privately at lunch that one of the junior programmers had found a new job and would be leaving. She advised me to update my résumé and make my move. I was very grateful and excited, but I was not sure what to do next. I did have many opportunities for interaction with the disliked manager, Randy, and decided to seize one when it came up to share with him my résumé and qualifications. I had decided not to reveal my insider's knowledge of the opening. My initial contact with Randy was not very good; he seemed to be holding out for experienced programmers. I kept my attitude positive. I was not going to give up after only one try.

When the programmer position became officially vacant, I was very excited and went to Randy's office promptly when he called. He spent a long time telling me about why he did not like to hire new graduates, but he was nevertheless ready to bend "the rules" and give me a chance. He explained that he would let me work under the watch of one of the programmers, and if my performance was unsatisfactory, they would let me go without any labor ramifications during the six month probation. In my puzzlement, I assumed he was trying very hard to make me say no. I replied that I had no problems with his proposal and was confident that I would satisfy whoever made the decision. As I was thanking him and getting up to leave, he stopped me and said he had forgotten to tell me that there would not be any change in my salary. I was speechless. He really was doing everything in his power to discourage me, but I was not going to let him be successful. I knew my salary was very low, even for a computer operator, and to do programming work for that amount was unheard of. I nevertheless said I was in full agreement with his proposal and left his office. I finally decided that I had made the best decision and that I would just let God take care of things. Most importantly, I was adding some experience to my résumé, which was the critical thing for me at that time.

It was now 1986. Just as things seemed to be going better, Karen told me that she had just about had it with her nursing home job. I said I shared her concerns and left the decision up to her but reminded her that a job move would require us to get a second car, with expenses like insurance, gas, and maintenance. None of that talk meant anything to her. I reluctantly agreed.

We bought her a car, which allowed her to search for jobs without interrupting my work schedule. This was the first time Karen and I had different opinions on anything, and it was the first time I realized that there was no compromising on her part. Within several weeks, she was hired at a nursing home in a city about ten miles from Excelsior called Hopkins. She was very happy about the facility and the level of care it provided. I was very excited for my wife and wished her the best. I began to think that soon I would also have enough experience to look for a new programming position, likely with a dramatic wage increase. I started to think of home ownership.

Time was flying by, and it seemed as if we were losing the meaning of everything while searching for the perfect jobs. Karen was still raving about her new nursing home job. She had to work every other weekend (both Saturday and Sunday), which did not help our social lives, but she was happy, and that was what mattered at the time.

One Saturday I got a call from Karen's oldest sister from a KOA campground near the Wisconsin border. She, her husband, and their three children had left their home in Underwood, North Dakota, to look for work. They were traveling with a pickup that had a small camper on top. She asked me if we would come and visit them. Karen was working, so I went alone. It was a bit of a drive, but I found them. I was amazed to see five people living in such a small camper, but I never said anything. I spent a few hours with them and wished them well. A few weeks later, we learned that they had decided to stop traveling and had rented an apartment in St. Paul.

I was very happy to have more of Karen's relatives close by. With no relatives of my own to visit, I welcomed all of hers. I missed the family connection. In fact, maybe that was one of the primary reasons I had rushed into getting married without being romantically in love. I did not consider my brother as a relative after how he treated me in Minot. Using all my money for a one-way flight to see him and coming back without a car was something not easy to forgive, especially since I later found out that he had sold his car to someone else. And my cousin and his drama with his wife and being pushed out of his apartment without any means to move was another thing that was very hard to forgive and forget at that time.

I was very surprised one day to get a call from the lead analyst at Health Risk Management. He told me that he had heard from my friend, Karen, about my good work ethic. He offered me a job and hired me on the spot. I went home very happy, as I would be getting a slight salary increase and my work commute was reduced by fifteen miles. It did not take long to find a good real estate agent to help us find out what we needed to purchase a home. In spite of our employment situation and the fact that we both did not have a long employment history, there were many homes that we could qualify for. The problem was that we liked Minnetonka and Excelsior, and both were considered two of the most expensive areas in the state.

As 1986 was coming to an end, we were ready to welcome a new year full of promise. My work at Health Risk Management was going very well. I was only twenty minutes away from home. The programmers at work were very relaxed, and at least once a week we all went out to lunch and had fun together. My manager was telling me he saw things in me that I was not seeing in myself.

The home-showing process in the Excelsior area was very long, tiring, and confusing. We ended up finding a small house in Minnetonka only about two miles away from our apartment in Excelsior. It needed many updates and did not have a garage, but the location made us over-look many of its issues. We decided to make an offer and wait for either a counteroffer or an acceptance.

After a couple of counteroffers, we finally had an agreement, and all of sudden, we owned our first home! Although happy to own a home, I was scared to death. I had never been around anyone fixing anything or doing any maintenance on appliances, furnaces, or the like. Despite my fears, I knew that I had no choice but to learn—somehow. I was hoping that when my in-laws found out that we had just bought a home, they would be very proud of me and come to visit and show me what I needed to do. I hoped to prove to them that I was worthy of marrying their daughter, if anyone had any doubts. Their acceptance and approval had been an issue for me from the beginning, especially after Karen's oldest brother and his family had not attended the wedding and no one had given a reason. We had no gifts from him, not even a card. He had planted the seeds of doubt in my mind right from the beginning, and it never went away in the days and years that followed.

Owning a home slowly turned me into a handyman. One of the first things that I wanted to change about the house was its electrical fixtures and outlets. It had no ceiling lights—it was designed to have only table lamps as light sources. I did not like that, and I also wanted ceiling fans. When I called electricians for estimates, I quickly gave up the idea of hiring contractors and decided to learn to do it myself.

I started buying books and going to home center suppliers and asking questions. I started my work in one room. Taking the electrical power from any outlet to the middle of the ceiling behind finished walls seemed a little challenging at first, especially working in the dark attic. Making mistakes was not an option. It took me a long time to do one room, but that gave me the confidence to tackle the entire house. I utilized every free moment to update the electrical system.

House in Minnetonka

Home projects proved to be very expensive. I never stopped buying the Sunday version of the *Star Tribune* to monitor the trends and the market and never stopped applying for any promising jobs. Karen's job was still going fine, and I did not hear any complaints from her about anything. So 1987 was moving in a busy, yet uneventful, fashion.

One of the many places where I applied was a local government branch, which was looking for several computer programmers. The location was near the airport, which was the same as my prior job at CC Systems. I was attracted to that particular job because during that time there was a huge demand for a type of software that I did not have any experience in. Becoming more marketable was my main incentive at that time, besides a potential increase in salary.

In those days, I was either at my job working or in the attic working on my remodeling projects. Karen was not interested in any of that. It seemed as though I was doing it all for myself. I truly had issues with the way Karen was in general. She never suggested any initiatives— anything to do, places to go—none of that. Right from the beginning, it seemed as if we were more roommates than husband and wife.

It was also during this time that I developed a love for dogs. Since we had our own home, I decided to get one—a cocker spaniel. Since my work was close by, I came home during lunch just to check on the dog and let him out for a few minutes. The entire neighborhood, except the lady next door (a single lady living alone), loved our dog and wanted to see it. This neighbor did not seem to be interested in socializing or even being nice to us, though this was not an issue at that time. I was busy with remodeling, and we were not spending a lot of time outside anyway.

One great thing that happened in 1987 was when I learned that Neil Diamond was coming to Minnesota. I knew my friend, Linda, from the Medical Arts Clinic, loved Neil Diamond and that her dream was to see him in concert. I called her, and she was very excited. I was able to get tickets for all four of us. We picked her and her husband up at the airport on the day of the concert. I could never forget what Linda had done for me during my citizenship and for being a great friend. This was my first live concert, and I was glad to share the experience with two true friends. It was now 1988. I had loved the idea of having children for a long time, but whenever the thought came up, I always found myself choosing to wait, despite coming from a big family. I was just not sure about Karen, and even after a couple years of being married, I was not madly and passionately in love with her—not really in love at all. I knew I was married and was honoring the vows, but something was missing. I kept moving ahead, pretending that everything was great.

In January 1988, I received what might be called a blast from the past. The local government office called me for an interview for a position lesser in grade and salary than what was initially advertised. My response was nevertheless positive, because it was an opportunity to learn the software that I was looking to learn. I was hired to start in February. Despite the lower grade, my new salary was more than what I was getting at Health Risk Management, and I was very happy about that. By this time, I had remodeled most of the house, including the kitchen, and painted inside and out. Now I could afford to pay attention to some of the things that were luxuries earlier. I began to think that we needed a garage to keep the car and garden tools in. I did not know what to do or how to do it, so I hired a contractor. It cost a lot of money and time and dealings about building permits, but it was finally ready. A new garage deserved a new vehicle, so I celebrated the occasion by purchasing a brand-new small pickup. This was the first new vehicle Karen and I had purchased together.

The garage celebration did not last very long. Soon we heard a complaint from the lady next door claiming that the garage was built on her property. The lady's name, not to be forgotten, was Dee Dee. We explained the long process we had gone through to get the permit including a complete survey to our house and the property lines. Dee Dee was not interested in being reasonable and threatened to take us to court. The following week while I came home during lunch to check on my puppy, I saw Dee Dee had hired her own surveyor checking on the property lines. I just shook my head.

It was clear that the surveyor had not provided her satisfactory results, because she never went to court or filed any complaints. Instead, she made it her life's purpose to make our lives very miserable. Every time we let our dog outside, Dee Dee called the police to complain. The police kindly advised us to keep the dog on a leash. However, the calls continued and irritated even the police department to the point where they suggested free mediation. Karen and I welcomed this. However, it proved worthless, as Dee Dee was very stubborn and did not want to come to any solution. I had spent a lot of time and money to remodel the home, and the thought of moving was very frustrating. Karen and I decided to go about our business and try to ignore this unhappy person. Having the garage built and then the Dee Dee situation made the year go by like a flash. I passed the probation period at the local government office. The entire neighborhood liked us and our dog, but they could not help us resolve the problems with Dee Dee. She was very lonely and never had anyone visiting her, and unfortunately, we became her only game to play.

Karen and I hoped for a peaceful 1989. Early that year we had visits from my in-laws and my sister-in-law and her boyfriend. It seemed as if Dee Dee knew when we had company and picked those times to call the police and embarrass us in front of our company. This went on regardless of who was visiting us. The police were very sensitive to what we were going through and often came inside to give us comforting words, but they were required to respond.

We decided that it would be best to look for another home to avoid any serious issues. I was very afraid that I might lose my temper and cause myself problems. We did not know how to start this process, but our peace of mind was all that mattered. I had fallen in love with the Minnetonka and Excelsior area and did not see any other areas that could make me as happy. Karen was not coming up with any ideas regarding this matter or anything else, even though I was very emotional about the idea of moving away and leaving our first home where I had done all the remodeling work. Karen had never helped with any of that, so she was emotionally unattached to the house.

My love for my dog was unconditional, and I had just added another cocker spaniel to keep the first one company. To avoid any further dog problems, I decided to limit our search to homes built on at least five acres so we would have running room for the dogs. However, I was well aware that any home in our area with five acres would be an impossible task financially, so I decided to look farther west, possibly in a country setting. We went many miles west of Excelsior to towns like Waconia and even farther.

CHAPTER SEVENTEEN
· ·

Putting Down Roots

I found a friendly realtor, Craig, and told him about our situation, the type of home we were looking for, and our budget limits. He showed us three or four homes in the Delano area. They were not to our liking, but he was taking notes about our preferences and said he would continue the search. We told no one of our home search, including the neighbors whom we loved. We did not want anyone to try changing our minds, wanting only to escape Dee Dee's harassment. All of our Saturdays were spent either looking at homes or hosting Karen's sister and her family, and we were driving many miles. It was taking a toll on us, and we had yet to see a home that we really liked. Most were old country homes that required a lot of remodeling and updates and had floor plans not to our liking. Craig finally suggested we start looking for "bare land." I had never heard this term before, so I simply asked him, "And what would I do with bare land?" He said we could build the home we liked. I had no idea how and what one would need to build a home, so I said I would think about his suggestion. I talked to a few friends, and they all said building a home was easy—find a contractor, and they will do everything. So I called Craig and told him to start looking for bare land.

By this time, I had received a promotion that brought me up to the grade I had initially applied for. Karen's job was also going very well. We continued to discuss having children, but despite my desire for it, I was still not ready and still not sure about Karen. Also, she expressed no thoughts or ideas. I clearly did not know what exactly I needed to do to make her display any loving emotions. The longer we went on with our marriage, the more questions I had about Karen. But I never thought of ending it, just because of who I was and what I thought about marriage and relationships. I was always hopeful that someday I would discover what was missing to make Karen more passionate and loving.

Craig soon found some bare land to show us. My jaw was almost on the ground when I saw it. I asked him, "Craig, is five acres really that big?" He laughed and said that it was not five acres but rather forty acres. "Forty acres?" I responded. "What do you think I will do with forty acres?" I wanted only five acres. Craig had thought I was aware of the common knowledge of this area, which is that the smallest parcel of land was forty acres. He said that by law, one cannot divide agricultural land into less than forty-acre lots and that a forty-acre lot can have only one house built on it. Craig truly liked me as a person, and he wanted to help as much as he could. It was clear that he did not want me to be scared of the forty acres, but for me, it was a lot to comprehend. I promised him I would keep an open mind and was willing to continue looking. He had several parcels in mind to show us. I was not happy with any of them. The more homes and land we saw, the more I revised and improved my wish list of things I wanted Craig to look for.

One of the properties had one very appealing and unique feature—the Crow River at its edge. I liked it so much that I asked Craig to start looking only for properties with access to rivers or ponds. He said that would narrow the selection, but they were out there; he agreed to show us only property with water access in order not to waste anybody's time.

We narrowed it down to two properties and then to one. The seller was open to a contract for deed with a small down payment and reasonable monthly payments. The forty acres was in a city called Waverly, about thirty miles west of Excelsior. The biggest problem was its fifty-mile distance from my work. I thought very hard about that, but the chance to be free from Dee Dee made the decision a little easier, and we made an offer. After a counteroffer from the seller, we signed off on the deal.

Now it was time to select a home plan. I did all the research. As usual, Karen never seemed at all interested and took everything for granted. I was able to find a builder who could work within the amount preapproved by the mortgage company. We found a willing buyer for our Minnetonka home who needed to close and move in within two months. That was not enough time for us to build anything, so we decided to rent a house near our property and store most of our furniture. It was sad to know our days were almost over in the home I had spent so much time remodeling.

We spent the next few weekends loading our pickup with furniture, dropping it at the storage facility, and looking for rental houses in Waverly. Our lack of familiarity with the area made the search difficult, especially because we needed a place where they would allow us to have two small dogs. I was becoming desperate to the point where I even considered going to a hotel, despite the cost. I tried to negotiate something where I could leave the dogs in a crate outside during the night and tie them up during the day, but to no avail, not even at a small motel. We had just about given up hope when I noticed a sign at a gas station in Delano about a home for rent. The house was behind the station and belonged to the owner. He said it was an old home that had been flooded some years ago, and the floors were all uneven. After I told him that we would not have a lot of furniture, that we both worked, and that we needed only a place to sleep, he said he would rent it to us. The only hitch was that it was on a month-to-month basis, which meant he could ask us to leave any time. I was surprised, since the home was truly unlivable, but we signed the rental agreement. Now at least we could relax.

———

On our last day in the Minnetonka house, I went alone to clean up and collect our few remaining belonging. This day would truly be burned into my memory. I was having a very difficult time and was emotionally exhausted, knowing this was it. I loaded the truck and drove away feeling defeated. I knew Dee Dee was watching from behind her curtains. I wondered why she had done the things she did. I always knew that there had to be a reason behind her troubles but did not know exactly what. At the end of the day, she had been able to drive us away from my favorite area, and I now had to do what I needed to do to get over this hurt.

As I drove away for the last time, I looked over and recognized a Minnetonka officer in his police car heading in the same direction as I was going. I knew the officer recognized me, and he must have known about our move. I truly expected him to stop me any minute to give me some encouraging words, but he did not. I just knew that he wanted to. For many years, I considered this day to be one of the worst days of my life because it was our last day in Minnetonka. That is how I was feeling then, but was it really the worst day?

Karen and I started driving to work together in the morning from Delano, with me at the wheel. It seemed safer and cheaper to do that, given our recently extended commute. I dropped her off in the morning and picked her up in the evening. This drive gave us a sense of what the Waverly commute would be like. I contacted the home builder to see what he needed to start the work on which he had already given us an estimate. When he saw our property, he added several thousand to his original estimate, which made it impossible to be approved for a mortgage. He explained that his estimate had been based on building in the city. In a rural area, he would have to add the cost of a water well, a septic tank, extension of the electricity from the town road to the house, and, of course, a long driveway. I could not argue with him, but I had not considered all these extra expenses. Based on the new estimate, I had to rethink what we needed to do.

Temporary mobile home

Digging the water well

At the same time I received this bad news, the landlord gave us notice to leave the house at the end of the month. I tried to learn if we had done anything wrong, but he simply said, "I need the home, and you must leave." I accepted this, as I did not want any trouble. However, we could not find anywhere to move. I offered another month's rent to the landlord, but he refused my money and threatened to take me to court and evict me that way. I had no choice but to tell him nicely to do whatever he wanted, because I was trying everything I could do to accommodate his wishes.

We soon received a notice to appear in court in ten days. I assumed the worst, that we might be forced to leave, so I asked everyone about our situation. I learned about a used mobile home that I could buy very cheaply and move to the property. If we could get a permit, we could live there temporarily.

Soon it was time to go to court for the rented house case. I decided not to hire an attorney, as I did not feel that I had done anything wrong. The judge asked everyone to state their position and then asked if I had given the landlord the rent. I responded that I made several attempts to give him the check on time, but he refused. I even showed the judge the check with the date on it. Then he asked if I was looking for another place. I said yes and told him the full story, including my application to the county for a mobile home permit. The judge glared at the landlord and said angrily, "What else do you need from this young man? He gave you the rent, and he is looking for a place. Don't you have any compassion in your heart?" He dismissed the case and wished me luck.

I left the court very inspired by the judge and the justice system. In the process I had learned that the landlord had promised to rent the house to one of his relatives who was not quite ready to leave his current place, so he had decided to rent month to month until the relative made his move. He had done this without regard to anyone's feelings or possible hardship. The house shouldn't even have been allowed to be occupied, based on its condition. For years after this incident, whenever I drove through Delano and saw the gas station on Highway 12, I remembered Mr. Theis and his greedy nature.

It was December 1989, and the weather was getting cold. My permit application for a mobile home was approved. The next day I paid the mobile home seller. He was a very kind person and said he would help with the move without any charge. He also asked me if I had a water well, electricity, and a septic tank. I said no, and he replied that I would need that to be able to live in the mobile home. He then introduced me to his builder, a local man who I trusted immediately. I asked him how close I could build to the adjacent lake, and we were able to settle on a location within two hundred feet. We also determined where the driveway, water well, and septic tank would be in relation to our future house. The cost for these three items was a little high but very necessary. When they were done, we moved in. The mobile home was actually very nice—much nicer than the house in Delano. It had two bedrooms, a kitchen, and a large, comfortable living room.

The biggest problem was the wind and cold. Because everything had happened so fast, no work had been done to keep the water pipes from freezing. But even despite the occasional water stoppages, living on our own land without anyone causing us any trouble was well worth it. My dogs loved running around and stayed dirty—they enjoyed running after everything, coming home with their long hair tangled with all sorts of debris. I spent many hours brushing, but it was a losing battle.

Karen and I continued to use one car for our long commute. The first winter seemed to be beyond challenging. When it snowed, our long driveway was impassable. We had to park at the far end and walk almost seven hundred feet to our mobile home. We occasionally asked people to plow our driveway, but that got very expensive. When spring was finally upon us, it seemed no easier than the long winter. The melting snow turned our driveway into an impassable mud pool—again, a long walk to our home, this time through mud. I quickly learned to keep a clean pair of shoes in the car for work.

Our property was nothing more than level agricultural land, but I immediately saw the potential of what it could be. In the spring of 1990, I contacted the Department of Natural Resources (DNR) and others to try to find tree seedlings to plant. I found a lot of help and started to plan what type of seedlings I could buy. Many friends discouraged me. They said it would take many years for a seedling to mature, and they would require a lot of watering and care. But I have always believed that I have to do what I think it is best and that God will provide and take care of what I am trying to do.

⌒⌒

That summer I talked to the builder regarding the house, saying that financially it would be best to wait until the following spring to start building. I asked him how early we could start. He said that because of local regulations, we could not start digging for the basement until May because of the frost line in the ground. I thought that might be a little later than what I liked. I asked if we could start in the fall by digging the basement. He had reservations about leaving the basement all winter and thought we would have to somehow heat it. Saying he was not one hundred percent sure, he asked me to go to the county zoning department and see what they had to say.

At the zoning department in the county, I asked the same question: "Do we need to do anything special if we build the basement now and wait for the following spring to build the house?" The person I was talking to started to tell me all the things I needed to do to be able to live in the basement, but it took me several minutes before I realized what he was talking about. I finally asked: "You mean I can do the things you listed and actually *live* in the basement?" He explained that it was like building a full house, and we must pass all inspections and finish it completely in order to live in it. It would be a walkout basement, meaning it would have a door from the outside, so I was fine with the idea.

Also that summer, the news broke that Saddam Hussein had sent his troops to invade Kuwait. He had ended his long eight-year war with Iran in late 1988 and apparently was ready to start a new one. I knew from having been part of the Iraqi army that Hussein did not trust his own troops, and he always wanted to keep them busy and occupied. He never cared about any casualties as long as he felt safe and secure by keeping his army busy with conflicts. The Kuwait invasion soon became an international conflict against Saddam Hussein and Iraq, which led into the Gulf War; it was also called "the mother of all wars" or Operation Desert Storm. This was one of the most difficult periods of my life. I was happy to think of the end of Saddam Hussein, and I volunteered my services to any government agency I could think of, but when I saw the heavy bombardments on Baghdad and the destructions of all bridges and water purification facilities, I often wondered how Nadia was and how her family was faring. I was truly feeling guilty not to be there with them and suffering as they were suffering. I did not like enjoying the things I was supposed to enjoy while Nadia and her family were without any electricity or power. I spent a lot of time crying for Iraq and the people of Iraq while Saddam

Hussein was safe and secure. The war ended in early 1991 with the destruction of Iraq, but Saddam Hussein had survived, much to my complete disappointment.

Also, Karen and I found out that she was expecting. This was not planned. I was surprised but also happy and eager to see what God would give us as a child. I did not know what we had to do, but Karen knew, and she bought announcement cards once we knew our baby was a girl. I would have loved a son, of course, but I was happy nonetheless because I had my own ulterior motive, which was to make all efforts to name her Nadia, despite that being an uncommon name. Karen sent the announcements to all of her relatives. Karen selected the big, reputable Methodist Hospital for the birth. Soon we started to get many cards from Karen's relatives wishing us well, except from Karen's oldest brother, Ron, and his family. Karen even sent him a second announcement in case the first one had been lost in the mail, but we still did not receive anything. Karen had apparently noticed my displeasure with her oldest brother's behavior and talked to her mother about it. Her mother said that Ron had moved to Idaho and maybe he never received her card, so Karen sent a third one. He did not reply to that one either.

Of course, now it was even more urgent to build the basement and avoid all the problems with frozen water lines. The builder began work. Once the blocks were in place, they built the flooring on top of it, which would normally be the main-level flooring. Then on top of the flooring, they built a temporary roof. An electrician, plumber, and sheetrock person were hired. We ended up with a nice bedroom, bathroom, and living and dining areas. Both the living area and the bedroom had legal-size windows, and the front door was also a window that allowed a lot of light to come through. We were truly amazed at what we received. It was like a brand-new home. It was built so tight that the temperature inside was as steady as could be—we did not even have awareness of how cold or warm it was outside, unlike the mobile home. We then had to sell the mobile home, according to the agreement with the county.

Building the basement

Basement home

By fall 1990, Karen's pregnancy started to show. We took part in several classes and bought a crib and a few other necessities. Karen also received many gifts at a baby shower at her workplace. When we discussed naming our daughter, we had our first big argument. I insisted on Nadia, no matter what. Karen did not like the name at all and kept suggesting others, but I stood my ground and said I had to have the choice of the first name. Several hours into our discussion, Karen asked me what was so special about the name Nadia. I kept referring to Nadia Comaneci the Romanian gymnast, winner of three Olympic gold medals in 1976. After a while Karen agreed, but she wanted to choose the middle name. I did not care what that would be as long as I could give her the first name Nadia. Karen finally decided on the middle name. I was looking forward to calling my daughter Nadia, as that is a name I will never forget—ever. I have kept the reasons for wanting that name to myself until now.

My in-laws visited us to check out our new basement home, and we accommodated them nicely with our sleeper couch. Karen's sister, Cindy, and her boyfriend were becoming regular visitors also, and they were welcome anytime they wanted to visit. Even so, I always felt that I did not belong, no matter what I did for them. I kept hoping that I was wrong. On March 16, 1991, everything was still as normal as could be, but as we were watching television after dinner, Karen said it was time to go to the hospital. At first, I thought it was a false alarm, and I was reluctant to load up the car. I kept asking Karen to check with the nurse as she had in the past. Angrily, she described her current condition. This time the nurse finally said the magic words—come as fast as you can. Though the hospital was at least forty miles away, I drove at a very normal speed, as I did not want to be stopped at a moment like this by the police. My heart was beating very fast. When we arrived at the hospital, the nurses were ready and helped Karen climb into a wheelchair as I went to park the car. I came running with my suitcase and video camera, ready to spend a night or two.

By the time I had my camera turned on, however, Nadia was born—a little after ten o'clock that night, very healthy, with a normal weight. We brought her home the next day. I was full of joy. She was a truly beautiful baby with a head full of dark hair. I was so happy to see my little Nadia looking like my other Nadia. I was truly hoping that the birth of Nadia would change Karen and bring out the passion—the enthusiasm that I had yet to see in her. Now I knew we had to make this relationship work. I owed it to my daughter; there was no other way around that, according to my personal values.

<hr />

We made a lot of phone calls that day, listening and talking together on separate phone handsets to save everyone time and long-distance charges. All the calls went great, but one of them made me stop and think. After that call, I had to step outside and shake my head, wondering exactly what everyone was thinking. My mother-in-law had been on the line, but she had not been aware that I was on it, too. I had only jumped into the calls when it was appropriate or when someone asked to talk to me. In this case, I had been very excited, but quiet, while Karen told her mother the whole labor and birth story—how easy labor had been and how healthy the baby was. Her mother had stopped her to ask an "important question"—what were Nadia's "complications"? Karen did not answer at first, either not knowing what to say or not understanding. Karen's mother clarified: "Is Nadia as dark as her father?"

When I heard that, I think I shut down emotionally and did not hear anything more. I do not remember if I stayed on the call until the end, but I do remember stepping outside to breathe some fresh air. The only thing that came to mind at that moment was that my darker skin color was a problem to my mother-in-law and possibly other relatives of Karen. I knew they were very regular churchgoers. I asked myself, *Do they know where Jesus came from? Jesus came from the same area*

I came from, so why do they think Jesus looked any different than I do? How could anyone claim to be Christian while at the same time judging people based on their skin color? I had a tough time with that phone call to the point where, twenty-two years later as I am writing this, it is still a source of discomfort to me.

During Karen's maternity leave, the in-laws and Karen's sister, Cindy, and her boyfriend were regular fixtures almost every weekend. I enjoyed the family connection and wanted to believe that I was accepted and considered part of the family, despite what I was feeling inside. Karen had two other brothers besides the older one who had seemingly had cut his ties with us. They had taken part in the wedding but were no-shows since we moved to Minnesota. We also traveled to North Dakota to visit as many of Karen's relatives as we could possibly see in a few days' visit, including some I had never met before, in small towns like Center and Mandan. I was bending over backward just to feel a part of Karen's family, but I was beginning to realize that no matter which relatives we visited, the cold reception for me was the same.

It usually started with warm greetings—until everyone sat down. Then all the attention went to Karen or other family members—who had passed away, who had gotten married, or who'd had a child. I was just another stranger occupying a seat. No one ever wanted to learn about me or my family. No one ever asked how we met or who made the first move. I was not sure if they already knew these things, or if they simply did not care. As time went by, I began to believe they did not care and did not look at me as an equal human being.

Once it was time for Karen to go back to work, we needed to find a day care provider. We looked carefully at many and finally decided on someone who lived only three miles from our house in a small town called Montrose. She took care of her own children and a few others. We felt very comfortable with everything she was providing. Her husband owned a local body shop and was a volunteer firefighter. We thought we had found the best situation for our baby.

For the first few days, parting with Nadia was very difficult, and as the weeks went by, I started to feel uncomfortable with Nadia spending most of the day at day care. Our round-trip commute alone was two hours minimum, and with work time added, we were away from her for more than twelve hours. In the evenings, after trying to rest, cook dinner, and do household chores, we were left with hardly any quality time with Nadia. A further complication was Karen's schedule, where she had to work every other Saturday and Sunday. My concerns got even bigger as fall approached, because on a snowy day, the commute could easily expand from two hours to three or four. I did not want my baby being raised by a day care provider. I had not been brought up that way.

I suggested to Karen staying home to care for Nadia until she was older, but she wanted no part of that. Karen had never been a person who could sit, look me in the eye, and exchange thoughts and ideas. When she heard any suggestion not to her liking, she usually took herself to the bedroom, closed the door, and stayed for hours. What made this situation even more difficult was that I was the opposite of Karen in this area. I liked to debate, exchange, and come up with the best solution. The more Karen insisted on putting her work over caring for Nadia, the more I was beginning to grow away from her. Keep in mind that Karen and I had never felt very close to start with.

I was feeling more and more frustrated. I did not know what to do and had no one to share my feelings with. I had lost all contact with my Minot friends, and I had no friends locally. My cousin was still having issues with his wife and was becoming reckless in everything he did, so I did not have very strong ties with him and stayed free of him and his problems. I felt very lonely and shut down and tried to find things to keep me busy.

I began to wonder where Denise might be. I looked at Minot, North Dakota, as my second home after my native Baghdad. By the same token, I considered Denise my "first love" in my second home. These feelings were real, and I was going to do whatever was required to keep my friendship with Denise, no matter how far we were from one another. Before the Internet and Google, there was no way to find where she had gone other than calling the directory for each state to see if they had a listing for her name. In my lonely situation, I listened to music and began to love scanning and manipulating pictures and images on my computer, which I kept in a small office-like room. I also kept my books there, including the yearbooks from Minot State University. I found myself looking at Denise's pictures, no bigger than one inch square. I often thought of scanning and enlarging them but never did, as I did not feel that would have been appropriate as a married man. But I did wonder if our paths would ever cross again.

As to my brother, he had left the country. He had finally graduated from Minot State but had given up on finding a soul mate in the United States. I had made many unsuccessful attempts to convince him to move to another state and give himself a chance. I was afraid for him, as going to Iran with an American passport could have been dangerous. But he went there anyway and reconnected with my father, brothers and sisters, and some distant relatives. He got married there but had a very difficult time getting out. A childhood friend of his was living in Sweden, and he had heard some good things about Sweden, so he ended up there instead of returning to the United States.

I now had phone numbers for some of my sisters in Iran and was able to connect with them occasionally over the unreliable Iranian phone lines. When we did manage to talk, it was very difficult to hear, and I knew I had to be careful about saying anything that might cause them any problems. They were in desperate need of help and asked me if I could send them money. This made me feel sad and powerless, because it was against the law to send money to Iran. They wanted to know if I had any news about our brothers who were being kept in jail by Saddam Hussein, but I did not. I was filled with guilt for being free while they were having such a rough time. They asked me to come visit them. I really wanted to, but I could not imagine putting myself in such danger—not so much for myself but rather for the possibility of leaving Nadia fatherless.

My job was going well, and I had received another small promotion and small salary increase. Nadia's first birthday was upon us, and Karen and I made sure we took many professional photographs of beautiful Nadia at the JC Penney studio. I truly enjoyed visits from Karen's sister, Cindy, and her boyfriend during this time, because it gave me a chance to take them places to shop and eat. Without company, Karen and I did nothing together other than our daily routine activities. We had never learned to sit down peacefully and discuss or plan anything. The only planning we did concerned when to go to visit her family in North Dakota. I believe if they had lived closer, we wouldn't have even talked about that—she would have just gone to visit them without having to plan anything or even tell me or invite me.

<hr />

Our basement was very comfortable and spacious, and we had everything we needed. The idea of building the rest of the house went on the back burner. Planting tree seedlings in the spring and finding ways to water them in the summer was consuming most of my free time. Life was normal, but the truth was that Karen and I were never connected, never on the same page. I thought about our situation a lot but always saw it as my fate and felt that I had to submit to whatever that fate dealt me. Nadia was growing and very healthy. The weekends when Karen had to work, I spent with the baby, and it was truly quality time to bond with my Nadia. But Nadia was spending a lot more time at the day care than with us at home. Other working couples might have been okay with that, but for me it was terrible. I always knew that I was very capable of providing for us if Karen took a few years off from work to raise Nadia. When I tried to discuss this with her, she always turned the tables on me by saying, "Why don't *you* take time off from work?" Karen never used any logic with anything. She never understood that I was bringing in a lot more income than she was and, most importantly, that I was at the beginning of a career that had a lot of potential, while there was little hope of advancement in her line of work. She would not discuss anything and was always defensive for no apparent reason. Karen never looked at my suggestions as a way to build a better environment for Nadia.

The DNR was very helpful regarding my plan to plant trees. They came by and recommended several types of trees that would thrive in our property's soil type. All that service was free of charge, and I was very grateful. I ordered several hundred young seedlings from them at very reasonable prices. I kept the roots wrapped and moist, and every day after work I would take thirty or forty seedlings and plant them randomly; I planted even more on weekends. This was a difficult job, and it kept me busy for a long time. The surprising thing was that no one ever encouraged me. In fact, most everyone laughed at me and discouraged me from "wasting my time," saying it would take many years before I saw the seedlings become trees. None of that hindered me, and I kept planting year after year, knowing that someone would enjoy them, even if it was not going to be me. When I started the project, I was totally grossed out by finding strange insects on my clothes. I learned they were called ticks, and I made sure to spray myself so that they would not attach to my skin. I eventually got used to them, figuring it was part of the price for being able to plant my seedlings.

CHAPTER EIGHTEEN

Life Gets Real

Because of Karen's constant rejection of my ideas, I started to think of other possibilities to make a living with some kind of small business. One of my first attempts was making personalized videotape stories for children that were no more than five minutes long. I used my computer to enter the name of the child and produced the videotape on the spot. I called it All-Star Video and created business cards. I was under no illusion that this would enable me to leave my full-time job, but I used it to learn more about business and what I could do in the days ahead. I leased a booth in Knollwood Mall to try it out for a few weekends. Soon it was Nadia's second birthday, and Karen and I celebrated it with gifts, family visits, and our annual portrait. Because Karen still had to work every other weekend and I now had commitments to be at Knollwood, we needed someone to care for Nadia on an occasional basis. After an extensive search, we found a fifteen-year-old girl named Sarah living on a small farm only about four miles away who agreed to do the day care at her house with the help of her mother. I liked Sarah and her parents. They had a lot of farm animals around the house that I thought would be good for Nadia.

Sunday morning, April 18, 1993, I was ready to go to Knollwood. Karen had already left for work. The sun was shining brightly, and the temperature was moderate. I was very happy knowing that the weather was not going to be a factor and looking forward to an easy, leisurely trip to Sarah's house and visiting with her parents before they left for church. The route to Sarah's house crossed Highway 12 onto an unpaved gravel road which elevated slightly just before some railroad tracks and then descended just after. The trees and the farms on both sides of the tracks limited visibility of anything coming down them to just a few feet on either side of the road crossing. At that time, the railroad tracks did not even have drop-down guards to warn of a train's approach. I did not hear any train siren, so I continued moving up the hill toward the tracks. When I was about fifteen feet away, I was shocked to see the train emerging from all the trees.

There was no time to consider any options other than turning to the left or right or stopping. I knew instantly that I could not turn, as the road was very high and driving off it would have guaranteed death to both Nadia and me. I slammed on the brakes as hard as I possibly could and closed my eyes, hoping and praying for a miracle. The impact occurred seconds later. I could not open my eyes for a minute or so, and I had only one thing on my mind—Nadia.

When I finally opened my eyes and looked over at her, she appeared to be fine. I felt a little bit better, but it was not over yet. The train was still rushing by only a few inches from the windshield. I closed my eyes again and continued praying. The sound was deafening, and it felt as if the train were going right through me. I was not sure if I was alive or dead. After what seemed like years, the sound of the train finally disappeared.

My eyes were still closed, and I was still intensely praying. Suddenly I felt a hand on my left shoulder and heard voices. I opened my eyes. It was a police officer asking me if I was okay. I was too shaken to speak. He asked me to get out of the van, but I could not take my foot off the brakes.

Finally, using all his strength, the officer was able to release me. I got out, but I was screaming at him to help Nadia first. Another officer was there and took Nadia out. He looked at me and said that it was a miracle we were alive—they had come to "collect body parts."

I looked at the van. The entire front end and the engine were gone. If I had driven one more foot, both Nadia and I would have been in the path of the train and there would not have been any body parts to collect. The van had been pulled by the train right to the edge of the road and let go just before it would have fallen several feet into the ditch. It was still smoking heavily, and I was thankful that it had not caught fire. The tow truck driver wanted to take it away to a junkyard somewhere, but I begged him to just take it to my house. The police officer took us home, followed by the tow truck. After making sure we were really okay, the officer left us alone. I hugged Nadia and kissed her, not really believing that we were still alive.

Van eaten by train

I reviewed the events, still in complete shock. I knew I had been saved from death by a miracle yet again. This was my third "close brush with death" or "escape from death" encounter. I was not enlightened enough yet to know that I had been saved by the angels. After finally convincing myself that I had survived, I called Karen at her work and asked her to come home immediately. She asked me what was wrong. I just said, "Come home—now." She finally agreed. The sight of the van left her utterly horrified, but she soon realized that Nadia and I were fine. I told her the whole story and said we needed to have a celebration. I did not care about losing the van or anything else other than realizing that I must appreciate the gift I had been given. On our way to the restaurant, I drove the car without any problems and was just grateful and looking ahead to the future. The celebration continued all day. When Karen told her parents the story, they immediately made plans to come and visit us.

The next day I got up early, and we all went to work and day care as usual. Sitting at my desk, I started to recall the accident on a different level and began to realize how close we had come to losing Nadia. I began to sweat to the point where my friends realized I was not well. My supervisor decided to send me home and asked me to rest and not come back until I was fully ready. I left the office, but I knew I had to wait to go home until Karen finished her shift. I decided to go to a café near her workplace. For the first time, I was having a very difficult time driving. When I saw anything, even a bird, I would automatically and uncontrollably slam on the brakes, endangering everyone behind me.

As days went by, my condition became worse and worse. Even sitting at the dinner table I would get accident images and begin to sweat and shake. This went on for more than six months. Needless to say, this accident ended my little video business efforts. Those railroad tracks are still in place today, but with major differences. Now there is a guard with lights that prevents anyone from crossing before the arrival of the train. All trees and buildings on both sides of the tracks are completely gone. It is much safer now.

The months after the accident passed very quietly. The van was totaled by the insurance company because it was so old. I decided to buy it back for very little money. Initially I wanted it just as a reminder of how blessed I had been to survive such an accident. Later, my father-in-law offered to take it to his body shop in Underwood to try to fix it with used parts. I had no problem with that and told him that I would pay whatever it cost. He took it away on a two-wheeled car dolly and rebuilt it within a few months. We took the train to Minot to visit the in-laws and drove the van back to Minnesota.

One day in the fall of 1993, as I was driving to pick up Karen from her work, I realized I was ten minutes early, so I decided to stop on the way at my favorite building supply store, Knox, to buy some small item. As I was waiting for my change, I glanced two counters over and noticed something familiar about the back of another cashier. Hesitantly, I asked my cashier for the name of her coworker. To my great astonishment, she replied, "Denise." I finished my transaction and slowly walked away, not knowing what to do. I did not want to shout out her name. What if she did not even remember me? I finally decided to just stand by the door right in front of her, wait until she looked my way, and watch her reaction. As soon as Denise finished with her customer, she looked up and recognized me right away. She jumped out of her station, ran over, and gave me a huge hug. I was so happy! I left after a couple of minutes, because I did not want her to get into any trouble at work. We exchanged phone numbers, and I promised to call her.

Throughout the entire drive home, I was thinking, *what were the odds of Denise moving to Minnesota instead some other state? And what were the odds that Denise would work in a store that I shop at regularly? And what had made me decide to make this particular stop at this particular time?* I could not wait for the next day to call Denise and get some answers. Denise's primary job was as an accountant, and I talked to her at her office. I kept the phone call very brief, respecting her wishes. She was very excited to talk to me and invited me to an upcoming house-warming party for her and her boyfriend. I told her we would be there.

I bought a gift and told Karen we were invited to a housewarming party for a friend of mine. Karen and I never talked or shared stories, and this was no different. I never told her about the encounter in the store, and Karen never asked about this friend or where or how I had become friends with her. After all these years, it still seemed that Karen was not at all interested in knowing anything about me.

It was a very lively party with a lot of people. I met Denise's boyfriend and then took a corner with Karen and Nadia. This was not the time to catch up with Denise, as she was busy hosting. I was not acting myself either, because Karen was clearly uncomfortable.

She never asked me anything about Denise, but I couldn't imagine she was worried, especially since Denise and her boyfriend had just bought a house together, and I was married. Even so, the entire time seemed somewhat awkward in every way possible, and after a while, we excused ourselves and left.

The next week Denise and I arranged over the phone to meet for lunch on her day off. I took off a half day from work. Seeing Denise took me back to our days of sitting together in the student union at Minot State. Just like any two old friends would do, we had our lunch and then continued to talk and catch up with one another. We were very comfortable together, and I laughed as I had not done in years. Denise reminded me of the days at the North Hill Bowl restaurant where we first met. She recalled the baker saying to me, "David, your girlfriend is here," whenever Denise came in the door. I laughed and told Denise that I had been very shy and did not know what to say to those comments. After a while, all the other lunch customers had left, but Denise and I were still catching up. At an amazing moment, quite casually, Denise asked me if I remembered the college article written about me in the *Red & Green*. I said, "Of course I remember, Denise. In fact, I still have copies of it. Why do you ask?" She responded that she still had a copy, too. I was very taken aback and honestly did not know what to say.

As we were leaving, Denise asked for her leftover lunch to be boxed up, saying it was for Rob, her boyfriend. That made me comfortable and told me that Rob knew about our lunch and trusted his girlfriend. We agreed to keep meeting for lunch from time to time to continue our friendship. In the car heading home, I grew teary and actually cried a little. Denise still had a copy of the article? I realized then that she actually had cared for me in a time when I cared for her also. But I had never actually asked her out. Even now, I was angry at myself for being such a coward. I also began to wonder if Denise had moved to Minnesota because she knew from the article that I had been planning to move to Minnesota, or was it a total coincidence? I pondered and pondered and blamed myself over, over, and over again.

———

One day an incident occurred, something I have never been able to forget. Life was never the same afterward. I was sitting in my car outside the nursing home waiting for Karen when one of her coworkers stopped by to chat, as by this time I had become a well-known face. I don't recall every detail, but the coworker mentioned that Karen had been saying that she was worried about me and what I might do, that I might take our daughter away from her, similar to events in a recent book called *Not Without My Daughter* that had later been made into a movie starring Sally Field. I had not read or seen either, but I was aware of them. It is very difficult to describe what I felt. I can say only that I felt very hurt, angry, and betrayed that Karen could even think something like that. Karen got in the car, but I said nothing to her right away. I was trying to figure out the best time and way to open up to her about what I had just heard. But after only a few minutes of driving and boiling inside, I could not hold it in any longer. I did not reveal who exactly had told me what she had said, and she never asked. And as usual, Karen did not give a good reason why she had felt that way or said those things. Karen had never appeared to know the meaning of apology—not even when she knew she had made a mistake. She began to give me excuse after excuse, and truly she was just making me more upset. I angrily asked her if she even knew my story and the fact that I had no other place to go except right where I was. I asked her if she was even aware that I would be killed at the airport if I attempted to go back to Iraq. Karen's ignorance about my story was even worse than I had thought. I asked her why she was still married to me if that was how she was feeling. I never received any answers, but then again, I never really expected any either.

What a year it had been! Surviving a collision with a train, then meeting Denise again when I was least expecting it. Entering 1994, I was feeling truly trapped. I could not possibly think of doing anything to disturb Nadia's life—I was more than willing to sacrifice my entire life for Nadia. I had never been happy with my marriage, not even at the beginning. Seeing Denise again reminded me how much joy I could feel being around her. That was something I had never experienced with Karen. I was beginning to think that Karen would never change, simply because she had never been exposed to anything outside her family and a very small town in North Dakota. I was making excuses in my mind for Karen to justify her behavior and her total lack of interest and passion. But I had submitted to my fate and started to think of expanding our family, despite its dysfunction. The thought of another child was solely in my own head. Karen and I had never discussed anything in a civil manner up to that point.

Christmas of 1993, and Nadia's third birthday, was a very special time. I was videotaping Nadia in almost everything she did. I did it without telling anyone that I was still celebrating getting a second chance at life. No one knew how much the accident had changed me and how much it still occupied my thoughts. As I was getting closer to the first anniversary of the accident, I celebrated the day alone by listening to my music, mostly Abdel Halim Hafez. It took me back many years to when I was among my family—my brothers and sisters. I reflected on my marriage relationship, in which no one cared enough about my family to even just casually ask about them. And I was feeling guilty about so many things. I was always blaming myself for things that I had no control over. I was feeling guilty for living in freedom while my entire family was in a foreign land or in jail, for not asking Denise to go out before I was married, for marrying someone who I knew I did not have any connection to, for having a young, beautiful daughter but no one to use my other languages with in order to teach them to my child. I knew how easy it is for children to naturally learn languages when they are exposed to them. Now I was adding that guilt, too.

In the spring of 1994, I received several hundred more tree seedlings. By that time, I had bought an old tractor for the unpleasant job of clearing snow from our long driveway. I planted seedlings on both sides of the driveway in the hope that someday they would grow tall enough to prevent snowdrifts. Karen had just tested positive for pregnancy, and so we were officially expecting our second child. I couldn't wait to find out its gender. I was hoping for a brother for Nadia to grow up with, but was ready and grateful for whatever God would give us.

Denise and I continued to see each other once every three or four months for lunch. We always had a great time together. Denise never once asked me about Karen or my private life. Our entire conversation was about our days at North Hill Bowl and Minot State University and the people we knew together. I was feeling comfortable enough to ask Denise about Rob. How and when had they met? What did Rob do for a living? Were they planning to take their relationship to the next level and get married? Denise was very comfortable discussing all this. I took the role of older brother who wanted the best for her, and she understood my intentions. I shared with her our expectation of a new child. Denise was very excited for me and wanted me to keep her updated with anything new.

We soon learned that Karen and I were going to have another baby girl in December. Because I still wanted a boy, I took this as a sign that we needed to have more than two babies. We both came from large families, so that was not going to be an issue, or so I thought, anyway. I was grateful that everything looked fine, and our daughter was healthy. This time I would surrender the choice of names to Karen.

Karen's sister, Cindy, in South Dakota, had finally married her boyfriend, and they were all seemingly very happy and excited for us. Cindy had a daughter called Mariah, so Karen picked Miranda. We both liked that name, too. I never, ever shared with them what Karen had said to her coworkers regarding the *Not Without My Daughter* movie. I figured if she had said those things to near-strangers at work, there was a very good chance that she had said them to her parents, sisters, and other relatives.

By early December 1994, we were all ready for a sudden trip to Buffalo Hospital. The Christmas tree was up and decorated earlier than usual, and a new stocking was already in place. Labor began on December 19. When we arrived at the hospital, we were told to relax and "feel at home," as Karen was not completely ready. I slept in a very uncomfortable chair all night right next to Karen. It was not until the next evening that her doctor, Dr. Ibrahimi, was called. He was a very nice and down-to-earth man whose native country was Iran. I had a chance to tell him about my family and how they had been deported to Iran for several years. After a very smooth labor, Miranda was born on December 20, 1994. She was very healthy, normal, and beautiful. Miranda's complexion and eye color were a copy of my mother's complexion and eyes. I felt great joy and gratitude, knowing that Nadia would soon have a baby sister to play with.

Once things had settled down at the hospital and Karen was resting comfortably, she shattered my world when she gave me a piece of paper to sign.

"What is this?" I asked.

"It's just a release," she replied.

I was getting a little angry as I read the paper and asked, "Release for what?"

Karen replied that the doctor could not perform the procedure without my consent.

"Procedure for what?" I asked again.

Karen very calmly responded that it was the procedure for tying her tubes.

"Did we even discuss this?" I responded angrily.

Her reply to my question was astonishing. "I didn't think you wanted any more children."

"Did I ever tell you this? What made you think I do not want more children when we never discussed this topic or any topic, for that matter?" Karen ignored my concerns and kept saying she just didn't want any more children. Our argument just kept going on, on, and on, though the day was supposed to be filled with joy. She was getting very loud, and the situation was very embarrassing, especially when one of the nurses came in to check on things. I wondered how and when she had talked to the doctor about this. When did she get the release paper? What had I gotten myself into? I had just assumed that because she came from a large family and was supposedly a Catholic, she would not believe in doing this procedure.

Because I wanted to end this argument with Karen, I repeated my desire for more children, especially how I wanted to have a boy before considering stopping. Karen just turned her face the other way and pretended she was not hearing me. I told her that I did not want her to be able to tell anyone that I was holding her hostage by not signing the paper. I angrily signed it, while repeating my desire for more children, and told her I wanted her to prove to me that I could trust her by respecting that desire.

I left the hospital to take care of my dogs, steaming and furious. I just wanted to let the anger out of my system so I could refocus on our new daughter, Miranda. I was not in a big hurry to find out what Karen would do. I spent as much time as I could playing with the dogs and visiting Nadia at the day care before returning to the hospital. I pretended that Karen and I had not even had our argument, while in reality I was still living it. I did not ask Karen, but it did seem as if she had not had the procedure after all. We went home the next day.

The Christmas tree was ready and decorated, and we truly felt blessed and ready to celebrate. Karen called everyone to tell them about Miranda. I decided to stay away from the phone this time, recalling the painful conversation with Karen's mother after Nadia's birth when she had asked about "complications." My in-laws told Karen that they would come to visit us in the following weeks and months.

Christmas Eve was truly glorious, and we exchanged gifts early on Christmas morning. I recorded every move on video. I went back to work on Tuesday and shared pictures and my joy with my friends there. One day the following week, soon after New Year's Day, I came home from work and was shocked to find no one at home, only a note from Karen telling me that she had called on a friend of hers to take her to the hospital to have the procedure. I could not believe my eyes. I was very angry. For the first time, divorce became an option. It was hard to think straight, but I was angry enough to not go and see Karen at the hospital. I had no plans to bring her home either. I figured if she had friends to take her to the hospital, they could also bring her back.

When Karen, Nadia, and Miranda came home the next day, I was still very mad but elected not to acknowledge Karen at all or open any conversation. Karen had done what she wanted to do and ignored and disrespected my wishes. There was no longer any use for discussion, because the damage had already been done. I attended only to Nadia and Miranda. I stayed in my room during dinner working on the computer and listening to my music. My dreams of having a boy had been shattered by Karen for no apparent reason.

Both of her deliveries had been very easy and uneventful. This was a family decision made only by Karen without any regard to my wishes. I began to wonder. If the doctor had not requested a signature, Karen would have probably gone through the procedure without my knowledge and without even feeling the need to tell me. I was very confused. I began to withdraw completely from her, even avoiding the dinner table, and I began sleeping on the couch. When I had to answer to any question, I often replied to her with only a nod.

I seriously wanted to divorce Karen, but it seemed that no matter what I was thinking, my thoughts would come back to what was best for our girls, according to my understanding at the time. I never discussed or sought any help. I had always been very private and did not have many close friends with whom to share my thoughts and feelings. I tried to think of how I could do it but was feeling trapped, because I knew Karen's communications and reactions to things were very unpredictable. Whenever we had visitors, I usually acted like there was no problem at all and tried to be a perfect host. The awkward thing for me with overnight visitors was that I had to sleep in the bedroom and surrender the couch to them.

Soon it was Nadia's fourth birthday, and we celebrated it, as always, by taking professional pictures. That year was even more special, because many of the pictures included baby sister, Miranda. My silence occasionally came to a temporary end when I felt the urge to revisit Karen's selfish decision. If she felt like giving an answer, it would be something like, "I knew you did not like children," or "When I come home from work on weekends, you look like you couldn't wait for my arrival because you did not like being with the girls." Karen was very good at giving answers based upon what she thought I was thinking. No matter how much I tried to tell her that she was wrong in her assessments or perceptions, my words always fell on deaf ears.

Unfortunately, by this time I had completely lost trust in Karen. I began to reexamine the cold reception and being completely ignored whenever we visited her family. I wondered what she was saying to them behind my back. Most importantly, if she had truly meant the *Not Without My Daughter* remarks, why was she still married to me, someone she did not trust? I was very confused.

I kept up my happy face with everyone and still saw Denise every few months. Denise came by one day while Karen was at home and brought some gifts for Miranda. Karen never asked me about Denise, but I always felt that she had a lot of issues with her, despite her silence on the subject. I would have been very happy to answer all of Karen's questions frankly and honestly, but she never asked any. I did not feel comfortable volunteering information, as her actions spoke louder than anything else. Karen had never been able to tell me how she felt, regardless of the situation. This was very troubling, but I had to deal with it.

———

My work surprised me with an opportunity to be part of a project in its Washington, DC headquarters. It would require me to fly to Washington for the entire work week and would also be a great opportunity to be away from Karen, a person who neither trusted nor loved me. So, even though being away from my daughters would be a big sacrifice, I accepted the offer. I bought some new suits and ties, wanting to fit into the Washington scene. I loved the hotel room and all the complimentary services and great food. I was alone, but I needed to learn how to deal with it. I went down to the bar during happy hour to watch television and be around people. After a few hours of snacking, I felt fine. Once settled in on Monday, I called home to speak to Nadia and tell her that I was safe. Friday came; I flew back to Minnesota and drove home. I was so happy to see my little girls. It seemed Miranda had blossomed in just the few days I was away from her.

Week after week I followed that same routine. By the fall of 1995, I was getting really tired of traveling and sleeping in hotels and missing not only my children, but my dogs and attending to the seedlings I had planted. One day while sitting helplessly in the airport during a major flight delay, I began to think about a career change. My priority was having the opportunity to stay close to my children. I began to rethink starting my own business. I wanted it to be a true business this time, where I would have a location and be open every day. After several months, the Washington project ended, and I was back to my regular work.

I must mention here that all those commuting annoyances came with a silver lining that I will cherish forever. Most Mondays I boarded the plane in Minneapolis with the Minnesota senator, the late Paul Wellstone. Sometimes his wife, Sheila, flew with him. On each flight he behaved the same way. I never saw him fly first class, ever. After the seat belts came off, Mr. Wellstone would usually greet all the passengers, going from the back of the airplane to the front. I had many opportunities to shake his hand and talk with him. I grew to like him very much. A couple of years later I attended the Delano Fourth of July parade with my daughter and saw Mr. Wellstone walking in the parade with the usual banners and staff. When he passed by us, he immediately recognized me and stepped out of the parade for a moment to greet me warmly. I will never forget that moment and was very saddened when I heard on that snowy October day in 2002 of his plane crash. May you rest in peace, Paul and Sheila Wellstone.

I thought about my career dilemma day and night. I had a strong desire to be a businessman. My main problem was that I did not know the first thing about business. One of my friends suggested I look at franchises. He explained that once you bought a franchise, you would receive guidance about everything you needed to do. I loved my friend's idea a lot and decided to pursue it. I began to be alert everywhere I went for businesses that appealed to me. High start-up funding requirements did not stop me from searching. My ultimate goal was to raise my girls properly, meaning not by a day care. Since Karen's job was very important to her, I had no choice but to pursue something where I could be with my children, make an income, and be able to hire employees to do the day-to-day work while I managed it from anywhere, including home. By late fall of 1995, I had begun talking with the owners of a dollar store business out of Nevada. The numbers they gave me made it all look amazing and profitable. Most importantly, the employees would not need any special skills, so I could hire anyone. I decided to fly to Nevada and check it out in person. We went over all aspects of the business. They would help me find the right location to lease and then send someone to set it up, train me, and bring enough merchandise to open up. It required several thousands of dollars that I did not have, so I borrowed from my 401(k) plan, sent it as quickly as I could, and waited for the whole process to start.

Soon it was Miranda's first birthday, which meant Christmas was right behind. By now, I had accepted that my marriage to Karen was beyond any repair, but I was still committed to do anything for the sake of my two daughters. I had given up on the idea of divorce and wondered whether getting the business going might be of some help to the relationship. So my efforts were concentrated on the business. We had the usual Christmas celebration and combined it with Miranda's birthday. I was starting to dislike that combination. I was hoping that it would not be an issue as she grew up.

In January 1996, someone local who had been hired by the Nevada group helped me find a location for my business. I had my mind set on Buffalo, even though it was a small town, as I needed the business to be close to home if I had to go back and forth. The franchise representative helped me sort out all the terms, and we decided to take it. We were told to lease it starting several months in the future, as it would take time to design the store and send all the required fixtures.

CHAPTER NINETEEN
. . . .

Big-time Karma Kicks In

N adia's fifth birthday was upon us in March 1995. It was extra special because she was becoming a beautiful young lady. Karen and I talked about preschools and beyond. I was not affiliated with any specific religion or denomination, but I always believed that as a parent I must provide to our children a path to God. As they grew older, they could decide on a religion or denomination for themselves. I suggested the St. Francis Catholic schools in Buffalo, and Karen agreed.

While waiting for the official store opening in May, I created a business name and applied for state and federal tax IDs. I also hired an accounting firm. I was very busy, as I was still working at my full-time job. I was also very nervous, as I had spent a lot of borrowed money and signed a three-year lease. Karen never expressed any interest or curiosity about what I was doing. When I would get impatient and ask her for an opinion, she would just make a childish face and turn away. If I was lucky, she would give her famous answer that she used for most everything. It was very simple: "I did not want this." At first, I would argue and say things like, "You may not want this business, but as a couple, we have it, and we have to help each other to make it successful." No matter what I said, she would end the conversation by storming into the bedroom and slamming the door.

Karen's attitude was frustrating, but I was getting used to it. I really had no idea what she wanted me to do. I knew she was from a small town and saw her father doing the same thing year after year, which was admirable. Perhaps my open mind for different things was a source of issues to her. Karen never knew how to sit down peacefully and discuss any matter. I was feeling all alone, just doing my best. Like always, I was trying, and I was never afraid of failure.

One evening in early May 1996, shortly before the arrival of the store fixtures and merchandise, I was in the back room checking some of my papers regarding the business. Karen had been growing more and more impatient and showing her displeasure in just about everything.

That evening, she began to shout and scream at me, about what, I was not sure. I ignored her and closed the door so I could do my paperwork in peace, hoping she would soon be quiet. I could not really hear what she was saying, but I did hear the words "the police." I shook my head and continued doing my work. I could still hear her voice, but she was not shouting anymore. I assumed that she was on the phone with her parents or her sister in St. Paul. While she was still talking, I heard the dogs barking outside, which told me that someone was approaching. While checking on the dogs, I saw two police officers by the door wanting to come in. Karen had actually called them, complaining that I had threatened her.

One of the officers talked to Karen, while the other one took me to the other side of the room and began asking me questions. I was very honest and told him exactly what had happened, but he somehow did not believe my version of the story. He did not believe a mere argument could cause someone to call the police, which I did not believe either. He asked me why I had hit Karen and threatened her. I completely denied the allegations. I told them that I was planning to start a business, and she was not happy about it. While I was talking, they told me to turn around and put my hands behind me. Then they handcuffed me and told me to go with them to the police car.

I will never forget those moments. I can still feel the handcuffs against my wrists. It made no sense. My mind immediately took me back to my childhood in Iraq to the time when both my brother and I were taken away for no apparent reason. After ten or fifteen minutes, which seemed like a lifetime, the police car arrived at the county building.

I was led down hallways and into rooms where they took my mug shot and asked many questions. I was given a tiny blanket, led into a small room with a metal bed attached to the wall, given a short instruction on how to fold my blanket, and told when the door would be locked and unlocked. I sat on the tiny bed, and for the first time in my life, I wished I were dead. I did not want to see or socialize with anyone.

After a couple of hours, a guard took me into a room where there was a man in civilian clothes waiting for me. He read from a paper that stated what I was accused of. He then asked me to sign the paper and told me that I would be seeing the judge in a few days, or sooner, depending on the judge's schedule. I was then taken back to my little room. Soon I heard the doors automatically lock, but the lights in the room were still on, apparently so the guards could monitor all activities in each cell.

I did lie down on the so-called bed, and the springs felt like they went right through my back. It was very uncomfortable, but I lay there and covered my eyes and cried and cried. I could not believe how easy it had been for Karen to call the police and convince them to take me away. Was it because I was a man, or because I was a man from the Middle East, or was it both? I was thinking about my girls, not knowing what this incident would do to them. I do not remember sleeping at all. The next morning the other prisoners got out of the rooms and stood in a row waiting to be handed breakfast. I told the guard via the speaker in my cell that I did not feel like eating anything. What had Nadia thought when she saw her father taken away in front of her eyes? Most worrisome, I had spent all my retirement money on a business that I was now not sure would even happen.

I stayed in my room after the mandatory morning cleanup feeling depressed, betrayed, and deeply hurt. I had no one to call who could help me. I had no idea what to do or what was going to happen to me. I began to question myself and all I had fought for all those years. Was it really this easy to take me away from my own home for something I had not even done? Finally, a guard came and asked me and several others to follow him to the courtroom. We were told to be seated, and one by one we were called to stand in front of the judge. Most of the people sitting with me had lawyers waiting for them. I was by myself, as I had not had the chance to see a lawyer yet.

Some of the cases ahead of me were very complicated and involved drugs or driving while under the influence of alcohol. They took a lot of time. At last I was called. The judge read the charges and asked me, "How do you plead?" I did not know what my alternatives were other than speaking the truth, and I replied "Not guilty, your honor." He spoke briefly to a lady sitting next to him about his calendar and then stated that he would release me without a bond because I did not have any prior incidents, but I would be required to come to a trial on a certain date. He went on to say many things that, frankly, I did not understand. Then the guard came to take me out of the courtroom and took me into an area where I could change back into my own clothes.

He handed me a piece of paper. It was a restraining order, or order for protection, and told me that I could not attempt to contact my wife and was supposed to be a certain number of miles away from her.

I replied, "Stay away from her? How am I supposed to be at home?" He then explained that I was not allowed to go home, and if I needed anything from the house, they would send a police officer to witness my arrival. I would only have thirty minutes to take what I needed and leave. He also told me that they could not release me until they got in touch with my wife. I was surprised and did not know what this meant, but I did not ask any questions. After about an hour, the officer said that they had talked to my wife, and I could go home for thirty minutes. An officer would be waiting for me.

I did not have any money with me, as I had been taken with just a shirt and pajamas the night before. Fortunately the taxi driver believed me when I told him I would pay him at the end of the ten-mile drive. The officer was already waiting by the house. I quickly collected a few personal items and made sure that my dogs had enough food and water, as they were outside dogs. I got in my car and drove and drove, not knowing where I was going or what to do, or even if I would be coming back. I finally grew tired and went to a hotel in Buffalo to shower and clean up. I ate dinner in a café and returned to my room very sad, and not in the spirit of seeing any other human beings. I sat down and cried like a baby. I asked myself, *Where are my daughters? Where are they living? How could my wife do anything like this?* The *Not Without My Daughter* incident and the tube tying filled my mind as if they just had happened. Were they just clues that I had not fully understood? I began to blame myself for not having left the relationship in a more timely fashion. I also started to reproach myself for bringing Nadia and Miranda to life and putting them through this terrible situation.

I was missing my daughters a lot and was not sure when I would ever be able to see them. I just could not make sense of the last twenty-four hours. What made the situation worse was a lack of any friends to open up to and exchange ideas and get advice. I had not spent any time making local friendships, as all of my attention had been on my family and ways to get ahead.

The next day I went to work. After taking care of work business, I called several attorneys and finally found one in Buffalo and told him I needed to engage him right away, as it involved seeing my children. He agreed to see me after work. He explained that my not guilty plea would automatically involve a trial, and no matter what attorney I had, it would cost me a lot of money that I did not have. He also said that if the case was proven against me after the trial, I would be facing some serious jail time, up to three months or more.

On the other hand, if I pled guilty, because it was my first case, I would probably be fined only a couple hundred dollars. He equated pleading guilty to getting a traffic ticket. Once he had put things in those terms, I told him I had no money and would have no problem in pleading guilty and putting this episode behind me. As far as the restraining order was concerned, he said that most judges approve and sign them without knowing the facts, due to the increase in women's abuse. He said that once they are approved and issued, there is a hearing for both sides to decide if the restraining order is warranted. I hired the attorney and paid him what he called a retainer. He told me that I needed to meet him the following week at the courthouse before the restraining order hearing. The other trial, for domestic abuse, was several weeks away.

My business trucks would arrive in two or three weeks. I truly did not know what to think about what I had done. What was I thinking, spending that kind of money when I did not have any support at home? Once again, I blamed myself, over and over. The uncertainty surrounding my children was clouding my mind. I looked only to the day when I would find out the judge's decision on the restraining order. I took that day off from work and went to court early to see my attorney. The attorney simply said that judges were becoming very sensitive to women's issues, and they usually granted most of their requests for restraining orders. He went on to say that seeing my children was my right, and I would be granted that right, regardless of what my wife might say or want.

At the courtroom, there was my wife, surrounded by a group of women who I later learned were members of a women's advocacy group called Rivers of Hope. After a lot of give and take, the judge ordered visitation rights in my favor. He ordered my wife to let me see the children every Wednesday and every other weekend. Since it was Tuesday, I would see my children the next day. Despite the difficult circumstances, I was very hopeful and happy. For some reason, my wife had decided that the meeting place to hand off our children would be the Knollwood Mall, which was thirty-five miles away. I did not care where, as long as I could see them and spend a night with them.

Later that evening, I began to wonder: why would Karen want to exchange the children at Knollwood and not any place closer? Maybe they were not living at home. I did not understand. Why would Karen prevent me from going home if she was not living there? I then thought of the dogs and wondered who was feeding them. I did not know anyone to send home to check on the dogs, and my heart was in pain for my helpless animals. I had no answers, but I was not going to be silent and do nothing, so I decided to take a big risk and check on them myself. I did not want to drive my car in case my wife was home; it would be easy for her to see the car and get me in more trouble. I decided to wait until dark and park at a gas station about three miles away. The first mile was walking on the highway, which was easy. The last two miles, I did not take the roads. No one ever walked those roads, and I knew I would attract a lot of attention if I did, so I went through farm fields instead. I did not take my long driveway either, but approached the house sideways through a field. I saw no lights on, indicating no one was home. My dogs jumped for joy when they saw me. I hugged them and gave them food and water. Instead of just leaving, I decided to check on the house. The voice mail indicator was flashing, and the caller ID showed the number of Karen's sister in St. Paul. I assumed that the sister was aware of what had happened, and because we were seemingly on good terms, I decided to call her and learn what she thought of all this. I tried several times, but no one answered. I decided to turn the lights off and go to sleep in my own bed but leave very early in the morning using the normal roads to go back to my car.

While trying to sleep, I heard my dogs barking, which indicated someone was coming. I was very scared and made sure all lights were off. My heart was pounding as I stood in the dark behind the bathroom door looking at the front door to see who might be coming. Someone with a flashlight was approaching. I realized that it was a police officer, and I prayed he would not force his way in. He flashed his light around for a while and then left. The officer was looking through the door while projecting his flashlight inside and decided to leave. I was breathing very heavily. I was not sure if the officer had actually left or had just decided to get into his car and wait. I could not sleep anymore and just stood there in the dark, waiting and waiting. I waited three or four hours and then crept out the front door, locked it, and took a path as far from my own driveway as I could, fearing a police officer was waiting. It was still dark as I crossed the farm fields to the highway. I then felt somewhat comfortable and walked another mile to reach my car and drove away to my hotel.

Karen gave me our girls at Knollwood that evening. I was very excited, feeling as though I had not seen my girls in years, but Miranda was coughing and not feeling well and Nadia was very quiet and probably very confused about all she had been through. I tried to do everything to entertain Nadia while also tending to Miranda.

Though pondering deeply about what my wife had put us through, I surprised myself by also beginning to wonder what Karen was thinking and feeling about her own separation from them and impulsively dialed her number so Nadia could to talk to her. I told Nadia to tell her mother that Miranda was sick, and she was welcome to come and see her if she wanted. Much to my surprise, Karen agreed. After seeing Miranda, she decided to stay for the night and told me that she would go to the court and drop the restraining order. I was very pleased by that. I did not blame anyone and just wanted to look ahead for the children's sake. I had made the call out of concern for Karen's feelings. I never thought of feeding Karen the same medicine she had given me. I never believed in the "an eye for an eye" mantra. I was hoping to help Karen see how different we were and hoping she might try to change, but that never happened.

The judge signed the reversal of the order a day later, and I was able to live in my own house again. I wondered if Karen was even aware of the genuine compassion I had shown her. I was very hurt but more than ready to put the whole affair behind us. It then came out that when I had called Karen's sister from our home, they were both actually at the sister's house but had decided not to answer. Karen knew from the caller ID that I was home, and she had called the police to catch me violating the restraining order.

As I awaited the arrival of my business fixtures and equipment, the day to face my fate in court came up. Though I had promised my attorney that I would plead guilty, I was having serious second thoughts. Despite the money and time a truthful plea would cost, I felt ready to face the consequences. At the last minute, however, I put the principle aside, realizing that no matter what, I was still a man from the Middle East. No one would ever believe me. I assured my attorney that we still had a deal. When my name was called, my attorney beckoned me to the front of the courtroom. The judge read the charges and asked me how I pled.

"Guilty, your honor," I replied. When he asked me if I understood the charges and whether anyone had pushed me to plead guilty, I said I understood and no one had pushed me. He then read out my punishment: First, I was sentenced to ninety days in jail, which was stayed eighty-eight days with credit for the two days I had already served. I was fined seven hundred dollars, with six hundred of that stayed. I was required to attend weekly anger management classes for a full year, and I was under a supervised, two-year probation.

As I was hearing all of this, my knees were failing me. I could not breathe or even speak, wanting only to have some private time with my attorney. I asked him what had just happened. He was far more relaxed than I and wondered why I was being so emotional.

I replied, "Didn't you hear the ninety days in jail?"

He laughed and said, "Yes, ninety days, but eighty-eight days were *stayed*, which means you will not serve any time unless you fail to obey the terms."

I relaxed a little bit but still was not sure about the weekly anger management class. I told him I hardly had enough hours in my day as it was. But the damage was done, and he took me to pay the hundred-dollar fine and outlined for me exactly what I needed to do. I was somewhat at peace, as I no longer needed to worry about what was going to happen to me. The next day I made arrangements to start both the classes and the supervised probation in the next few weeks.

I also received a call that day telling me that the delivery of my business fixtures and products was hours away. Instead of being happy, I was very depressed about having gotten myself into something that I might regret. It was Friday and I was off work, so the timing was perfect. Two big trucks arrived at the store location, and I met the main person who was going to build out the store and furnish it according to our plan. The company had sent out all of the material with only one person. That person would then hire local help to assist him. This was cheaper for the company than sending a lot of people. I did not even need to be there for that if I did not want to, so I gave him the keys and told him that I would stay in touch. Three days later, the store was completed and stocked. I took the entire week off from work to be trained, and I hired a company to work on a lighted sign for its name: Mighty Buck.

Sarah, our babysitter, had agreed to work at the store when it was open and ready. She was not sure she could do it, but I trained her and stayed in touch with her to develop her confidence. After working ten hours, I went straight to the store. Sarah then went home, and I attended to the store until closing at eight. I went home very tired.

I was trying very hard to put the trials and tragedy of the past two years behind me. I avoided all discussion about anger management and probation at home. I knew these were my issues to deal with and prove to myself that I could move on. The timing of my first class during the store's opening week was very awkward and forced me to close before 7:00 p.m. I was hoping I could soon hire more employees to cover for me whenever I couldn't be there. I knew that a new store needed to be open longer, not shorter, hours.

The class was very difficult in the beginning. Some of my classmates had committed horrible crimes, while I had not done anything. From the start, we were told to never say things like "I never did anything," because we had to "own up" to what we had done. Owning up to something that didn't even exist was very difficult, but I knew that I must survive these weekly meetings for a full year. I was very quiet in the first meeting and did not feel that I could relate to anyone in the class. I related to the instructor very well, however, and she was truly inspirational—patient, very understanding, and kind.

After several classes, I began to revisit the lessons I had taught myself while serving in the Iraqi army. I reminded myself how I had ironed my uniforms, unlike anyone else, which made many of my friends very upset at me for being so positive. I decided to be positive here too and make a difference. I read, prepared, shared my thoughts, and spoke at every opportunity. The instructor was amazed and viewed me as a leader after only a few classes.

The other required punishment seemed less hectic. The meeting with the lady at the courthouse for my two-year supervised probation lasted only about thirty minutes. I discussed openly what had happened to give me this "police record," and she seemed very understanding. The meetings were to be monthly or even further apart, very much to my liking, especially since I had to take off work to attend.

It was a very busy year. I had involved myself in a business that was not making any money and giving me a lot of responsibilities and very little free time to enjoy life. Communication between Karen and me was worse than ever. There was little of it, even on so-called good days, and any exchanges were very negative. Not only was I not happy with my marriage, I was indeed depressed. I was working many hours for the sole purpose of providing for my family and felt that my wife was throwing obstacles in my way instead of helping me. The short separation from my children, however, had taught me a lesson in tolerance.

In late summer of 1996, after several months of operation, I decided to have a grand opening on a Saturday. I invited many people from my work and also my friend, Denise. My work friends who came to check out my new adventure were happy for me. Karen and Nadia were inflating helium balloons to give away, and I had also paid for an ice cream truck for more giveaways. I was inside attending to customers. Toward the end of the event, Denise came by with more balloons and gifts for me. I was not expecting anyone to bring anything, and so Denise, my good friend, was truly a class act. She stopped by the cash register to talk to me. Denise did not know anyone there, so we kept up a friendly chat as best we could while I waited on customers. As I glanced out the window to check on the activities, I found myself eye to eye with Karen. I realized at that moment that Karen was watching Denise and me instead of filling balloons. I also could tell what was going on in Karen's mind. I knew that she had no basis for her concerns, but I was not about to convince her of that. I wondered if trust had always been an issue in Karen's life.

The grand opening had brought many people to the store, but I did not sell enough to even cover the ice cream and balloon expenses. I did know that any new business would need some time to let word get around. I was told before opening to have enough money on reserve for six months. The dollar store was the first of its kind in Buffalo and all the surrounding areas. Buffalo was a low-income community that I knew would appreciate a store like mine.

Miranda's second birthday arrived, December 20, 1996. We celebrated in the usual way, but this birthday meant a lot more to me than ever. Being together with my daughters was a joy with the knowledge that they were doing well. But the future was very frightening because of my concerns over how the children might end up being raised. I always had doubts that my marriage would survive without a major change in Karen. Not only were we not a good couple, we were not even friends, and I needed a friend like I needed air to breathe.

My demanding schedule was taking a toll on me. From work I drove directly to my business and stayed until eight, except Wednesdays, when I attended anger management class. I never made it back home before nine, when I would fall into bed, only to get up and repeat the routine all over again.

One Friday, several weeks before Nadia's sixth birthday in March 1997, was my day off. I normally would have been at the store, but I had some errands to attend to, including a visit to my probation officer and a meeting with an attorney over some matters related to my employment. I had made plans for Sarah to work in the morning and Karen to take over until I finished with the officer. Returning to the store, I was surprised to see Sarah still behind the counter, not Karen. I did not suspect anything, however, and sent Sarah home.

I called Karen, but there was no answer. I began to get a little worried. Was she at the hospital? Were the girls okay? It was not a busy night, so I closed up shop early. When I arrived home, it did not appear that anyone was there. I went to the bedroom and was shocked to find many things gone. I kept calling Karen, but she was not answering. I called Sarah to find out exactly what had happened. Sarah did not want to tell me a lot but did say that Karen was going to move out, and I was not supposed to look for them. If I did, she would file a restraining order. I asked Sarah many times if she knew where Karen had gone, but she claimed she did not know.

I was very upset, confused—and clueless. What exactly had I done to trigger Karen's departure? I had phoned her at the store barely an hour before I arrived there, and she hadn't said a thing. I was beginning to feel like a hostage to my wife. She knew how much I loved my children, yet she felt free to take them away from me whenever she was feeling in need of any attention.

The next day, I spent the day going from place to place, unable to focus. I went to see the attorney who had defended me in my recent case and told him what had just happened. He was very honest with me, but I knew he also did not want to be unethical. I sensed that he was trying to tell me that it was best to divorce, even though he never said it directly. I had often pondered divorce myself, but so much had been holding me back. I was fearful of losing my children. I had no one to support me. And I always feared the courts would treat me, a man from the Middle East, less than fairly. And no matter what happened, I was always thinking about what more I could do to please Karen and make her happy. It was almost time to start sending Nadia to the Catholic school at the St. Francis Church in Buffalo that we had chosen for her as a means of spiritual direction. It went only up to sixth grade, which I viewed as a better spiritual foundation than public school. The other advantage was that the school was close to our store in Buffalo. Nadia was able to wait at the business after school until either Karen or I could take her home. The dollar store was losing money, and I was going deeper in debt. I asked myself if I should have chosen some other business. My regular job was getting harder because of all the time I had to take off to attend to the situations Karen had set in motion. Despite all that, I still kept asking myself what more I could have done to please her. I began to explore the idea of finishing the upper level of our dream home. I still did not know where Karen was, and most important to me, our children, but I kept trying to find out. Because I feared Sarah could quit any minute, I hired one more person and gave her different hours. This was an added expense that I really could not afford, but I wasn't thinking clearly.

Ten days after Karen's departure, I was surprised to receive a call from her asking for money, as her paycheck was being deposited directly into our joint banking account. My first response concerned only the children—I said I must see them. She continued on about the money, saying she wanted to file for divorce. I told her she was free to do what she wanted to do but asked that she put the children first.

She replied, "If you think it is so important to put the children first, why did you hire a divorce attorney?" Before I could even reply, she threatened me by saying that, with my "police record," it was a sure thing that she would gain full custody of our children and I would never see them again. I tried to calm her and asked her to tell me when I had hired any divorce attorney. She said I had told her myself that I was hiring an attorney the day I was heading to the probation officer.

My jaw dropped to the floor. I said, "Karen, I hired an attorney for my case against my employer, not for divorce. Why didn't you ask me to clarify things before you moved out?" Karen had now revealed to me one of her cards with her threat about winning full custody of our children and preventing me from ever seeing them again. Was that the reason she called the police?

She came back home in a few days and expected me to act like nothing had happened. I never said anything to her, even though I was bleeding inside for being a coward. But I was a coward only because I felt I was doing the best for our children. That was all that mattered to me at the time.

And I still hadn't given up trying to do more to please Karen. One day while getting a haircut, it occurred to me that Buffalo could use a Great Clips. It turned out that Minnesota was closed for new Great Clips franchises, but I moved on to check out other companies. I found one in another state that was willing. I did not investigate the pros and cons of being that company's one and only franchise in the state. Fear had overtaken me and my soul. I was desperate to do something, anything, that would enable me to keep my children.

After many calls and borrowing more money and charging all my credit cards to their limits, I was able to buy a haircut franchise and bring it to the space next to the dollar store. I was hoping for a complete reversal of financial fortune. I did not know anything about hair or cutting hair, and thought it was a business like any other business.

I learned some quick lessons. I found out that no salon can open its doors without a stylist who has a manager's license. The hired manager was well aware of that, and she was also aware that I did not know anything about hair. Those facts translated into the reality that if I did not do what the manager told me to do, she could walk away and force me to close the business. I was beginning to understand the hostage theme. I was a hostage for my wife, hostage for my salon business, and all of this after running away from being a hostage for Saddam Hussein. I surely did not feel free, even though I appeared to be. I knew that the struggle must continue.

The salon turned into another nightmare when I tried to hire stylists. I was an unknown in the business, and many did not want to risk working for me. I had many money problems. Everything I spent was feeding only failure, simply because I did not have the support at home. What made it even worse was that I did not know if, or when, my wife was going to take our children away from me again. The fear was consuming me every moment of every day. Karen had not expressed any opinion when I was searching for a salon franchise, but the minute she learned that I was having problems, she made it known that she "did not want a salon." Karen never knew how to say something like, "David, this is our business, and we will try to make it work." Hearing something like that would have been heaven, instead of what she really said.

I continued my friendship with Denise at lunch meetings. We never discussed my troubles at home, and she never asked me about any personal issues. I asked her every time I saw her if there were any wedding plans. I was acting like a pure, true good friend who wanted the best for her. I also continued to call my sisters in Iran, but calling and getting through were two completely different things. When we did manage to talk, I felt sadder than I had before the call, as I only learned more about my sisters' struggles and my inability to help.

CHAPTER TWENTY

· ·

Disintegration

In November 1997, Karen filed, and then later canceled, another restraining order and again disappeared with the girls. I was not sure what had triggered her this time. Now I had two dysfunctional businesses, a full-time job, and a wife who filed restraining orders as readily as she breathed air. I knew I was being abused and held as a hostage because she knew I loved my daughters, but I did not know any way out. Sometime in early 1998, I decided to close the dollar store, as my credit cards were completely maxed out. We followed the accountant's and attorney's advice to seek relief by filing a business bankruptcy and getting a fresh start. At the same time, I realized that the haircut franchise management was not giving me the help I needed, because I was their only store in the state of Minnesota. They were restricting me from performing certain services, like hair color. I decided to work out a deal by forfeiting all the money I had given the franchise and just leaving it. I had a limited time to register my own salon name and remove all references to the franchise. My first registered name was Style City. Now I was officially someone who owned a salon yet did not know a thing about hair and had no one to call on for help. Despite all my struggles with the hair salon business, for some unknown reason, I felt a great connection to it and was determined to make it work somehow.

Despite our constantly tense and mistrustful relationship, I still tried to get Karen involved in the salon. A kind product representative advised me one day that it was best to have an owner present at the salon most of the time. She made us aware that most stylists would find ways to not report services when the owner was not present. She suggested we put Karen on the premises by sending her to school for nails. It would take less than two months to get a nail license, and after that, she might like to do more, like getting a hair license. Karen was standing next to me when that suggestion was made, and surprisingly, she was in agreement with it.

Initially, this was a financial burden, but I was somewhat hopeful that it would be a permanent solution to my business problems. Karen seemed excited too, and it seemed that she was starting to see the big picture of running a salon.

The representative began trying to convince me to go to school too—for hair. She told me that once I finished, I could, after some practice, apply for the manager's license myself. I was very resistant to the idea, despite my awareness of the great benefits of knowing the business. I was an educated person, and it would be very hard for me to relate to fellow students who had only high school diplomas. I finally promised the representative that I would look into it. But there was another, even bigger issue, for me—my awareness of the general image of male stylists and that they had a different lifestyle than mine. I had nothing against any lifestyle, but that one was not me.

In spite of my doubts, I finally decided to register at the Scott Lewis School. I had many weeks of earned vacation time to use. The first four months were classroom lessons in cutting, coloring, and perming, as well as pedicures and manicures.

In no time Karen was ready to get her license. I added a nail table and everything Karen needed to become part of the salon. In the beginning, there was hardly any nail business, because it usually takes a lot of time to build a client base. I had very little time for sleep or anything else. I used my Fridays off to recharge my energy.

In the spring of 1998, I learned from Denise that she was getting married to Rob in early September. I was very excited and wanted to be of help to her in any way I could. Denise's family was somewhat dysfunctional, and Denise was not even sure her father was going to attend. She asked me if I could design the wedding invitations on my computer, and I was happy to do so. She loved them, and I even printed labels and handled the mailing.

One evening as I was printing labels, not bothering to hide my work, Karen stood over me and asked, "What the hell are you doing all of this for?" I was taken aback. Karen had never been this bold. She had always moved silently behind my back, doing things like going through my computer and books while I was at work.

I responded honestly and said, "Denise is my friend, and for crying out loud, she is getting married. I am helping her. If Denise asked me for the shirt off my back, I would give it to her." Karen went into the bedroom and slammed the door. I finished my work, expecting another restraining order in the days ahead. It was all a big mystery to me. What kind of bad intentions could an engaged person possibly have?

One day the product representative visited the salon and asked Karen if she liked going to school for nails, and Karen answered very positively. Her next question to Karen was, "Why don't you consider going for hair also?" She said that all nail study hours could be counted and that she would be done in no time. Karen liked the idea very much, and I decided to send her to school again.

As though I was not busy enough with my full-time computer job, going to school for hair, and managing a salon, I also began a search for a builder who was willing to finish our house. This was very difficult, as many refused to take the risk involved in removing the temporary roof and building on the basement that we were living in. If there was rain, the basement and our belongings would be damaged. When I found one who said he was ready, I wasted no time. What made it even crazier was my decision to be the general building manager, which meant hiring all subcontractors and arranging their schedules. How did I do all of that at the same time? I truly have no idea. I just wanted to please Karen and make her change her ways in dealing with issues in general.

Building began in June 1998, beginning with the house framer. Karen never participated in any phase of this process, acting like a complete stranger. I had the full responsibility for everything. Several times I was with the builders discussing different things when Karen drove up. She just walked by us without even saying hello and went inside. None of the contractors ever said anything, but I could read everything in their minds and see their facial expressions asking me, "Is *this* who you are building this home for?" I was asking myself the same thing.

I used every time-saving opportunity to finish school. Karen had gone full-time, and her schooling was done. She began to work at the salon, which did help to stabilize it. But I still needed the manager's license to feel completely free of employee manipulation. I knew I was headed in the right direction, but deep inside I was not sure which one was better: being a hostage to employees or being a hostage to Karen's irrational moods.

Denise and I met for lunch and I asked whether everything was on track for the wedding. She said it was, except for the videotaping, which would be quite costly. I immediately said I would do it. Denise was very happy to agree to that. I even offered to "give the bride away" if her father didn't show up, but she politely declined.

I took the day off from school and closed the salon at two to get all four of us dressed up and ready. I filmed the entire ceremony, Denise and her family greeting the guests, and even the reception. I planned to put it all on a DVD for the best wedding gift ever. It was very important to me to prove to myself that I was able to be a pure friend to someone whom I had loved so much for so many years.

Our two-story house was all framed up by this time, and the windows and doors were installed. It was now time to hire the rest of the contractors, especially for the stucco, my favorite siding, to protect the house frame before the snow. I found a contractor who promised, at minimum, to wrap the house with felt, which would be enough to keep any water away. The home was becoming a beautiful sight and attracted many positive comments. Was this enough to make Karen act like a responsible wife and mother? I had my fingers crossed.

By early 1999 I had graduated from the Scott Lewis School and was officially a stylist. Things were seemingly going well. During my school months, I had many regulars who asked for my services. One lady in particular enjoyed my pedicure, and another young lady named Jackie loved how I did her hair highlights. Jackie also enjoyed talking to me and told me everything about her family and her boyfriend. She promised to follow me to my salon. I was happy to hear that, but I did not think she would, as it was about thirty miles from her home.

I felt that things with the salon were starting to go my way. I worked very hard to establish it as a great salon to go to. I took appointments at any hour, late or early. Regardless of how hard I worked, I wanted Karen to feel comfortable and appreciate the salon as her salon too and be proud of it. But she never showed any interest in checking out new products or suggested any changes to the salon or the layout. I was the one who had to do all orders, interviews, and decorating. I never heard Karen tell me that she liked her job, and I never asked, fearing I might upset her.

The salon, however, was still not making enough money to cover the rent and operating expenses. The main reason was that I had to pay someone for being on staff with a manager's license in order to stay open. Also, we did not have enough clients to keep us busy and enable us to hire more stylists. It was hard to hear clients telling us how hard it was to find us. Even if they found us on the highway, there was no easy way to turn back, and often people just drove past to other salons. When I tried to discuss these issues with Karen and tell her that the salon was not making enough money, rather than engaging in a civilized conversation, Karen always became defensive and heard what I said as faulting her personally. I always thought that Karen was a great worker and performed great services, but she was very lousy at promotion and making any business decisions.

Several months after Denise's wedding, I called her to arrange one of our lunches. I had mailed her the wedding DVD but never heard back from her, which was very surprising. After three unreturned messages, I started to worry. I wondered whether Karen had said something to her, or maybe Rob was getting jealous, though that was unlikely. I finally wrote more letters wondering what might have been the problem. After no replies to any of them, I decided I had done enough, and no one could blame me for not trying. I did not understand why Denise could not even bother to call me and say something like, "Thank you for your friendship, but I must move on." I dared not ask Karen if she had said anything or mailed Denise a letter without my knowledge.

I was beginning to have trouble with the landlord for the salon, as he was continually making improvements to the entire building and passing the expense on to all tenants. These unexpected expenses were making paying the rent difficult or impossible. I did tell him that I would not renew my lease when it was time, even though I never knew for sure when that time would be.

The house was being completed very slowly, but nicely, and I even ended up doing some of the finishing work myself. There was no deadline as long as I was doing it the way I wanted. I ended up painting the entire house on my own. Karen never gave any opinion regarding the colors. I was very frustrated that Karen was so blind to all my efforts, but I was very cautious about upsetting her, as I knew I might have my children separated from me for weeks if I did.

In the midst of a discussion with my cousin, he told me that he had heard through his contacts of the passing of my father in Iran. I had no one to call and did not know what to do. I had not even applied for an American passport yet and was not sure how long it would take. Even if I had one, would I dare travel with it to Iran? Most importantly I did not know how much time had gone by before my cousin learned of my dear father's passing.

I was feeling very guilty for not being there for my father's funeral. What were my sisters doing? I was crushed, and cried for hours and days. Karen never once tried to comfort me, acting as though she did not even see me cry. My children came to me and comforted me, but not my wife. I was expecting her to call her parents and relatives to tell them the news, but even if she did, I never heard comforting words from any of them either. Sadly, I have never forgotten these acts of unkindness.

The year 1999 was coming to end, and I was working hard everywhere. We were getting ready for Y2K at work, busily changing and testing our computer programs. My youngest daughter, Miranda, was turning into a radiantly beautiful young lady, and I planned to let her follow the same path as we did with Nadia at the St. Francis Catholic School.

At the salon, Karen was very silent each time I cut or colored a lady's hair. It was a hair salon, I was a stylist, and women go to salons. What was I supposed to do?

Jackie, my friend from hair school, was coming once every four or five months for a highlight. The first time I colored Jackie's hair I charged her the full price, but I felt very guilty doing that. Jackie, a young lady who went to hair schools for services to save money, was driving sixty miles round trip to see me. How could I charge her full price? I decided to give her a discount in the future. But Karen's reactions were making me very uncomfortable.

It was a typical Saturday at the salon in the fall of 2000, with both Karen and me working and Nadia and Miranda in the massage room playing on a computer I had loaded with games. Karen started to style Nadia's and Miranda's hair. I loved to see our daughters with updos, but I had to ask what the occasion was. Karen answered without looking at me. "We are going to Sarah's wedding." I had forgotten that I had given my permission to Nadia several months earlier to be the flower girl in our babysitter Sarah's wedding. I was surprised that Karen was not reminding me to get ready. In front of my other stylists, I asked Karen, "Going to the wedding? Aren't I invited?"

Karen looked at me in a very angry way and snapped, "Nope."

I froze. This was a moment that I will never forget for the rest of my life. Karen's face said a lot more than just a "nope." It was full of pure hate. Stunned, I walked to the back of the salon and kept myself busy acting like nothing had happened. Soon Karen was ready to leave. Nadia and Miranda were not aware of any of this, and they innocently came to the back of the room to give Daddy a goodbye kiss. I came out to the front of the salon after they left with teary eyes. My stylist, Lisa, asked me, "What the f——? How could she do that? How could any mother do that to her children?"

I did not know what to say and just went to the back of the salon to cry. About half an hour later, I washed my face and went to the front of the salon as if nothing had happened. I now realized why Karen's schedule for the day had been nearly empty. This had all been well planned and executed by her. I could not wait until it was four in the afternoon so I could close the salon.

The ten-minute drive home seemed like it took ten years. I looked around at the beautiful home I was building as I entered. We had not moved to the upper level yet, and when I went to the basement to change into something comfortable, I noticed an envelope on the green Formica table in the kitchen. It was addressed to "Karen, Nadia, and Miranda Haaland." I opened it. It was a wedding invitation from Sarah's parents inviting only the three of them. I put the envelope in my briefcase. I have kept that envelope in a drawer until just recently, when I decided to destroy it to help heal myself from this very dark encounter.

I had no question in my mind that Karen was either too stupid to realize what she was doing or she just simply hated me beyond my imagination. Why would Sarah's church-going parents go along with this game? When Karen came home, I confronted her. "You were behind that invitation. No one would dare invite only one parent." Karen dismissed everything I was saying. Then I said, "It is clear our marriage is not working. Can we please try to divorce peacefully and do it in a civil manner?" Karen did not respond; she just rushed into the bedroom and slammed the door. Why was I always seeking a "civil" solution when she never did anything civil?

I did find out how and why Sarah's parents had gone along with Karen and sent the invitation without including me. One day when Sarah had still been working for me at the dollar store, I found her playing outside the store with several young people of her age while other kids were inside stealing various items. I did not say a word to Sarah, but that evening I shared the story with Karen as normal husband and wife talk. It turned out that Karen had told Sarah and her parents many lies about me. Sarah's parents, rather than asking me about the accuracy of the things Karen had told them, had just believed her and decided to boycott me. I also found out that Karen had stayed with them most of the time while the restraining orders were in effect. Why Karen said those things, I will never know.

By the end of the week, Karen and the girls were gone again. I did not receive a restraining order this time. However, I did receive a threat that if I started to look for the girls or go to Sarah's parents' house, Sarah's mother would call the police on me. Within ten days, Karen and the girls returned to the house. I was heartbroken and full of guilt for having two beautiful children who must be confused by what their mother was doing. I asked myself, *How are they going to cope with future difficulties considering what their mother is teaching them? Where had I gone wrong? Was this what I fought for all these years? Is this what I left my family, country, girlfriend for?*

Two views of current home

Karen's parents continued to visit us about once a year. I had hoped her brothers, sisters, and other relatives would come as well to celebrate and shower us with housewarming gifts. That never happened— not even a simple card or word of congratulation. Even so, I was always very happy to host her parents and spend as much time with them as possible. I always prepared breakfast for them. I learned that my father-in-law loved one of my dishes made with eggplant, tomato, and onions, so I tried to make it for him whenever I could. Karen's parents never once spoke to me about anything, especially all the troubles Karen was causing me and blaming me for. I never talked to them about the problems either, because, ultimately, they were our problems. During their visit in December 2000, I was very surprised when Karen's father talked to me in a very hostile tone and asked me why I was not buying his daughter any clothes. I was taken aback but smiled and said, "I was not sure that I was supposed to buy Karen any clothes." Was he truly serious? I was spending more than fifty hours a week on my full-time job and the commute, managing and working at the salon, building and finishing a new home, and I was supposed to go shop for clothes for Karen? Why would Karen complain to her father about something like that? What was she expecting to accomplish?

By January 2001, the house was completed, and we had moved up from the basement. Everything turned out great except the floor tile work. I had built a big master bathroom and used expensive tile throughout, but the work quality was unsatisfactory, and I was planning to redo it soon. I was overjoyed that Nadia and Miranda had their own rooms, painted according to their preferences, with matching carpets. Seeing them so happy helped me forget about the complete indifference of my in-laws.

CHAPTER TWENTY-ONE
· ·

The Way Back Home

I was in the office one spring day working on a computer problem with the radio tuned to my favorite AM station, WCCO 830, mostly for white noise. I wasn't paying much attention as I worked away, but when a call-in program came on, I heard some of the callers crying. This did grab my attention, and I started to listen. The guest was Kathryn Harwig, and the callers were asking about people or animals in their lives that had passed on. Kathryn was "connecting" the callers to their loved ones, even providing information and messages from them. Most of the crying was actually from joy. I was very skeptical but curious at the same time. As the show went on, I became more and more curious and wrote down Kathryn's phone number. I later called Kathryn and made a private appointment with her.

Kathryn was a very sweet, friendly person, and she put me at ease right away. As she was explaining the ground rules—I could not ask for anyone specific, she would connect me with whomever presented themselves to Kathryn wanting to connect—she stopped and began describing someone who was ready to communicate with me. I knew right away that it was my mother. Kathryn was telling me things that no one but me could have ever known. I was crying as Kathryn became the medium between my mother and me. While these messages were coming, Kathryn began to describe my father and said he had also decided to join and talk to me. As the session went on, the general theme became the abiding wish of my parents that I stop feeling guilty for them. My father's specific messages were that I was his favorite son, and he loved me. Before he was deported, he had hidden some valuables that still had not been found. I was crying throughout the entire session, and Kathryn handed me one tissue after another. As our time came to an end, I could not help mentioning my former girlfriend, Nadia, and the guilt I was feeling for not doing better by her. Kathryn almost shushed me and told me to stop feeling guilty. She said that Nadia still loved me and thought of me positively; she was married and had given birth to three children, but one of them had passed away. She told me to rest assured that Nadia had no regrets, but I probably would not see her again in this lifetime.

A particularly strong message from my parents stuck in my mind. Even though Kathryn had never come out and said it directly, I somehow understood the message anyway. My parents were recommending that I divorce. I cried while driving home. I was very happy to be connected with my parents and happy that I needed to learn to stop feeling guilty. Of course, I was very happy to know that Nadia was doing fine and that she was also thinking of me.

This was the beginning of my intuition journey, and I have kept up a very close friendship with Kathryn. I have seen her many times since our first meeting, even after her decision to halt her private readings. She always told me that I was very intuitive, that I had inherited this gift from my mother, and that I must sharpen my skills.

Kathryn Harwig is a graduate of William Mitchell College of Law and has been a practicing attorney for many years. She appears on many radio shows, does local and regional presentations, and holds monthly meetings of local like-minded individuals near her residence. She has written or co-written eight books and is planning to write more. Her current titles are as follows:

Analysis System of Self-Discovery (1994)

Your Life in the Palm of Your Hand,
a Hand Analysis System of Self-Discovery (1994)

The Millennium Effect (1996)

The Intuitive Advantage (2000)

The Angel in the Big Pink Hat (2005)

Palm Visions: Your Life Is Still in the Palm of Your Hand (2008)

The Eight Principles to Inner Peace (with Dorothy Lee) (2009)

The Return of Intuition: Awakening Psychic
Gifts in the Second Half of Life (2010).

By 2001 I had put to rest my thoughts of asking Karen that we try to divorce peacefully. Her tactic of stripping my children away from me had created a fear like no other. I never stopped thinking of divorcing but just did not know how. The salon was limping along. I loved the services I was providing, but I did not enjoy being questioned every time I talked to a female stylist or customer. Though I would occasionally hire a new stylist to help me with the hours, I came to realize that I would never be able to have a full staff, as every time I hired someone, one of two things happened. Either Karen would tell the stylist all our dirty laundry, including many lies, to the point the stylist would quit, or she would file a restraining order and I would lose the stylist when Karen failed to keep the salon open.

One slow Saturday afternoon in June 2001, near closing time, someone called the salon for a pedicure. Since the pedicure room was in the back of the salon and no one was at the desk, I locked the door during the appointment because I would not be able to hear if anyone was coming in. I thought Karen had left, but fifteen minutes later, she showed up in the room from nowhere, pretending that she had forgotten something. She found nothing and left. I could not wait to get home to confront her and ask her what she had been expecting to see. I knew she had spied on me while I was doing a service for a complete stranger. I knew exactly what she had hoped to see me doing; instead, she found me scrubbing someone's feet to bring in income.

When I arrived home, I found the front door locked and a box on the steps full of my favorite CDs and a couple of shirts. The big question was whether I should unlock the house and go inside or just leave and check into a hotel. I waited a few minutes and decided to go inside. I was fully expecting Karen to call the police. She had to call the police every few months to build up that "history of abuse." I lived in fear of the police, becoming worried even when I saw a police car simply driving behind me on the highway. What a way to live! I picked up the box, went inside, and set it down. I then pretended to relax, but without saying a single word. Karen did not call the police, but she wouldn't face my questions regarding her mistrust and the spying either.

On another Saturday a few months later, I was in the massage room to be with Nadia and Miranda as they played computer games. Karen came in and told the girls to get ready to go. I knew it was not yet time to close, so I asked where they were going. When she said they were going to visit her sister in St. Paul, I immediately knew I was not invited. I jokingly said, "They are with *me*, and they are not going." At that, Karen shoved the door against me, scratched my face with her long nails, and stormed out the door with the girls. The stylist was shocked to see my bloody face and asked me if I was going to call the police. I simply said, "No, Karen probably already did." After the stylist took pictures of my bloody face and bruised arm, she helped me clean up with alcohol. I decided to close up for the day, as I was in no shape to face clients.

I ended up going to work on Monday despite my scratched face, mostly to give myself a chance to think of what I should do. I did not call the salon all day, just to avoid talking to Karen. At the end of the day when I went to the salon to pick up the girls, I again found it closed and the lights out. This time, I did not even get out of the car, as I knew exactly what had happened. I drove home expecting the furniture to be gone, and I was correct. This was becoming very old. I wondered if I should just give up on everything. I was feeling more hopeless and alone than ever. I ended up calling the therapy center where I had endured a year's worth of anger management classes to find someone who could help me cope, someone with whom I could talk freely.

Within a couple of days, I was served yet again with a restraining order preventing me from talking to Karen. I was becoming very familiar with these restraining orders; by now, they were a big part of my life. This time was somewhat different, as it was not just a restraining order. Karen had separately filed a police report of my abusing her the Saturday before. I was charged with domestic abuse, even though I was the one with the bloody, scratched face. If Karen had made her report on that same Saturday, I would have been taken to county jail without any question, but because it was reported later, an officer was assigned to investigate the charges. No matter what I said or did, the officer did not believe me. I even showed him the pictures, all to no avail. I wasn't informed of any results or charges.

This time, Karen decided to stay away from the house for weeks. The salon would stay closed unless I took a lot of time from work just to open it. I did not have a lot of business at the time, but I wanted to keep it open anyway, if only to avoid any rumors that I was closed forever. My job was becoming very difficult, as the manager was fed up with my irregular schedule. I was confused and missing my children very much. My business was becoming frailer by the week because Karen was no longer working there. My girls were living at Sarah's parents' house, and I tried to contact them several times. Sarah's mother was becoming worse than Karen and threatened me several times. Both women reported my contact attempts twice to the police, and I was served on two separate occasions with "violating the protection order" and notices that I had to face them in court.

I will not forget Tuesday, September 11, 2001, until the day I die. As I was driving to the courthouse for my hearing, I heard reports of a major accident in New York City. A plane had crashed into the World Trade Center building. The building was on fire, and the situation was chaotic. Then I heard the report of another plane hitting the other tower. The consensus became that it was not an accident but a terrorist attack. I was feeling horrible for all the victims, but a fear for my own life upon entering the courthouse was starting to creep in. Of course, I had no choice but to go inside. The building seemed empty as people were gathered at televisions in every office. I eventually closed out my violation cases, paid the fines, and went home to watch more horrific news from New York.

We were all at home that evening watching television when the phone rang. Karen answered it. After a few minutes, she handed it to me and said that Diane wanted to talk to me. Diane was Karen's sister in St. Paul. She had recently left her husband and their three children for another man. I had not talked to her since that had happened, because I strongly disapproved of her behavior. Diane was obviously calling from a bar, based on the loud music in the background. She was crying, and asked me if I was okay. Surprised, I said I was fine and wondered why she would ask me that. Still crying, she exclaimed, "Dave, I hope you are not one of them!"

My jaw almost hit the floor. Of course, she was referring to the hijackers, whose identities were not known at the time but who had all been killed during the terror attacks. I had to work hard to contain my emotions.

I responded only, "No, Diane, I am not one of them." I then ended the call. I have not talked to Diane since, but her call explained everything I had suspected, going back to our wedding day. Karen and her family never tried to know my story, and they must have fabricated and then believed their own "information" about me. This was even harder to take than what Karen was doing by piling police records on me. If they all felt that way, why didn't Karen just agree to divorce peacefully? Was her mission in life to destroy my life? I had done more for her in a short time than most people do for another person in an entire lifetime. If I could talk about only one thing in this book, it would be that phone call. That is how powerful it was. I always wondered what Diane had asked Karen at the beginning of the call. I suspect it was something like: "Is David home? Was he home yesterday?" But I never asked, and I shall never know. Regardless of how much Diane cried and tried to show me some sympathy, she had projected her true feelings and those of her entire family onto a big screen. Things were very clear to me from that moment on. Sadly, to this day September 11 has a completely different meaning to me than the entire world. I am not sure which one is more tragic.

As the days moved past the September 11 attacks, talk began of the possibility of war against Afghanistan and all responsible and sponsoring countries behind the attack. It became a reality in October 2001 under the name Operation Enduring Freedom. I tried to cope and move on with my life. As Miranda's seventh birthday neared, I prepared and mailed my usual Christmas cards for everyone in Karen's family. I still had heard nothing from Denise, but I decided to include her too, hoping that someday she would realize how much she meant to me as a friend. In January 2002, a business envelope arrived in my mailbox addressed to "the Haaland Family" but with no return address. I assumed it was some sort of advertisement but opened it anyway. It contained only a Christmas card made from a photograph of Denise, her husband Rob, and a baby dressed in pink. There was nothing written on the back of the picture at all. Was this how she returned a favor? But I did not let anger consume me and began thinking of the bigger picture, which was the birth of Denise's baby.

The next day, I tried to estimate the baby girl's age and size, went shopping for gifts, and boxed and mailed them. Several days later, I was very surprised to receive a thank you card from Denise. This time she actually wrote a few words expressing her gratitude. I was very excited and happy and began to think that this could be a new beginning. I sent a reply, but I never heard from Denise ever again. This marked my last attempt to contact her, and I never tried again. I cannot recall what Denise said in the card, because it disappeared for no apparent reason right after I read it. Karen did refer to the card several times after that by saying, "Denise said this or that in the card, so you must have tried something with her." I ignored her words and was amazed at her childish behavior. I knew she had taken the card. I was always very confused when I observed how jealous Karen was when she saw me connecting with any other female, yet at the same time was doing everything possible to destroy our troubled relationship. Analyzing that someday will require a person with very high psychology credentials.

As Nadia's twelfth birthday, Saturday, March 16, 2002, approached, I purchased her birthday gifts and got ready to celebrate. Jackie, my friend from hair school, called to schedule her regular appointment. Jackie arrived on time, and as expected, Karen became very quiet, with her face reflecting major dissatisfaction. I was used to this behavior, however, so I ignored it and tried to engage Jackie in conversation. I knew Karen had seen the appointment in the book, so I did not feel that I was hiding anything or doing anything wrong. Because of Karen's presence, I could not give Jackie any personal advice or ask her about her boyfriend like we used to do, so we kept the conversation very general. After the highlighting, wash, and style, Jackie was happy with the results, as usual. As I led Jackie to the front counter to check her out, Karen did something unusual. She rushed up to the counter from the back of the salon and sat very close to me. Her face was ready to explode, and I asked her if she wanted anything. She shrugged her shoulders and just said "Nope." I thought it was very weird and felt uncomfortable as I completed Jackie's transaction. Because of the weirdness, I forgot to apply Jackie's usual discount for making the long trip just for my services. The normal charge for highlights was seventy dollars, but I always charged her either forty or fifty. This was not hidden; anyone could see what I charged at any time. I called Jackie back and returned twenty dollars to her. Before Jackie could get out the door, Karen started to shout at me and say I was ripping the salon off. She used every possible nasty word in an unacceptable tone. Jackie left the salon frowning and shaking her head. I tried to calm Karen, telling her that regardless of how much of a discount I gave Jackie, I still made enough profit, and it was my prerogative as a business owner to make those types of calls. Karen was not listening and was shouting so loudly that the print shop owner from next door looked in to see what was going on. Karen was not slowing down in her name calling, and other business owners began to gather at the window. I tried to guide Karen to the back of the salon and away from all the eyes. Karen was emotionally pushing my hands away and refusing to move. I was very embarrassed but kept trying to quiet her and lead her away to the back of the salon. At some point, she fell down. As I was trying to help her stand up, the Buffalo police rushed in. The chief was himself present at this raid instead of letting his officers take care of business as they do everywhere else. The chief had a score to settle with me and once I saw him, I knew I was in big trouble.

The police chief himself took me to the side while another officer took Karen to the back of the room. I explained in great detail what had happened. When the chief and other officer compared notes, they asked me to go with them to the police car. I started to argue that I had not done anything that would require me to be taken away, and I was especially upset because Nadia's birthday was the next day. They did not care to listen and pushed me into the police car right in front of my own children and all the business owners. They took me to the courthouse and county jail just around the corner. I was led to a holding cell, processed, and handed a tray with something inedible on it. I was so humiliated and upset that I wished for something to take my life away. The tray had plastic wrap over it, and I took that little plastic cover and attempted to suffocate myself with it. I ended up vomiting it out. I was hoping no one would notice. No one did.

Still wishing to die, I sat down on the uncomfortable bed feeling my life was over. After a few hours, an officer led me to a person who explained to me that Karen had told the officers that I had pushed her to the ground, which had resulted in a broken wrist. I was officially charged with assault. I realized that I was now in big trouble, probably much bigger than I could imagine. Even so, I was as much concerned about missing Nadia's birthday the next day as I was about the charges. I cried all night in my lonely cell and spoke only when I had to help clean up. The following Monday, I was taken to see the judge and be formally charged. When asked how I pled, I said, "Not guilty." Because the charge was assault, the judge set the bail higher than I could afford.

Several days went by without talking to anyone, and I was becoming very desperate. I found the telephone number for Sarah's parents and called them. I knew that Sarah's parents were siding with Karen, but in my desperation, I was ready to reach out to anyone. I did manage to reach Sarah's mother on one of our very limited collect calls, but after accepting the call and hearing my plea for help, she hung up on me and actually said, *"I am late for Church"*. I was talking to myself as I was talking to Sarah's mother and said, "Do you think you are going to fool God by being at Church? God already knows that you refused to help a desperate person. God would have preferred if you had missed Church to help me." I returned to my cell. Later that day, I was contacted by a bail bond lady. Apparently, she had access to information about who was eligible for bail but had not yet asked for it. She knew the amount I needed and said she could bail me out if I paid her an exorbitant amount. I told her I could probably borrow the three thousand or four thousand dollars in a few days. She was fine with that and began the bail process.

I walked back to the salon and realized it had been closed since the Friday incident. I cleaned myself up, locked the door, and left to get some coffee and ponder my situation. I knew that the first thing I had to do was go to work in the morning and justify my absence. I did not have enough money to check into a hotel for some unknown number of days. I knew that it was illegal to sleep in the salon. If the police or the landlord found out I was doing that, I would have caused myself many more problems than I needed. I decided to do it anyway to save money, but in a very careful and creative way. I went to Walmart for toothpaste, a toothbrush, shaving essentials, and an extra shirt and pants. The salon was not a good place to sleep, but it was not any worse than what was called a mattress in the county jail. I went to work after placing a note in the salon window that I would be open that evening. The feeling of hiding and sleeping on an uncomfortable chair at the salon after completing the dream home for our family is truly a feeling that cannot be described or forgotten.

As the days went by without my daughters or any support system, I ended up with a prescription for depression medication. I was seriously considering taking my life and was open to the doctor's suggestion for therapy in addition to the medication.

Karen served me with divorce papers. She had hired a divorce attorney, but I could not afford an attorney for myself and was prepared to accept whatever was handed to me. Everyone had told me that Karen's accusation of assault prior to filing had been nothing but an attempt to seek the maximum advantage when divorcing in terms of custody and other benefits. I went to the first divorce hearing by myself, while Karen and her attorney were present. When the judge asked if I was represented, I responded, "No, because I cannot afford it." The judge did not do anything except reschedule the hearing and asked me to find a representative. I left the courtroom not sure if I was going to be present the next time, as my suicidal thoughts were increasing. I was in a deep depression.

I went back to the salon, mainly as a place to be alone, as I had hardly any customers. Why would I have customers when I was closed more than I was open? My attorney had asked the court to reschedule my assault case because of his own personal issues, even as he was asking me to pay more of the remaining money I owed him. It was now April 2002. My depression was getting worse, and the day arrived for going back to the courthouse for the divorce hearing. I closed the salon door but left the radio and lights on, as I was not expecting to be gone long. Karen and her sister Cindy were standing outside the courtroom. I was not sure why they were not inside, so I did not go in until others began to enter. The judge asked me if I had an attorney yet, and I said no. The judge made some orders very quickly and rescheduled the hearing for a future date. As I was leaving the courtroom to go back to the salon, from nowhere the police chief himself yet again confronted me about why I was trying to talk to Karen and her sister Cindy when I had a restraining order against me. My jaw dropped to the floor. "When and where?" I asked. The police chief told me that Karen's sister was the one who had made the complaint. As I was trying to deny this new charge, the police chief decided to take me to the attached building, which was the county jail, and put me in a cell. The Buffalo police chief, yet again, was able to score another victory against me and must have been the happiest man on earth at that time.

I had been very depressed before this false accusation, but by now my depression was at its greatest depth. I was processed along with others who had done different things. One lady was very cheerful and carefree, but when she looked at my face, she started to cry. I knew then that my face must be advertising death. I did not care about anything at that moment and was determined to take my own life the first chance I got. The next day the judge let me leave on a small bail, but I was handed another charge for violating the protection order. Cindy was living up to my worst fears about her and the entire family. I had hosted her and her husband, thinking that we were family. I realized that I was not going to survive these evil attempts by my wife and her family. I began to think about ways to end my life. I was one hundred percent serious. It was just a matter of when and where.

Karen must have gone to visit my cousin and his family at some point, because my cousin called me and asked me how I was doing. I did not take anything he said very seriously, because I thought if he really cared, he would have rushed to see me and let me go to sleep at his house instead of the salon. If he had done that, he would have done a great thing for my depression, because I would have had a chance to talk to someone and actually sleep without the fear of illegally sleeping in the salon. I think I made the mistake of telling him goodbye, and I must have told him that I was for sure taking my own life.

A couple of days later, I was at the salon, having decided that I would hang myself there, between two columns that were only four feet apart. My plan was to buy a piece of wood to nail between the two columns horizontally that the rope could come down from. I would put the rope around my neck while standing on a chair and then kick the chair away. It was now just a matter of getting the rope and the wood. Before going ahead with my plans and only a day after I had told my cousin Tony of my plan, I was actually doing a haircut on a customer of mine. I was enjoying the activity and expecting to follow it with another cut for our friend, Gail, who was waiting. As I was doing all this, the Buffalo police chief, with another officer, came in and just stood there looking at me. I asked them, "How can I help you?" The police chief with a big grin on his face told me to just finish my job. I was not sure what it was all about and was getting very frustrated as I finished the haircut. I went to clean my scissors so I could take Gail next, but the police chief did not give me a chance and took the scissors out of my hands.

"You are coming with us," they said. "

Going with you? Where and why?" I asked.

The chief and the officer were not in the mood to answer me. They let me lock the doors and then took me to their car and drove me to the hospital, which was only a mile away. They took me to a room and summoned a specific doctor. After a long wait, the doctor and a nurse came in and began to question me. Apparently my cousin had told Karen that I was going to take my life, and Karen had called the police. After several minutes, the doctor decided that I was not a threat to myself and could leave. I demanded that the officers drive me back to the salon, and they did. I started to wonder if the police chief was somehow watching or had nothing else to do other than magically show up when he had a chance to harass me. I knew that this could not be a common practice for the chief. For someone like a police chief, he must have sworn the oath to protect. He definitely was not protecting, instead was after David Haaland any chance he had. I can honestly say that today when I drive to or through Buffalo, I hope to God that I do not have even a car accident because the same chief is still in Buffalo and he would love to make up an excuse to get me in trouble.

Gail had witnessed everything because she would have been next if the police chief had not taken me away. Gail apparently had called Karen and told her that the police had taken me away. Both Gail and Karen were at the salon when I was returned. As Gail was trying to reason with Karen and mend the bridges between us, Karen was on the phone with her sister Cindy. I could hear Cindy yelling and ordering Karen to leave the salon immediately. Apparently Cindy and her husband were calling from my house, enjoying staying there in my absence. Cindy's demands that night were so loud that I can still hear them in my head, even after so many years. After twenty minutes, Karen and Gail left, and I decided to go to the hotel, as I needed to relax after such a night.

During this time and while at the salon and being away from my daughters for weeks, I called my father-in-law and begged him for help, telling him I was losing my mind from not seeing my girls. I had never heard my father-in-law use any bad words before, but that day he called me more bad things than I could handle. "Call me Son, Dad," I begged him, but he never stopped yelling at me. I ended up telling him that my plans were set and that I was going to be taking my life and would make him sorry for the rest of his life.

His response was, "What are you waiting for? Do it now."

Those words are still ringing in my ears. When we hung up, I was left wondering when I should go and buy the rope.

Karen finally decided to cancel the restraining order and let me go back home against her sister's wishes. I remember very well that evening and how I felt. I drove home feeling for the first time very scared and unsure about entering my own home. As I entered the place I had worked so very hard to design and build, I felt as if I was entering somewhere unfamiliar. I could not even bring myself to go into the living room. I merely sat on a chair in the kitchen near the entryway. I was very tired and feeling very uneasy. Karen was on the telephone when I came in and continued to talk to someone. From my chair I could hear that it was Cindy, shouting very loudly and angrily. I did not say or do anything, just listened to Cindy trashing me with all possible nasty words. After a while, she began to threaten Karen by telling her that if she did not change her mind and kick me out, she would call all of their relatives and ban them from ever talking to her or us. Cindy's tone was making me even more scared.

After twenty minutes of this, Cindy hung up, and I began to feel a little bit better as Karen made coffee. A few minutes later, Karen's parents called. I heard Karen's father repeating Cindy's threats. His voice was as loud as Cindy's, if not louder, but then he went above and beyond Cindy with his words. He told Karen that she would be all on her own if she did not change her mind and that he would make sure that all of the family would follow in those footsteps. I made the mistake of asking Karen for the telephone to try to reason with him. Before I could even speak, my father-in-law started to call me every bad word he knew. I gave the handset back to Karen, not sure if I should stay or just leave.

There were several calls from Karen's family after this call and basically by the end of it, Karen's family proved their point of how much they disliked and did not want me. Why? I will never know. Sadly, when Karen's father became ill and later passed away, no one ever called me or invited me to take part. In fact, to this day no one from her family ever called and said anything. I never was in the picture from the early days of my marriage and will remain that way. I have surrendered everything to God our creator and trust in the master plan.

CHAPTER TWENTY-TWO

Let the Flag Soar

O ur mutual friend, Gail, had been making efforts to calm things down, and that had helped somewhat. They put a pause on my decision to take my own life, and I started to deal with daily events. In the fall of 2002, Karen's parents came to visit. I was not sure how they would act or what they would say. When they arrived, I acted as if nothing had happened and extended my hands to Karen's father. The tension was obvious, but I did everything as I had always done. For the first time, we were able to let Karen's parents occupy Miranda's room, which was fully furnished. Miranda shared Nadia's room during their visit. I made an extra effort to attend to Karen's parents by cooking a big breakfast for them every morning. I also made sure I prepared her father's favorite eggplant dish.

Something happened during their visit that engraved itself in my memory and became a part of me. A year earlier I had purchased a twenty-foot flagpole. I had always wanted a good flagpole and found one at the state fair. I was very proud of it and mounted it to the side of the house. I had also purchased an American flag and a Minnesota Twins baseball flag at the fair. The American flag had become weathered because it was displayed all the time. Whenever Karen's father visited, I always made sure I took them to stores he liked, such as Menards and Fleet Farm. During our visit to Fleet Farm, I noticed that they were selling an American flag the same size as the one I had at home, so I purchased one. I was very excited to lower the weathered flag and install the new one. I was trying hard to show my in-laws how proud I was of my flagpole and American flag. After the new flag was raised to its highest point, I asked my father-in-law a very simple and innocent question: "What should we do with the old flag?" He shrugged and made a face to say he did not know the answer. No one else said anything, but I knew that you could not just throw it in the garbage or leave it lying around to collect dust and dirt. I remembered that some people cremate their loved ones when they pass away, and I was aware of some Indian ceremonies where things were burned to honor them, so I immediately said, "We should burn it." My suggestion came out of total respect for the flag, but as soon as I made it, my mother-in-law, who had not said anything to that point, loudly said, "No sirree! *We* don't desecrate the flag." I went very silent. I was completing in my mind what my mother-in-law was trying to say but hadn't: "No sirree. *We* don't desecrate the flag, *but you and your kind sure do.*" Why would she ever think I wanted to desecrate the flag, when, in fact, I had paid a lot of money for the flagpole and had just purchased a new flag? Had I gone through all that trouble only to desecrate my beloved Old Glory? I was very sad when I realized her comment only reflected what she thought of me. It was nothing new to me but was still very sad. This is the first time I have talked about that incident, and releasing it from my memory is helping me heal. I always think of that day whenever I replace the flag.

In January 2003, the court date for the assault charge was finally fixed for March 18, almost a full year since the first incident that led to it. The attorney suggested that I should plead guilty. He had already collected several thousand dollars to defend me. His other choice was to pay him many thousands more for a trial. Feeling scammed by the attorney, I pled guilty and wanted to put the entire episode behind me. The penalty my attorney had explained to me was read out in detail. I was given an extended period of time to serve my few weeks of work release jail time. I paid the fine amount before we left the courthouse. I will never forget how these attorneys can easily scam and take advantage of desperate people like I was.

In the fall of 2003, I began looking into the cost of continuing my higher education. My employer offered only limited assistance, but I wanted to take advantage of it regardless. I decided to pursue a master's degree in information technology and leadership. I was not in a big rush to take many classes at the same time and wanted to set up a schedule to maximize my employer's contribution. It had been twenty years since my last college class, and the wheels of my brain were very rusty. I enrolled mostly to show my own children the importance of education and that no matter how old a person is, he (or she) must always try to learn.

At the salon, I had brought in many new services in hopes of breaking through to actually making money. The only problem was that I was not able to retain any employees. For a long time, I did not even know why, because I was never there during the day. I learned only later from one of them, after she got to know me, that Karen was trashing me all day long in front of the employees and customers. At some point she stopped trusting Karen and decided to leave. I knew I had to find a solution for this. I could not understand why Karen was doing this. Didn't she realize that having more employees would give us more flexibility and also enable her to be a true manager or even seek the nursing opportunities she always said she preferred?

My cousin called me and told me that he was going to Iraq in a few days, despite the dangerous situation. I wanted to send gifts with him, but there was no shopping time. I quickly scanned many pictures and put them on a CD to give to Nadia and made a sketch for him based on my memory of where our house and Nadia's house were. After a horrible experience, my cousin managed to come back home safely. He did manage to get to Nadia's house and talk to her sister. Nadia's mother had passed away, and Nadia was married and living in a different area. He gave the sister the CD of photos and brought back phone nmbers for some of our relatives. My cousin also took a picture of what used to be our home, which was now occupied by strangers.

Saddam Hussein had been in the custody of the United States/ UK since December 2003. I was hoping for the day when there would be a free Iraq, and I could visit at least one last time as a closure for unfinished business. I applied for a passport and was full of hope that I could use it sometime soon. I was very happy to know that Nadia was fine, she had received the CD, and the war had not affected her. That was more than enough good news to last a lifetime.

Unfortunately, along with the happiness of the connection to some of my friends and relatives came news of sadness, anger, and heartache. More than 250 mass grave sites had been discovered in Iraq. Each site contained remains of thousands of people killed by the ousted Hussein regime. It was said that the total was in the millions, but there was no accurate estimate of the number of mass graves. One of my brothers, Jamal, was identified in one of them. To date, there has been no accounting for my other brother, Jamel. Both had been kept behind when Saddam Hussein deported the rest of my family to Iran.

Our home in Baghdad occupied by strangers – Picture taken by my cousin

The deportation of many Kurdish families had preceded the Iran-Iraq War, also known as the First Persian Gulf War or the Eight Years' War, from 1980 to 1988. It was said that Saddam Hussein was planning that war when he deported the Kurdish families without the young men. His intentions were to deprive Iran of any young Kurdish men who could be used to fight against him. One of his tactics was to jail and kill these young Kurdish men, including two of my own brothers. This was not very different in shape or form from the Holocaust ordered by Adolf Hitler or the slaughter of the innocents by King Herod.

I had been working very hard to encourage and instill a "business mind" in Nadia since the early days. Every day, Nadia spent an hour or two at the salon after school answering the telephone and scheduling clients. I wanted to reward her, so I asked her to keep a sheet of her hours and present it to me for cash payment whenever she wanted. This incentive worked great. In no time, Nadia became good enough for a substitute front desk position and made money in the process. It was only $1.50 an hour to start, but I raised it to $3, and she was soon making at least $60 or more every two weeks. Yes, Nadia, even at her early age of fourteen, wanted to get paid more, but my main goal was to teach her important life lessons. In an effort to try to allow Karen to go back to her nursing job.

My brother Jamel – Jailed and later killed by Saddam

My brother Jamal – Jailed and later killed by Saddam depicted by Spirit Artist ~ Rita Berkowitz

I began looking to expand to another salon in a different area. My goal was to eventually find a manager who could be the "general manager" for both salons. I had a good lead on a small salon in one of my chosen areas—Rogers, Minnesota. I decided to drive by and get a gut feeling before taking it any further. It looked good, and I expressed some interest. I ended up purchasing the salon in Rogers, but unfortunately the owner who sold the salon with the intention of staying as a manager quit shortly after and revealed her true unethical intentions.

I welcomed 2006 with a new outlook, and I was within three months of a master's degree in project management and leadership.

I graduated in March with a GPA of 3.8. I happily looked forward to attending the graduation ceremonies with Nadia and Miranda so that they could clearly see their father's commitment to continuing education.

Capella University

By its authority and upon recommendation of the faculty, the Board of Directors hereby confers upon

David Kariem Haaland

the degree of

Master of Science
in **Information Technology**

with a specialization in
Project Management and Leadership

with all rights, honors, privileges and responsibilities thereunto appertaining.
Given this thirty-first day of March, two thousand six.

Chair of the Board

President

Master's degree certificate

CHAPTER TWENTY-THREE

Unexpected Wake-up Call

In June 2007, I was served with a second set of divorce papers after Karen had left the house yet again with our girls. I could not understand what was making Karen think that she had the full control of our girls. Was it solely out of hate and a wish to punish me, or was there some stupidity involved? I was very angry and sad when I thought about how she was damaging the girls and their future ability to deal with issues.

The idea of suicide to end it all came rushing back. Some months earlier I had gone to Fleet Farm for the flexible pipes they sold to connect to the exhaust and run it outside the garage when working on the car with the garage doors closed to avoid carbon monoxide exposure. Now I was contemplating the complete opposite use: I would connect the flexible pipe to the exhaust and run it into the car through the window. I would sit and listen to my music while ending it all. All that remained was to decide exactly when. One day in early July, I purchased duct tape and actually secured the pipe through the car window. I sat in the car for a while looking out at the driveway, holding my girls' pictures. Then I turned on my music and started the engine. The car was a newer model, so I assumed it would take a bit of time before it produced enough carbon monoxide to kill me. After several minutes, I began to visualize a caring officer coming through the driveway as he had done many times and catching me just before I died. This image scared me very much, and I shut down the car and removed the pipe as quickly as possible before the officer arrived, which he never did.

I repeated that exact same scenario about three times. Why was I getting the officer's image every time? I have no idea. I have never thought of it before, but as I am writing this, I realize that no matter how kind an officer is, he would probably never make trips on his own to anywhere without being dispatched. Who exactly was this officer? Was he truly an officer, or was he an angel? I may never know. After three attempts, I gave up on the idea and placed the pipes in the garbage to get rid of them forever.

Karen was back in the home once again and moved all the furniture back. She said it had been in storage. That made me angry. The brand-new furniture was all scratched, treated poorly, and then taken to storage? I had bought all this furniture without any input from Karen. She had not even bothered to come with us when we purchased it. What was Karen thinking? I was becoming sure she had some kind of mental issue. I often wondered if any other person in the world would take a woman like Karen back after so much of her nonsense.

By August 2007, I had sold both salons at a great loss, hoping that Karen would finally realize that I had made a major sacrifice and given up my dream by literally giving the salons away. I was hoping I would finally find some peace and, more importantly, be able to pay attention to our daughters' well-being. I spent two or three days, free of charge, with the new owners of the Rogers salon to teach them the computer systems and other procedures. I even offered my help above and beyond those initial days, as I truly wanted them to be successful. I was already missing being with some of my clients and was hoping that the new owners would call on me for help.

I was using my newfound extra time to make up for lost time with my daughters. I promised Nadia I would buy a new car for her as a gift for her graduation from high school and a used car as soon as she received her driver's license. I was sad that Miranda had not had a chance like Nadia to work behind the salon desk and gain needed skills and cash.

Karen was soon offered a job as an LPN at a senior assisted-living residence in Buffalo. She seemed happy with it. I vowed that no matter what new venture I got into, I would not repeat the mistake of involving Karen, because of how quickly she could change her mind and how little she cared about the damage she caused. I was not seeing any improvement in Karen's judgment or maturity.

In December 2008, Miranda turned fourteen and was becoming more beautiful than ever. She was a very sensitive, gentle, and caring girl. As we entered 2009, I was very hopeful that I could put all of the salon issues behind me. I was hoping that if Karen would just keep doing what she was doing, I would have no reason to take any more emergency time off from work and could begin paying attention to my career.

Nadia had turned seventeen in March 2008, and on her birthday I gave her the car I was driving. She drove it very responsibly, and I was very pleased, as things were seemingly turning around. She was even taking college classes in her last year of high school. I now had more time to attend to my garden and trees and listen to music. In March

2009 she was ready to graduate from high school and seemed like an adult lady.

Not long after that, she reminded me that I had made a promise to purchase her a brand-new car when she graduated from high school. I said I did remember the deal, and even though financially I was in no position to purchase a new car, I would find a way to fulfill my promise. Most of my credit cards were at their limit, and I had no savings. So once again, I refinanced the house.

Karen, Nadia, Miranda, and I drove to St. Cloud, and Nadia selected a car. We were all happy for her. I gave her the option of driving either car, so at this early age, she already had two cars. When Nadia looked at the paperwork for the new car, she immediately noticed that it was in my name and not hers. She gave me a strange look, and I knew what she was thinking. I explained to her that legally I could not put the car in her name yet because the loan was in my name but assured her that I would put it in her name as soon as the loan was paid off.

By now Nadia had taken her graduation pictures, and I went with her to purchase the photo packages. When I asked her about having a graduation party, I was very surprised to hear her say she did not want one. When I asked Karen to talk to Nadia, I received the same answer, because not having a party was actually Karen's idea and not Nadia's. I was very disappointed, as I felt there had been a terrible shortage of fun events in our lives. Everything had been about restraining orders. I truly wanted to have a party and wanted Nadia to show everyone that her father bought a brand-new car for her, but that was not to be the case. Later I found out that Karen had sent many invitations for Nadia's graduation ceremony without sharing it as a family event. She even sent one to my friend, Linda, and her husband. When I asked her why, she responded in her normal way, just making a face and moving away from me like a little child.

Nadia was hired at the same senior assisted-living residence where Karen worked. I was happy for Nadia but was not happy that Nadia was following in her mother's footsteps. I was truly worried about what else she was going to model after her mother. Nadia seemed happy and adapted to her work and the courses she was taking at a college in Bloomington, a suburb of Minneapolis. I was very happy that Nadia was pursuing higher education, regardless of what it was. She never asked my opinion about college or anything related to it. Apparently, due to her mother's influence, she did not have any appreciation for what I had accomplished in my life. Much like her mother, Nadia never showed any interest in my background and how I was brought up and how I made it to where I was. I was not interested in forcing anything on my children and assumed that they would ask when they were ready.

On Thursday, October 28, 2009, I came home from work and found Miranda sitting in the living room as she normally did, doing her homework. There was a note on the table in Nadia's handwriting. I read the first line, which said that she had decided to move out. I went into a state of shock and almost fell on the floor.

When I recovered enough to read the rest of the note, I saw that she was asking me to keep up her car insurance and that she would pay me for this and that. This was a day that will not be erased from my memory any time soon.

I tried to contact Nadia many times. She had written a note asking me for financial help, but she would not even answer my telephone calls. I knew very well that Karen was aware of this master plan and had supported and planned it, but she always pretended that she was not aware of it.

It was now 2010. One day I came home and found Nadia's car parked in the driveway. I was very happy, as I thought Nadia had come to visit her sister. But Miranda did not know anything about Nadia and said the car was there when she got home from school. That is when I realized that Nadia had decided to give up the car and its insurance solely so she did not have to bring it once a month for an oil change. I was very sad about Nadia's behavior but did not want Miranda to see my sadness. I just told her, "It's okay. It looks like you have a car already, even before getting your driving permit." Miranda gave me her beautiful smile, and I turned away to hide my sadness.

Nadia's actions truly woke me up. My reason for the years of staying in a marriage that was clearly not working or getting better—the well-being of my children—had just been proven wrong by the way Nadia had cut off her contact with me. I began to feel angry at myself and guilty for not leaving the marriage soon enough to protect my children from the effects of all the abuse. How could my girls respect me when they saw me kicked out of the house time and time again? I just had to stay connected with my children and pray that they did not make the same mistakes their mother often did.

Nadia's actions made me pay even closer attention to Miranda to help her make better decisions for her life. I began to share my feelings with Miranda and treat her as an adult. Miranda was very open and seemingly cared more for me than her sister, Nadia, did.

One day at work, I walked over to a colleague's office to discuss some routine matter. I passed by many cubicles on the way, and as I walked by a particular cubicle, I had a very strange gut feeling without even seeing the face of the person sitting inside. I wondered briefly what the feeling was but soon dismissed it and went about my day. A few days later, the same thing happened with the same feeling. This time, I made an effort to see the woman's face. I had never seen her before, and she did not even have a nameplate on her cubicle. I finally learned that her name was Amy. She seemed pleasant during any of the three-second encounters we had, but I was feeling this strange feeling constantly. I was becoming very curious and intrigued about Amy and began to stop by for a minute or two once a week just to say hello. I never asked her about her present or past, as it was none of my business. I was just trying to figure out why I was feeling the way I was feeling.

One time as we were making small talk, I learned that she liked Porsches and BMWs, and I just happened to own a BMW. I rarely drove it unless I had a complete day off and the weather was perfect. I emailed Amy a picture of it, and she liked it. I told her I just might drive it to work someday. I also told her that if I did, she would have to see it in person. We had an innocent agreement, and I was very excited to think about the day when I would actually drive the car to work. I kept up the habit of stopping to say hello and chatting once a week for a minute or two.

One day I drove my BMW to work for the first time, hoping that Amy would be there. We decided that having her see the car at the work parking lot would not be appropriate and to avoid any rumors, we separately went to a sub restaurant nearby, and I kept the conversation very generic, except for one comment. I simply blurted out, without even thinking, "Amy, I do not know why, but I feel that we are related." Amy responded with a big smile and did not say anything. She must have thought something like, "I have never heard this pickup line before." Afterward, I berated myself, believing I had been really stupid to say something like that.

I connected with my intuitive circle as I always did, and one by one, each one told me the same thing in one form or another—Amy and I had been husband and wife, boyfriend and girlfriend, or secret lovers in our past life. I began to believe that Amy and I did have a past life connection. I recalled my stupid remark to Amy about feeling related. That was before I had talked to anyone. What had made me say that? Was I that intuitive without even knowing it?

Week after week went by, and I remained quite formal with Amy and respectful of her privacy. But the message that I was getting from my gut feeling and that was repeated by some of my intuitive friends was that Amy needed, or would need, my help. What kind of help? I was not sure. How could I help Amy when I did not even know what she needed? I had never talked to her with that kind of depth. I was not about to go up to her and say, "I am ready to help."

My interaction with Amy remained very limited, although if I learned that she would be gone for a period, I often sent her an email wishing her well. The strange thing was that I had never asked her anything about her personal life and just limited my talk to well wishes. She would reply to my emails with something like, "I am very private and want to limit our interaction to only work."

———

One day at work I was devastated to hear that Amy would shortly be rolled off—that is, her contract would not be renewed. I sent her an email of sympathy, and she immediately replied that it had been in the works for some time. I gave her a goodbye gift of a massage certificate. She accepted it but not as warmly as one might expect.

Weeks after she was gone, I continued sending her very short email well-wishes with a small message in the subject line. Most often she did not even respond. Several months later, I asked her if she had used the gift certificate and let her know that if she had lost it I could get her a replacement. This time I did receive a quick response. It was not anything like, "Thank you, David. Yes, I used it." or "How thoughtful of you." Her exact response was "Stop emailing me." Even if she had said, "David, please stop emailing me," that would have been acceptable to me. I respected her wishes and ended all my connections and to myself "I guess I can't offer her my or any help". She must have thought I was making some kind of romantic moves which was totally wrong. I later found out from a colleague that she was a married women from different state and romantically got involved with a married man from work. Later she divorced her husband and her new lover divorces his wife. Learning this little history about Amy, would have been enough for me to avoid her if I was aware of her past. As I said I completely stopped and sent her many healing prayers.

CHAPTER TWENTY-FOUR
· ·

Angelic Intervention

A big snowfall came down over the weekend of November 13, 2010, but I nevertheless decided to set out for work on Monday morning.

The roads were clear. Apparently, the weekend snow crew had been on top of things. I was very pleased and drove at normal speed. Just before Maple Plain, about fifteen miles from home, I hit an icy spot, and my car began to spin violently and uncontrollably. The highway at that spot was very narrow, with low guards, only two feet high, on both sides. I knew instantly that if I hit those guards at my speed, I would go over the rails and fall ten or fifteen feet below to die.

I held onto the steering wheel with both hands and closed my eyes. I was praying the entire time. After what seemed to be a year, the car stopped spinning, and I had not felt or heard any impact. That is when I opened my eyes and realized that I was in the opposite lane and my car was facing the opposite direction. There were no cars coming or going at that early hour. I quickly got out of the car to see what had happened. The car was only a few inches from the guards, but it had not hit anything. It was still running. My first instinct was to just go back home and celebrate my escape from another brush with death, because my car was already pointing in that direction. Instead, I decided to turn around on the narrow stretch of road and continue on to work. I did not leave right away. I was guided to stop for a moment in a safe area nearby to pray and thank God for the gift of life. I was shaking and was somehow getting an image from the movie *Angels in the Infield*. I felt something strange but was not sure what it was.

I realized that this had been my fourth "near escape from death" situation. I went to work a changed man. I worked a full day, and when I came home, I told Miranda what had happened that morning. The rest of the evening was normal. Miranda asked me if she could have Nadia's old room, because it was bigger than hers. I told her she could as soon as I repainted it. Nadia had painted one wall very beautifully but for some reason had left the others in a mess. I was not even aware she had done that much, as I never made it a practice to go into their rooms. I spent Monday evening finishing the job.

The next day started very normally. After a full day of work, as I was getting ready to finish painting Nadia's room, I checked my emails and found one from someone I did not know. It was a newsletter of some sort. Ordinarily, I would have deleted it without reading, but the lady's name, Insiah, was somewhat unusual, so I clicked it open. As I read, I became very intrigued. I had many intuitive friends whom I considered psychic. Insiah was also intuitive, but she was using her angel connections in her readings. I immediately thought of Amy and wondered if I could make an appointment with this new person to see what she thought of Amy or the reasons I was feeling the way I was toward her. I was able to schedule an appointment almost immediately for the upcoming Friday, my day off. When I called to schedule, Insiah asked me how I had heard about her, and I said that it was weird, but I received an email, even though I had never signed up for it. Insiah said, "Well, I will see you on Friday, and we can talk about it."

I arrived two hours early in case Insiah could meet sooner. She was busy and asked me to help myself to the living room and wait there if I wanted to instead of driving around aimlessly, which I did. I looked around, and everything I saw was about angels—pictures, statues, books. I had never seen anything like it before, although I had always believed in the angels and was aware that they are mentioned in all of God's books that I knew of—the Torah, the Bible, and the Quran. That was the extent of my knowledge.

The wait went by very quickly as I was immersed in looking at the angel statues. Then I heard someone coming down the stairs and stood up in respect of Insiah's arrival. Before she even reached the bottom of the staircase and before I could give her a proper greeting, I began, without thinking, to talk about my near accident on Monday. This was very unlike me, as I usually greet people in a polite way. Before I could even finish my story, Insiah stopped halfway down and said, "Archangel Michael is telling me that he was the one who saved you."

I was speechless. She then said, "Archangel Michael is telling me that it happened so fast that he had to intervene and save you. Archangel Michael is telling me that he is the one who brought you here." I did not know what to think. I knew Insiah had asked me how I found out about her, and I had told her only that I received an email. I asked myself *Did Archangel Michael do emails, too?*

After that amazing introduction, Insiah and I went on to talk about different things, including my unhappiness with my marriage.

We also talked about Nadia back home in Iraq and finally brought the conversation up about Amy. Everything I knew about Karen was confirmed: Karen had many issues growing up, and unfortunately, I was the one who had to experience all of her drama. I was also told that Nadia in Iraq was thinking of me (which I had never doubted) but that I might not see her in this lifetime (which I was also aware of). When we started to talk about Amy, Insiah told me that she and I were not even remotely at the same spiritual level. Insiah told me all about myself and who I truly was, while Amy was not even aware of herself. Insiah strongly recommended that I move on from Amy. I did not have anything with Amy to move on from but was compelled to find out why I was feeling what I was feeling whenever I was around her. It was not a physical attraction but something else that was very hard to explain. By the end of my meeting with Insiah, she had told me a little about the archangels, including Michael and Raphael.

I drove home in a state of total wonderment. I had been saved by Archangel Michael! Was he the one who had saved me in all my prior narrow escapes from death? How about the train incident with my daughter, Nadia? Or when I was a child and almost died trying to feed my pigeons? When I arrived home, I started to search the Internet for anything about Archangel Michael. I found books, pendants, and many other items. I eagerly ordered a number of them. They arrived within a week, and I began to wear the pendant. Two of the books particularly drew my attention:

Michael: Communicating with the Archangel for Guidance & Protection, by Richard Webster

The Miracles of Archangel Michael, by Doreen Virtue

I took these two books to work to glance over whenever possible, but soon, for some unknown reason, I narrowed my interest down to

My friend the late Insiah Beckman

Doreen Virtue's book. I was very intrigued and began searching to see what else this author had written. Much to my pleasant surprise, I found many books and something called oracle cards.

Without hesitation, I ordered more items. When I saw Insiah for the second time, I mentioned my book search and particularly Doreen Virtue. Insiah told me that she was good friends with Ms. Virtue. She also told me that Doreen had been to her house and mentioned Insiah in one of her books. I did not say anything to her, but I did wonder if all of these turns and twists were accidental or planned by some divine order. I had many books from many authors. Why did I focus on Doreen Virtue? Doreen's friendship with Insiah was another instance of divine order that I had to discover.

It was December 2010, and I was very excited to see what new surprises the New Year might bring. Early in January 2011, I received an email advertisement for something called "I Can Do It." I had never heard of anything like it before. Why had they sent me their email? I was not sure, because I had never registered on any websites that promoted that type of education and spiritual elevation. I looked and looked at this amazing ad. "I Can Do It" was a conference in Vancouver on March 12 and 13. I looked at all the presenters and recognized the name of Dr. Wayne Dyer, whom I had admired for years, and also Doreen Virtue, whom I had just learned about through a series of coincidences. I did not know any of the other six or seven presenters. I was very intrigued by the opportunity to actually meet these two people. The question was: was I intrigued enough to go to Vancouver for that chance? My gut feeling was telling me yes. I printed the schedule and placed it by my work computer to look at and think about. What would Karen accuse me of doing if I went? But my intuition prevailed, and so I called and made reservations.

Through Insiah I had met another local young lady who was also an angel communicator. This young lady was amazing. She told me that the angels were telling her that Amy had been sent my way on purpose. Amy was handpicked because she had been in my past lives—not just one past life but several. She told me that Amy's purpose was to wake me up and help me realize that I had a full life to live and was wasting my time with my wife. She went on to say that Amy was not meant to be in my current life, but I should not be surprised if someday Amy showed up in my life asking me for help. "Be careful," she said.

March 11 soon arrived, and it was time to fly to Vancouver. I did not know what to expect. I woke up early on Saturday so I could locate the Queen Elizabeth Theater, the conference site. It was raining, but I was so excited that I did not even go back to the hotel for my umbrella. It was still very early, but many others had already gathered by the main door. I made a few good friends, most of whom I still keep in touch with.

When the door finally opened, we all marched inside and were given a schedule and IDs on lanyards and found seats. Soon Louise Hay came onto the stage. I was very familiar with her book, *You Can Heal Your Life*, but it took me a few moments to realize that she was that same Louise Hay. Ms. Hay was the organizer for the entire event. She has written many books and has a long track record in the inspirational world. Soon Dr. Dyer appeared, and I was thrilled to see him in person after seeing him so many times on television. He treated us to a three-hour presentation and also introduced his daughter, Skye Dyer, who sang several beautiful songs.

The next presentation would not be until one thirty that afternoon, and I left the auditorium to look for Dr. Dyer's book-signing line. I went all over and asked many people but did not find him anywhere. I was very disappointed and wondered how this could be. Dr. Dyer had been half of my goal and manifestation practice. I hoped that I would at least see Ms. Virtue that evening. I had skipped breakfast, and the food service was quite a distance away. However, the rain was still coming down, so I decided to skip lunch also. I listened to Geneen Roth and Brian Weiss, and was grateful that I was learning about so many great spiritual leaders to follow. I had been uplifted all day with the thought I would get to see Doreen in a few hours.

By now it was five o'clock in the evening. I checked the schedule and realized that Doreen's presentation was at seven. I was so excited that I decided to skip dinner, too. Her topic was "The Angels of Health and Happiness." I enjoyed Doreen's words very much and truly felt a connection like I had never felt before. Somehow I knew that in my search for books on Archangel Michael, I had received a divine order to follow her over any other author.

At eight thirty that night, I was sad it was over but ready to run out of the auditorium to search for the book signing. Doreen was making an announcement that she would play her beautiful guitar music with her band, Obsidian, along with Mark Watson and his partner Tatiana. I loved her music and listening to the band, but I was becoming more worried that she might not sign books, as it was getting very late.

After the performance, I ran out and did find her book-signing table. As I got closer to Doreen, I was getting as excited and as nervous as a little boy—a feeling that I had absolutely never experienced before. I had the feeling that I had known Doreen for a very long time. I knew I always had "the intuition," but I was not good at interpreting my feelings and often questioned them. I had a very short chat with her. I asked her if she knew my friend, Insiah, and she said yes.

Doreen had said something at the end of her presentation that did not mean much to me at the time, but I took a mental note of it anyway to investigate later. She had announced that she would be teaching her last angel therapy class in June.

Doreen Virtue

Back at my hotel room, it was past ten o'clock at night. It was now too late to go out for dinner. My stomach growling, I went to bed, pondering the idea of skipping the first speaker on the next day so I could get some breakfast.

The first presenter on Sunday was someone named Caroline Myss. I had not heard of her either, which made the decision to skip easier. But was it really easy? No, it was not at all. I meditated the way I knew how at that time to see what to do, and three times I received "No, do not skip it." I decided to listen to my gut feeling. Her topic was "Loving Beyond Our Wounds: Exploring an Emerging Path of Human Intimacy." As soon as she started to speak, I sat up and paid attention. As I walked away, I asked myself, *And you were going to skip Caroline for breakfast?*

The eleven-thirty presentation was Robert Holden, "Be Happy! Release the Power of Happiness in *You*!" As soon as I heard his British accent, I said to myself, "Great, how much of the seminar will I understand?" But as soon as he told his story and talked about his first job in the United States, I was not able to contain myself. I was laughing like never before.

The next presentation, Marianne Williamson, would not be until two that afternoon. I had about an hour and a half and had not eaten in a day and a half. It was raining, and I was a little overdressed for the occasion, but I had my umbrella, so I was off to find the food quarter. I just followed the crowd, knowing that I had a lot of time. Because of my suit and tie, I carefully avoided any rain puddles. I soon located some fast food places. Actually, I smelled them before I saw them, as I was very hungry. Following my nose, I decided on one, and as I approached, I noticed that I was walking between two people: a very beautiful lady on my left and a handsome man on my right. They were both dressed much more nicely than anyone else, including myself. They looked as though they had just come from a wedding. I was too hungry to take notice of much of anything, but I did wonder why I was walking between them. Wouldn't it have been more normal for me to be walking alongside? I did not look at them and just continued walking, but the beautiful lady asked me, "So where did you come from?"

Caroline Myss

"Minnesota," I answered.

They both said something like, "Wow, that is a long way."

"Not really. It is not a long way for this kind of teaching," I replied. The man asked, "So who did you come here for mostly?"

I replied in a disappointed voice. "I mostly came for Doreen Virtue and Wayne Dyer, but unfortunately, I did not get to see Dr. Dyer. I only got to see Doreen."

Just outside the fast food place, the man and lady stepped in front of me and turned around to face me. I stopped walking. They both said, as though with one voice, "Do you know that Wayne Dyer is in the theater signing books right now?"

"No way," I exclaimed.

Again speaking as one voice, they said, "Yes, he is signing books right now."

I was full of energy and forgot how hungry I was. I replied, "You know what? The food can wait for now!" I closed my umbrella and ran back to the theater. I was not worried about any water puddles, either.

When I entered the theater, I saw Dr. Dyer surrounded by hundreds of fans. The circle around him was very large, and I was at its very edges. I was very happy to see him anyway and began taking pictures of him from a distance. After taking several, I told myself that was not good enough. I don't recall exactly what it was, but I did say something that immediately got Dr. Dyer's attention. He looked up at me and smiled and held up his right hand. Everyone moved away and allowed me to get in close, almost as though he had actually parted the crowd. I did not question or waste any time. I gave my camera to a complete stranger and asked him to take pictures of Dr. Dyer and me. We talked pleasantly for a few minutes, and then I moved away to allow all the other fans to get their turn. The pictures all turned out very well.

Dr. Wayne Dyer

It was two o'clock and time for the next speaker, Marianne Williamson. I was a little familiar with her but soon knew that a little familiarity was not enough. Her topic was "A Course in Weight Loss." I was completely amazed and taken by this energetic lady. I enjoyed every second of her talk and was determined to attend her book signing too, as I had bought some of her books and CDs. I raced to her line at three thirty and got pictures with her as well. By now, it was four o'clock in the afternoon and time for the final presentation by Cheryl Richardson, "Living, the Art of Extreme Self-Care." As with Marianne, I also knew a little about Cheryl's work but hardly enough. I learned many things, got another book signed, and had more pictures taken with an author.

Now there was no time to eat before the next presentation. On the way to the auditorium, I suddenly stopped and asked myself, *Wait! What did I exactly say to make Dr. Dyer pay attention to me?* I tried very hard but could not recall anything. Then I had other sudden thoughts:

Marianne Williamson

"Wait a minute. Who were those two—the beautiful lady and man who detoured me from eating to Dr. Dyer? Where did they come from? They seemed as if they had appeared from nowhere. Why did they walk with me in the middle? Were they people ... or angels?" Several months later while meditating, I learned and was told that they *were* angels—angels helping me manifest my wishes.

Before I left, I made sure to order a USB recording of the entire event. I said goodbye to some of the friends I had made and headed to the airport to go home. On the plane, I relived the amazing angelic way I had met Dr. Dyer. I had my camera with me on my lap instead of in its bag. I could afford losing the bag but never the camera with its precious pictures.

In the days following the event in Vancouver, I read all my new books. I was becoming increasingly aware of the angels and bought many more of Doreen's archangel books. Karen started coming home earlier than usual one night a week and then leaving without saying anything. She would return home quite late. I had never made it a habit to question Karen, but one time I had to ask where she went every week, because when she came in, she walked by my couch and interrupted my sleep. She said that she had to go to Bible study because I had "brought all the devils" home. I knew she was referring to the archangels.

I asked her, "Since when did Archangel Michael become the devil? And who do you think gave him the name Saint Michael the Archangel?" I was very upset at Karen, especially since she was supposed to be a Catholic. I was not going to let Karen come between me and my divine purpose of discovering my angels. Everything that had happened thus far was not accidental, and I was not going to let any of it go just to make Karen happy.

I continued to be a big part of Miranda's life, especially since Nadia had moved out. She was very supportive and wanted me to be happy. I dedicated as much time to giving Miranda driving lessons as I possibly could. By the test date, she was very comfortable with her skills, and I drove her in to the test site. She did great and received her license on the first try. Once again, we were both very happy. This daughter never asked for anything, and she was a very gentle and cheerful girl.

One day I asked Miranda to go with me to Walmart to do a little shopping. In reality, I did not need anything—it was just an excuse to do something with her. I stopped at the key chain rack and told Miranda to pick one out for me, as I liked her taste. I bought several other items, just for show. When we arrived home, I put the key for the car Nadia had returned onto the new chain, called Miranda over, and handed it to her, saying, "Congratulations on your first car!"

From the moment I arrived home from Vancouver, I kept thinking about the "last angel therapy class" Doreen Virtue had talked about. Of course, I couldn't be sure what Karen would be doing in June or if I would even be home, if she filed another restraining order. I decided to register anyway for the "last class" and pay for it right away to guarantee the space. If God and the angels wanted me to attend, they would make it happen. So I registered for the class, to be held June 20–23, 2011, in Kona, Hawaii. I had received a call from a very nice lady named Erin Solt several months earlier, shortly after I returned from Vancouver. She said she was from a publisher and asked me how I'd liked the conference. I responded very positively. She went on to ask me if I had my book transcript ready. I was very taken aback, as I did not remember filling out any forms or doing anything in Vancouver that would make her ask me this question. I did not respond exactly honestly. Instead of just saying no, I said, "It is not complete yet." She asked me if she could call again, and I said, "For sure, call me in two weeks." I assumed that she would forget and never call again. A week later, Erin called again, and I made up more excuses. These calls continued for a little longer than two months before they finally ended. Was there some kind of message directed by the angels from all these telephone calls? The seeds of writing a book had already been planted many years ago by all the ladies I had talked to at the Laundromat when I was in college. I seriously began to think about writing that book.

—————

I continued to talk to Karen about doing what was best for the children and finding a way to a peaceful divorce. Usually she would just walk away, but on the rare occasions she did not, she would demand, "Give me the numbers." I would say that it was not about my numbers or hers right now and that what we really needed was to find a neutral person to help us through the process. But Karen had no trust.

It was June 2011, and Doreen's last class was almost upon us. I had not told anyone about my plans to take part. By this time, I had bonded with Miranda and treated her as an adult. I opened up to her and told her that I was going to Hawaii to get certified as an angel practitioner. I said I was going alone and was not planning to "have fun" with anyone. Miranda fully understood, so I asked her to feed the dogs and my birds. I promised to call her every day and asked her to promise me not to tell Karen where exactly I was going. I trusted her with this confidence.

I arrived in Kona on June 19 and rented a car to drive to the resort in Keauhou. I was greeted very warmly, and the place was truly heavenly. The training facility was merely a beautiful walking distance away. When I found out we would be served a free breakfast, I decided to just relax in my room until the next day.

I woke up early on Monday, June 20, and decided to explore outdoors a bit before the restaurant opened. I found a majestic place overlooking the ocean to sit on the rocks and watch the sunrise. I meditated and took many pictures, then went on a walk and enjoyed seeing beautiful flowers and plants. I was ready to start a great day. At breakfast, I met many beautiful fellow training attendees. I made several friends and had an amazing time sharing stories for almost two hours with some great company.

Inside the large classroom, I looked around and realized that there were more than three hundred lucky people from all over the world in attendance. I also saw right away that I was in a very evident minority— there were only about ten males in the entire group.

Doreen had brought along many helpers, including her son, Grant, and his lovely wife, Melissa, and many others. At first, I wanted and in fact I included each and everyone's name as an honor, but I was guided to revise the book and delete their names. Unfortunately, I have found out that many of these so called "spiritual" people are doing it just to promote and benefit themselves financially through Doreen Virtue. I have discovered that many of them have only the financial benefits as the main goal and spirituality is just the mask they use to accomplish that goal. I have decided that they truly do not deserve to be mentioned in my humble little book.

Everyone had a great time learning many things and getting to know each other. We practiced many exercises in pairs. At lunch break, I called Miranda to see how she was doing. I asked her if her mother had asked about my whereabouts. She had not. I mingled with some of my friends, as we hardly needed lunch because of the great breakfast.

Angel Therapy conference in Hawaii

Being around Doreen Virtue was a truly divine experience. At the end of the day, my new friend, Monica Mitchell, and two others decided to reconnect after a short rest in our rooms, and we chatted for a while. Then I went back to my favorite spot on the volcanic rocks overlooking the ocean to meditate and watch the sunset. It was a very soothing and comforting place. Before drifting off to a peaceful sleep back in my room, I reflected on the magical day I'd had with beautiful, like-minded people.

The next day I went back to sit next to my rock. I felt a strong connection to that particular spot and just liked being alone to let my mind wander. I found a new group of friends at breakfast, and because seating in the class was not reserved, each day we could be in a different place and meet still more new people. I called Miranda to tell her I was doing well and learned that she was doing well also, without any problems from her mother.

At the end of that day, Doreen announced that there would a musical gathering after the classes the next day. It was not a mandatory part of the instruction, just a gift to us and a fun way for Doreen and her helpers to share their music. Doreen recommended that we show up with our angel's wings and outfits. Once again, I met with my three friends to relax and talk and enjoyed myself immensely. Then I went back to my rock. After the sun went down, I headed back to my room to reflect and rest.

CHAPTER TWENTY-FIVE

I See God in You

The next day began with yet another new group of classmates, and I was seated next to an attractive young lady whom I had never met before named Laura. We practiced all the morning exercises together and had a great time. Laura was from California, and she seemed very interested in me, but I had vowed to dedicate this trip to only the class. I was not interested in anything else, even dolphin watching and swimming. I respected Laura and was very polite with her. During the minibreak, I asked Laura if she was leaving on Thursday like most of the students or if she was leaving later. It turned out that we were both leaving on Friday, and I told her that I needed someone to go to dinner with Thursday night after class.

Laura seemed very happy to accept the invitation. I called Miranda at lunch and learned that she was still doing well. I spent the rest of the lunch break with my new beautiful, like-minded friends, but I was eager to get back to class. I am not sure if it was by design or mere accident, but Laura and I were seated next to each other again. We had a lot of fun. Laura continued to show an interest, and I continued to be very polite and attentive but was not ready to share her same type of interest. The class ended, and we were reminded of the optional get-together later in the evening. I was asked by many, including Laura, if I was going to attend, and I said I was. After the class, I dropped my notebooks in my room and went to my spot to meditate a little earlier than usual because of the gathering. I had my angel wings with me.

At the event, I stood there with my angel wings placed on my shoulders. Laura walked over to tell me that she would not be able to go to dinner with me on Thursday night after all. I tried to be understanding and asked her if everything was okay with her? Laura replied that she had said yes to me "too soon." Those were the exact words. She said that her girlfriend wanted her to go to dinner with her. I did not understand her logic but wanted her to know that I was fully accepting of her situation and simply told her, "Please don't worry, and enjoy your dinner with your girlfriend." I stepped to the side of the room to ponder our conversation. It was not supposed to have been a romantic dinner, only a friendly celebration of the completion of the class. Laura knew that I would have been more than happy to have her girlfriend come with us, but she had elected, for whatever reason, to cancel with me. My intuition was telling me that she had not been truthful at all with her excuse. As the party crowd got larger, I pulled aside to think about what I should do next.

For some weird reason, I did not want to be seen by Laura at the party. I was considering her feelings, thinking she might feel guilty every time she saw me and even leave the party. I then decided to spare her from the guilty feelings by not going to the party. As I started to slowly move away from the party location, I was greeted by many kind friends going toward it. They said things like, "Don't you dare leave; we want to dance with you." I lied to each one, saying that I would come back shortly.

Back in my hotel room, I took the angel wings off and sat down, wondering about exactly what had happened with Laura. At first I was happy that I had spared her from guilty feelings, but soon started to question what I had just done to myself. Why had I cared so much about her feelings when, in fact, she was the one who had hurt *my* feelings?

I questioned my judgment for putting the feelings of someone like Laura ahead of my own. By this time, it was too late to turn around and join the party, but I was very sad about missing a great opportunity to enjoy the music and my many friends (the ones I had lied to when they asked me to show up so they could dance with me). I was very sad in a place where I was supposed to have fun. I cried myself to sleep.

I woke up after a horrible night of guilt and sadness over my missed opportunity to enjoy Doreen's music with three hundred of my friends. I was still tired. On this morning, instead of walking with my friends, I decided to take my sadness back to the rocks and the ocean for more meditation. I was meditating, crying, and feeling guilty, and I was asking for guidance. On the way, I passed the resort swimming pool, where I saw an elderly couple enjoying themselves sitting by the poolside. I nodded at both of them and said, "*Good morning.*"

"*Good morning to you,*" they replied warmly.

Angel Therapy conference resort in Hawaii

I looked at them and said, *"Thank you very much."* I could tell from the man's face that he wanted to talk more with me.

I slowed down, and he said, *"What is that you have on your neck?"* *"Oh, this is just a lanyards identification that denotes we belong to the angel therapy class."*

The man was becoming more curious and asked me, *"What about angels do you learn?"*

"It is more than just learning about them; it is about connecting with them." I explained how angels are around us all the time and we must ask and give our permission to receive their help. I told him about the differences between archangels, angels, and guardian angels.

The man stopped me and said, *"Young man, I am sorry I missed going to church this Sunday. I never miss going to church, but we missed it because we are on vacation."*

At first, I was very surprised that this man needed to apologize to me for not going to church. I did not take what he said very lightly, and responded, *"Sir, you do not need to be in a church building to be with God. You can be anywhere—in your basement, on battle lines, or anywhere—and be with God. God is not open only on Sundays from nine to ten. God is with us 24/7, and he is with us everywhere."* I went on "preaching" without realizing that I was actually preaching.

The man then said, *"We saw you yesterday with your friends, and I really wanted to talk with you, but you were busy."*

I immediately apologized. *"I am truly sorry. I did not pay attention. Was there anything I could have done?"*

The man replied, *"Young man, when I see you, I see God in you."* I thanked them both, shook their hands, and walked away.

I went off to a secluded area and cried like a baby. I asked myself, *why did an older guy from Texas apologize to me for not going to church last Sunday? Why was he seeking me? Most importantly, who am I to be told I see God in you?* I was much moved emotionally—and very confused. I walked back toward the class location. I encountered a lady whom I thought was in the class, but I had not had the chance to talk to her. She was beautiful and tall and appeared to be Asian, maybe from Singapore. As we got closer to one another, she stopped me and asked, *"Why are you walking this way?"*

I was very surprised and did not know how to answer. I asked her, *"How was I walking?"*

She responded, *"Don't you know who you are? Don't you see the rainbow above your head? You are walking with your head and shoulders down! You should walk with open shoulders and recognize who you are."* I was speechless for a moment and then said, *"I am sorry. I just had an encounter that moved me deeply, and I was just thinking about it."* I then asked her permission to take a picture of her.

Apologetically, she replied, *"No pictures, please."* I respected her wishes and continued on to the classroom.

I spent some time before the beginning of the class to think about the two amazing encounters earlier that morning. I came to the conclusion that God and the angels knew I had been feeling sad all night, and that these people or angels had been sent to cheer me up. I could not ignore the strangeness of seeing the elderly couple by the pool before 7 a.m. and wondered if they were truly human or had been angels. They had been the only ones by the pool. I knew that these encounters were never to be forgotten. How about the Asian lady and her refusal to have her picture taken? Was she really in the class, or had she dropped from the sky?

When the doors to the classroom opened, I was able for the first time to sit in the front row and be that much closer to Doreen. That day I felt a deeper connection to everything Doreen was teaching. Because I was sitting in the front, I often felt as if I was the only one being taught by Doreen. As the last day was winding down, Doreen asked us to join her in praying loudly for the world. As the prayer went on, many people were touched and became very emotional, especially three Asian ladies sitting two rows behind me and to my left. Because of the horrible tsunami earlier in March, the ladies were very emotional and crying very loudly.

Doreen's assistants were running around handing out tissues to anyone who needed one. I did not think that the tissues would be enough for their needs. I was feeling the urge to go to the ladies and comfort them, but I was not sure if this would be appropriate or not. I finally decided to do it, no matter what it would cost me; I had to do what I was guided to do. I went over and gave each lady a comforting hug. One of them hung on to me tightly and cried on my shoulder. I truly did not want to leave her, but after a short while, I went back to my chair and started to cry myself, as I am very empathetic. I was thankful that no one said anything, and the class went on. This was yet another element of this very eventful, unforgettable day.

I called Miranda and told her I would be done that day and would be leaving on the next day, which was Friday. At lunch, I shared with my friend Monica the reason I had not gone to the music party. Monica pleasantly told me that she was not leaving that day and was planning to go out to dinner with two of our mutual friends. I was very happy for the news and told her I would join them all after class.

Our last class was very nice, but we were very sad to see this amazing event ending. We got in line to receive our certificates and received instructions on how to be listed on the angel therapy website. I exchanged email addresses with many friends and promised to stay in touch. Doreen's son was helping with the certificates. I took him aside and asked him a question: "Grant, I feel I am guided to write a book. What is your take?"

He simply said, "*One page a day. In a year, you will have a book.*" I thanked him for his wise advice. I then connected with Monica and the other two friends. We soon found a likely local-looking restaurant, where we had some terrific Hawaiian food. Monica and I joked about Laura and how her decision of canceling our dinner had turned out the best for me, as I truly was enjoying the company of good friends. We all bonded more and went back to our rooms with promises to stay in touch. After a sequence of flight cancellations and delays, I finally arrived home early in the evening of Saturday, June 25. I hugged Miranda, as I had missed her a lot. I had been gone a full week, my longest absence other than those forced by restraining orders from her mother. I placed my small suitcase on the kitchen counter and made some coffee to relax. I had purchased a few small things for Miranda from Hawaii, and I wanted to give them to her. Karen seemed to come out from nowhere and threw my suitcase open, saying in a loud and angry tone, "*Oh, Hawaii! Let's see what you have!*" Those were her exact words.

I was very tired and not in the mood for a fight, but I took hold of her hand and said, "*Karen, I have told you many times to not go through my stuff.*" I closed the suitcase up, took it to the car, and locked it inside.

I came back and said to Miranda, *"Did you see what your mother just did instead of making some coffee?"*

Miranda was silent, but Karen said, *"I was just helping you when I saw the luggage fall down."* I could not believe how quickly Karen had changed her story in a matter of a few minutes. I brought my suitcase inside and gave Miranda her little gifts, leaving it open in case Karen wanted to look further. I found out later that Karen had used all her tactics to make Miranda tell her everything.

I approached Karen one more time about meeting with her friend, Gail, for dinner to discuss finding a way to divorce peacefully and protect the house for the children. Karen still did not want any part of this talk. I had made up my mind before the trip to Hawaii to divorce, and I was even more determined to do so after the trip. I had been guided to talk to some angel therapists, and their advice was to move on with my life. I knew it was the best for everyone, and I was determined to put an end to Karen's putting out bogus restraining orders any time she wished. Karen never considered the emotional and financial impact of her childish acts, knowing that she was going to get her way every time. I told her that her refusal to talk would not change the fact that we were going to divorce, and I really had the best interests of everyone in mind. She still refused, over and over again. I decided it was time to file for divorce without further delay.

I continued to trust my little angel, Miranda, and treated her as though nothing had happened when I discovered that she had made Karen well aware of my trip to Hawaii. I shared with her that I had begun the divorce process. I told her that at her age her wishes would be counted heavily and that I would take care of her as I had always done. Miranda led me to think that there were no doubts that she would want to stay with me. A couple of days later, I found out that Karen had stopped her paycheck from going to our joint account, which was used for everything, including the mortgage payment. This was going to make it impossible to make the mortgage payment, but I never questioned Karen and avoided any conflicts. I suspected that

Miranda had told Karen about my seeing the attorney, but I did not want to confront her.

I soon received an email from my attorney that Karen had been served, and she would await Karen's response before she filed the divorce papers at the courthouse. Karen came home after she was served and did not want to talk. By this time, it was mid-July. I still had not made the mortgage payment, but I did not question Karen's intentions. She was coming and going as normal, and I wondered what her next move would be. I said to Miranda over and over again that I wanted her to stay with me. I would do everything possible to make sure her school and life would not suffer or change, and I was counting on her to be with me throughout this transition.

As days went by, I noticed that Karen was boxing dishes from the formal living room. I knew she was up to something, but I did not know what. I asked Miranda if she knew anything, but Miranda said she did not. I fully trusted Miranda, as I always had, and never had any doubts that she was not telling me the truth. I did not check our master bedroom, which had been Karen's room only. I did check in other rooms to see if she had taken anything from them. I never entered Karen or my daughters rooms without their permission, despite my full knowledge that Karen was always searching my belongings and briefcase.

On Monday, August 1, 2011, I left for work as usual at 4:30 a.m. I was not feeling very well all day but was not sure why. I even told my manager that I was not feeling well. She told me that I could go home if I wanted, but I decided to stay, hoping I would feel better. I ended up leaving at my regular time. I entered the house to find it upside down. The kitchen had been emptied; the dining room furniture and china hutch and all the dishes were gone. I did not see Miranda sitting in the living room as she usually did and assumed that she was upset and in her bedroom. I called out to her several times but did not hear any response, so I rushed back to the garage.

The car that I had given her not long ago was gone. Feeling I had lost my mind, I ran upstairs, only to find Miranda's room completely empty except for mounds of trash. I went to the master bedroom and found it completely empty also. The walk-in closet had a few things, but most everything was gone. I walked into the formal living room that I had designated as my angel room with a sign saying "Protected by Archangel St. Michael." I had put it up because I knew Karen periodically searched that room. The couch, love seat, and my iPod and stereo were gone. Even the computer modem and router were gone. I knew that the modem and router were useless to anyone else. Karen had taken them only to prevent me from listening to my favorite Hay House radio.

I felt betrayed, robbed, violated, and beaten. I was very upset and was having trouble breathing. How was this possible? Miranda was my little angel, and she was not going to leave me. What had happened?

I called the police and asked them to send an officer. While waiting, I assessed what else had been taken. Karen had collected all of our daughters' pictures! How was it possible that I had lived with this heartless person for so long? Even my alarm clock that I used to wake me up for work was gone. The police officer asked what I needed help with. I told him that my daughter had been taken against her will and that most of the furniture was gone. He said that he could not deal with the furniture, and I would have to deal with Karen in civil court. I replied that I did not care about the furniture; I just wanted my daughter. I gave him Miranda's telephone number, and he promised that he would call me as soon as he got in touch with either my wife or Miranda.

While waiting for word from the police officer, I started to pick up the trash left behind in the kitchen and dining room. I was a completely broken man and could not see clearly. A few hours later, the officer called me and said that he had located my daughter. He explained that she was with her mother and had not been taken against her will. I did not believe that Miranda was telling the truth, but continued to listen. The officer then said that Miranda had sent me an email, but because my modem and router were gone, I probably had not seen it. Based on the condition he had seen me in earlier, he advised me to not try to drive out just now to get a router. I promised the police officer that I would not try that, as I could still barely see.

I spent the evening and night going to Miranda's room and picked up all the trash left behind. There were a few items left behind that I have saved for my angel when she will make it back home, especially some pottery work she had completed for school. When I started to pick up the trash from the master bedroom and master bath, I immediately made the decision not to keep anything, even if they were in good condition. All items were to be tossed in the garbage as I had never seen them before. I had been sleeping on the couch for years and had never even bothered to check the master bedroom, unlike what Karen was doing to my briefcase. I then checked the huge closet in the bedroom that I had designed and built to be his and hers but it had become all hers instead. I was somewhat shocked to find out that my side of the closet was filled with all the magazines from the salons we owned. I had asked Karen to donate these magazines to a local library to get a good use out of them rather than throwing them away. Apparently, she had been keeping them at home knowing that I was not going to check the room. One thing worth mentioning was finding a small box of mine that contained some old tie accessories I had treasured from my younger days in Iraq, and my wedding ring. I had forgotten that I had placed that small box in the closet back when it was going to be "our" closet. The wedding ring had gotten smaller or more correctly, I had gained weight and I could not wear it and/ or did not want to wear it to display my displeasure with my marriage. I was happy to find the box after so many years. When I opened it, I found all tie accessories, but not the wedding ring. This is when I realized that Karen must have sold or exchanged my wedding ring many years before the divorce. I also imagined if I had discovered the disappearance of my wedding ring before the divorce how Karen would have responded. Of course, at first she would have denied knowing anything about my wedding ring, but if somehow I proved to her that I knew she had sold it or exchanged it, her response would have been something like, *"David, you are not wearing the ring and I did not think you needed it anyway"*.

This was harder than anything I could imagine. In the past when Karen took our children, I had not had the type of connection that I had developed with Miranda over the past few years. I was heartbroken but never blamed Miranda, as I knew how manipulative Karen could be. I walked in and out of Miranda's room all night, thinking she might appear from nowhere. I cried like I had never cried before but had no one to call or talk to.

I then went to the store to buy a router and modem and reconnected to the Internet. The email from Miranda was heartbreaking. I immediately knew that it had not been written by her. In fact, I did not think it had been written by Karen either. It was written by Karen's attorney in case I took the case to the courts. The email might have come from Miranda's email address, but the content was not Miranda's. I did not believe it was hers then, and I still do not believe it. I tried very hard to read the email, but I couldn't. The email began by saying *"Dear David"*. I was in tears and could not read another word.

My attorney went on to file the divorce papers, as she no longer expected Karen to come to the negotiating table. Within a week, a young inexperienced attorney identified himself as representing Karen. Day after day and week after week went by, and I did not see the mediation my attorney was talking about. All I saw was demand after demand to produce documents and financial statements, and all the while I was missing Miranda terribly.

I again began to ponder the idea of ending it all. I simply came to the conclusion that it must be me who was causing all these problems. I came very close several times to acting on these dark feelings, and there was no one nearby to stop me. I had no choice other than calling upon God and the angels for help. I asked Archangel Michael to help me and keep me safe from myself.

Soon the entire month of August 2011 had gone by without any messages from my angel, Miranda. I was sending emails but did not receive any in return. I thought maybe Karen was screening and limiting Miranda's messages. In the midst of all this turbulence, I found out that Doreen Virtue was planning to make a quick appearance in Ohio on September 10. I truly wanted to go and get energized, but how could I leave the dog, cat, and birds for two days? I had no one to ask to keep an eye on the house either, as I lived in the country. I meditated and trusted my intuition, which was telling me to take the trip. I fed the animals on Friday and flew to Ohio. I saw Doreen and many like-minded people, but I did not ask her for any insights on my situation, because I did not want to take time away from others who wanted to meet her. I was somewhat disappointed along with my excitement at seeing Doreen. How could she not see or feel what I was going through? How could she not see or feel what I had gone through just to see her? The animals were fine when I got home, protected by Archangel St. Michael.

September was ending, and there had been no progress or mediation in my divorce case. I was falling further behind in my mortgage payments, and my entire situation was getting worse. I could not share my loneliness with anyone at work. I called upon the angels to help me with my mortgage situation, as I had worked hard on the home and did not want to lose it. My two daughters were raised in this house and I was going to do everything to protect it. Fortunately, I was able to talk to a live person at the mortgage company. I asked for six months to resolve the divorce and find a permanent solution, and much to my surprise, my temporary solution was accepted. I now had some breathing room, until May of 2012. I thanked God and the angels for their help.

I was going through my days without hearing from my angel, Miranda, and it was nothing but heartbreaking. It was now mid-October, and there still had been no progress with my divorce or any mediation. I was getting very frustrated, but there was nothing I could do. Doreen was appearing in Philadelphia on Friday, October 28, and again I was guided to go and reenergize myself. I went to the airport very lightly packed on Friday, as I knew I was going to fly back in a few hours. Once again, it was an enjoyable conference with wonderful people. I also met a few gifted angel therapy practitioners like, Melissa Luddeni.

I was very grateful and lucky because I was able a little more to be with a group who had paid extra also. The group was given the chance to be in a room where they had served some appetizers with the promise that Doreen will make a special appearance and visit with us. I was lucky enough to be seated next to several young ladies including my dear friend Melissa Luddeni. Besides Doreen, we were very lucky to meet Mr. Don Miguel Ruiz, the author of *The Fifth Agreement* among other books. I asked my friend Melissa Luddeni to take a few pictures with me and Mr. Don Miguel Ruiz. Those are pictures that I will treasure for years to come. Again, I had many chances to ask Doreen for insight or a prayer for my situation but elected to preserve the time for her other fans. Just as before, I was disappointed that Doreen did not see or feel my situation and what I had done just to come and see her so many times in a very short period. One can say that I was only one in a big event, but the fact is that this event was not very big and I do not think I was just another fan. I know I was guided all along to meet Doreen whether she acknowledged it or not. I did not have any hard feelings and submitted that there was a reason behind everything.

Mr. Don Miguel Ruiz and me—Picture taken by Melissa Luddeni

It started to snow a little on the way back to the airport. I did not think it was enough to cause any delay problems, but I was wrong. My flight to Minnesota was canceled, and the next flight would not be until the next morning. I spent the night walking around in the airport, too cold to sit still. I kept reminding myself that it had all been worth it to connect with Doreen and many other friends. Everything at home was in perfect condition, and I was happy that I had listened to my intuition and gone on this short trip. I posted some of my pictures with Doreen on Facebook.

One day, as I was driving home from work, I suddenly began to think about all my earlier contacts with Erin Solt. (Erin Solt was the lady from Balboa Press who had contacted me several times after my trip to Vancouver.) I could not wait to get home to find her emails and call her back. I located her number and a gentleman answered. I was saddened when he told me that Erin was no longer there. His name was Dwight, and I told him how I had connected with Erin and my feeling that I was guided to write my book. He told me that he had all the emails between Erin and me, and he would be more than happy to work with me and make me the same offer Erin had made. I agreed on the spot but told Dwight that I would need a year to finish writing because I had not even started. Dwight told me not to worry, and I was signed with Balboa on November 3, 2011.

A week later, I went to Walmart on my day off for a shopping trip. Within a few seconds after driving out of the parking lot, I found my mind filled with an image of myself in a big conference, much like the "I Can Do It" gathering. I saw myself sitting in the audience with many mentors standing on the stage, among them Dr. Wayne Dyer and Doreen Virtue. All of sudden, Dr. Dyer pointed at me and asked me to speak for ten minutes about anything I would like to teach the audience. I vividly recall exactly what I said. At the end of my little speech, I looked to the side and saw Dr. Dyer and Doreen cheering and clapping for me. This vision occupied most of my ten-minute drive. As I entered the house, I stopped short and asked myself, *Wait, if you were daydreaming the entire distance, who exactly was driving?* I can truly and honestly say that I do not remember anything about the drive, only the daydreaming. I felt guided to mention this incident, and hopefully someday I will understand the real meaning of it.

I was very excited, after all those years, to finally fulfill a dream and a mission of writing a book. Day after day went by, and I still did not have any idea how to begin writing my story. But I was at peace and knew that I would begin writing in divine timing. I was never concerned or panicked.

In November 2011 I began my connection with another mentor, Ms. Deborah King, by taking her four-part online prayer certification class. The first two sessions were wonderful, and when Ms. King announced at the end of the second class that she would allow the participants to call in for ten minutes, I decided to try. Amazingly enough, I got through, and without even thinking, I moved away from the topic of prayer to this question: *"Deborah, I am guided to write a book. What do you see is blocking me?"*

Deborah responded, *"Absolutely nothing is blocking you. All you have to do is open your laptop and begin writing. The angels will be helping you write."* She finished by saying, *"I do see your book."* I was thrilled to hear her say that, and I still listen to the MP3 recording of the call to keep me motivated. That was the push I had been waiting for, and I began writing shortly thereafter.

By mid-November 2011, I finally received notification from my divorce attorney that we could arrange a mediation date. The mediators were selected and agreed upon by both parties. It would concern only parenting rights, as this had been at the top of my agenda since August. Miranda was not going to be at the mediation, but at least I was hopeful that after four full months, a decision would be reached so that I could see her soon.

Tuesday morning, November 29, I was in a room with my attorney and the two mediators. Karen and her attorney were in another room to prevent direct contact between us. My attorney had instructed me not to fight over things that did not matter. She told me that because Miranda was almost seventeen, regardless of who would have the physical custody; it would be effective for only one year. I did not care for the physical custody as long as I had visitation rights. After hours of mediation and going back and forth, we signed an agreement. It called for immediate reunification of Miranda and me in the presence of a therapist in the therapy office. The appointment was made for the next day. The rest of the agreement laid out the details of the visitation schedule. I left the mediation office very happy and thrilled, counting the hours and minutes until I could see my angel Miranda.

I could not sleep that night. Four months without Miranda had been longer and harder than anything I had ever experienced. I did not go to work, as the appointment was at one o'clock in the afternoon in St. Michael, Minnesota in the offices of Solution Counseling. I was very surprised to see how small the therapy office was as it was not like the flyer provided by the mediation attorneys. I gave the therapy office my insurance information and filled out all the forms. Miranda was not there yet. She had not called either. I did not mind waiting and was patient. After about thirty minutes, the clinic director called my attorney to see if she had any insights regarding Miranda, but she did not. He then called Karen's attorney, but he was nowhere to be found, so the director left him a voice message. He then called Karen at work and asked her if Miranda was coming. Karen replied that she was not aware that Miranda was supposed to be anywhere. I was shocked. How could she not know, when we had just signed the agreement the day before? I knew Karen was just playing another game. I called my attorney and asked her to get in touch with Karen's attorney and give them an ultimatum. I made another clinic appointment for the following week.

In the next few days, my attorney contacted Karen's attorney several times and finally received a confirmation that Miranda would attend the second appointment. I took the day off from work and entered the clinic feeling very excited. But before I could even close the door behind me, the director for Solution Counseling stopped me and said, *"You can't be here."*

At first, I thought he was joking and said, *"Pardon me?"*

His face was filled with anger, and he ordered me to leave the office immediately. I told him that he was mistaken. I said I was there for therapy reunification and that I had already given him a copy of the agreement. He replied, *"Karen called and asked to have the therapy just for Miranda alone. If you don't leave, I will call the police."*

I could not believe my ears. I got in my car and called my attorney. She asked me many questions, but I did not have any answers, as no one had told me anything or given me any good reasons for what had happened. She called the director herself but received no good answers either. She finally told me to just go home. I do not know how I was able to drive the twenty miles from St. Michael. I was shaking and crying and could not see the road very clearly. I shall never forget what kind of small mediocre therapy Solution Counseling of St. Michael, Minnesota was. I for sure will not forget the person who called himself the "director" of that small office and his ability to create problems instead of resolving them.

I wondered what kind of excuse Karen and her attorney would come up with this time. Miranda's seventeenth birthday was only two weeks away, and we needed to resolve whatever issues they might have. My attorney assured me that she would keep trying to find out the real story from Karen's attorney.

After a week, Karen's attorney claimed that the agreement we had was to have Miranda attend therapy alone. The signed agreement was very clear, but both Karen and her attorney were playing with my emotions. Karen was playing her last card to punish me but was punishing our children in the process. I asked my attorney to record the agreement in court so we could hold Karen in contempt of the court order. My attorney did not seem in a hurry to do that, as she was not feeling my pain. She recommended having a final mediation to resolve all other issues and file the divorce all at once, as that would be cheaper. Miranda's birthday was a week away. I did not care about cheap or expensive; I wanted results. She suggested finding a different clinic for a possibly better outcome, so I scheduled another appointment at a clinic in Buffalo on a date only four days before my daughter's seventeenth birthday. I was willing to do anything to be able to celebrate that occasion, but Karen did exactly the same thing with the Buffalo clinic. Once again, she had prevented my contact with Miranda. She was still able to play her games with no regard to Miranda's emotions and feelings. I was very vocal with my attorney when I stated my displeasure with her inability to resolve the parenting issue.

Now that the decree was final, I reminded my attorney that it was time for her to keep her promise to file a contempt order against Karen for not abiding by the legal agreement. The attorney did not seem very thrilled to be reminded and made one excuse after another, even though it seemed to me that I had already paid her to file the order. She sent me a new agreement to sign and demanded a new retainer. I would not sign and told her that I would either find a different attorney or pursue the case by myself. Not having found another attorney by February, I called the court administrator and asked if I could file the contempt charge on my own. The answer was positive if I followed all listed instructions. They seemed easy enough, so I filed the contempt order myself and paid all the fees.

I continued with my writing. In a few weeks I received an acceptance signed by the judge with a notice to appear at the courthouse in mid-March. I was confident that the judge would not have any problems with me representing myself, as I knew Karen would be coming with her attorney. I was hoping that she would change her mind before the court date and allow Miranda to contact me, but that did not happen. Karen's attorney provided his legally required response to my case in writing prior to the court date. He started out by listing all of the past cases Karen had accumulated against me and all of the restraining orders. I thought this was very unethical. None of those cases had anything to do with the real issue. Of course, he was trying to influence the judge's decision, but at what cost?

On the court date, my case was the only item on the agenda. As I presented it to the judge, I found him already aware of all the details, which indicated that he had read my case write-up. The judge then gave Karen's attorney a chance to speak, at which time the attorney demanded a hearing. The judge had no choice but to grant it. The earliest he could hear our case was Thursday, May 3. Before the judge let us leave, he wanted to talk to each one of us. He spoke to me first and told me that he was feeling my pain. He recommended that I come back with an attorney. He then talked to Karen and told her that if she was found in contempt, she would be facing jail time. Finally, he spoke to Karen's attorney and asked him if any of the therapy offices had ever recommended against the reunification of Miranda and me, and if there had ever been such a recommendation, he would like to see it. The judge then spoke to everybody in general, saying that this was a tragedy and that it was too bad that Miranda would soon become eighteen years old. He dismissed us, saying he would see us again in May.

I left the courthouse encouraged by the judge's words, but disappointed that I would have to wait until May to be heard. By then, it would have been a full nine months since I had seen Miranda or kissed her good night. I talked to God and the angels every morning and every night asking for help and giving them permission to help my situation. Every good attorney I knew of was willing to help but not available on May 3, and I was getting ready to go it alone. At the last minute I found someone who said yes. I was not very comfortable with this lawyer, who seemed inexperienced, but I had no choice, as time was running out. I paid her more money that I did not have and hoped for the best. I continued writing my story while waiting for the hearing date. My new attorney would occasionally call me into her office for things that could have easily been handled over the phone. I realized that she was doing this just so that she could charge me more money.

My attorney scheduled a meeting in her office the evening of May 2, just hours before the hearing, to tell me that the case would be very difficult to win. I was very upset with her and asked her why she waited so long to tell me, taking my money all the while. I felt betrayed. I told her that it was now too late to ask the judge to delay the hearing so I could prepare a defense myself and that she should still come to the hearing, regardless of how she felt about the outcome. I left the attorney's office very angry and went home. I was determined to try my best in court, regardless of the outcome. I wanted to prove to Miranda that I had fought for her and wanted to be with her. I knew that someday she would realize how hard I had tried. I was not trying to cause Karen any harm, only fighting for fairness and for our daughter's health and future.

I took the next day off from work to make sure I would not have to deal with any road delays. My attorney met with me before the hearing and coached me with answers for only a few simple questions. I felt that she had not really prepared anything and had surrendered even before we began. My attorney called me to the stand and asked me the questions that we had practiced. Then Karen's attorney questioned me. He had no real issues other than trying to prove that I was the one who wrote the initial complaint. He kept asking me the same question, and I kept answering him that I was the one who wrote it. He then asked me if I had tried to contact Miranda. I replied that I had, many times, but she was not allowed to respond to me. He was trying to show the judge that I had not been truthful when I made a statement in my complaint that I had not seen or contacted Miranda since August 1, 2011. I responded harshly to the attorney that an uninsured e-mail is not considered "contact." The hearing went on for several hours, and I only had one thought—why was Karen spending so much time and money to prevent me from seeing my own daughter? Was she truly that cruel? I walked away feeling that I had done everything I could. How could anyone or worse yet, any attorney, be so cruel to work so hard and tell lies to prevent a father from seeing his own daughter like what Karen and her attorney did?.

My attorney told me that the judge could take up to ninety days to make his decision and also observed that because Miranda was almost eighteen years old, the court would be reluctant to make many changes. I told her that I had done everything I could, and that was the most important thing. I would surrender the issue to God and the angels.

I sent Miranda an e-mail each week telling her I loved her, regardless of whether Karen was blocking it or not. The following week was my birthday. I did not hear from my daughters, but I had not expected Karen to allow them to contact me. I did receive a bill from the attorney, and she proved my intuition. She had charged me for a full hour for each of our meetings, even if it had lasted only a few minutes. I wrote her a letter of protest and asked her to inform the court that she was no longer representing me.

It was already June, and the judge had still not made his ruling. It was not easy waiting, living alone, knowing my daughters were only ten miles away but being blocked from contacting me, and knowing that my dream house was in great danger.

I took Friday, July 6, off work to write. I was nearing the end of the story. My dogs let me know that someone was outside the house. UPS had brought a package, which I was not expecting. It was a very large envelope from my mortgage company. I started to shake as I opened it. They were asking me for certain documents. I was very happy, taking it as a sign that my mortgage application had not been ignored, and they just needed more information to complete the process. Please keep in mind that after the temporary agreement was over, I asked the mortgage company to help me with a mortgage modification and expressed a genuine interest in keeping the house. I quickly found the needed documents, and as I left the house to go to the UPS store in Buffalo, I stopped to pick up my regular mail. There was an envelope from the courthouse. I was hoping its contents would add to my current happiness. But the judge had basically decided to do nothing. Although I was not surprised, I was still very disappointed. I had spent several thousand dollars on an attorney who had done nothing.

After mailing the envelope, I sat down to reflect on my divorce journey. I kept reminding myself that I had done everything according to my highest ethics. I had tried many times to exchange ideas with Karen on ways to divorce peacefully. I knew that Miranda would come to realize the truth, on the timetable of the divine.

I spent Tuesday, December 20, 2011, Miranda's birthday, grieving alone at home. I sent her a happy birthday email, but I did not know if she even received it. I could not believe that any human being could do something like this to her child just to hurt her soon-to-be ex-husband. If I had seen a movie depicting what Karen was doing, I would not have believed it.

The following Sunday was Christmas, and I was hoping for a miracle—hearing from my daughters. I had a Christmas tree with a few decorations and hung stockings for Nadia and Miranda as we used to do. I had to buy new stockings, as Karen had taken everything. I did not have anyone to call or visit on Christmas Eve or Christmas Day, so I spent it alone—a direct result of everything Karen had done.

On January 22, I received an email from my attorney indicating that the judge had signed the divorce decree on January 19, and she would be sending me a signed copy via mail. I received the signed copy of the divorce decree on January 25, just as it had been presented. I was very happy to be able to finally put the marriage behind me and start finding ways to connect with my children. Per our agreement, Karen had signed off all rights to the house. I took the document to the county planning and zoning office and reregistered the house in my name only. Wednesday, August 1, 2012 marked a full year since I had seen my angel, Miranda. I took the day off from work to just sit alone and reflect. What if someone wrote a story about what had happened in the last year? Would anyone believe it? How could a parent do this to her own children? How could anyone attend church every Sunday, yet act like this? Why wasn't this considered criminal? How could an attorney sworn under oath go along with this kind of crime without taking a moment to advise his client to do the right thing? Why hadn't the judge made a swift ruling instead of simply giving a speech about how tragic this case was? I already knew it was tragic! I just wanted him to help me.

In the midst of my sorrow, anger hit me, and I received a message through my angelic connection that put everything into perspective. The message had many facets to it, all having to do with what might have happened if Miranda had stayed with me. The main message was that there was a good chance that I would not have started telling my life story. Another was that her mother would have used Miranda to cancel the divorce. The biggest one was that I would have felt guilty and cancelled the divorce on my own, letting me see the hard way how different Karen is from me.

After all of this, there is just no way in the world that I would have any second thoughts about what I have done. I also received the message to be proud of finishing my life's story. Aside from any book publishing, I will be helping many people, and above all, I will have something for my own daughters to read. My daughters were brought up in an unhealthy environment, and they never had a chance to learn anything about their father. I was also reminded that in my entire marriage to Karen, I never once heard Karen say anything nice about me, not even one comforting word regarding me or my family in Iraq. I will never forget how I did not hear one kind word from Karen when I heard the words about the passing of my father. Most importantly, I do not recall even one passionate touch or kiss from Karen. There was not even one single happy moment between us ever. Even the happiest time of my life when Nadia was born had to be tarnished after hearing my mother-in-law wondering if she was as dark as I was.

Once I received this message and this insight, I was somewhat at peace and believed in my divine purpose. By August 2011, my writing had nearly caught up with my current, day-to-day life. I found it to be ironic that without any planning, my worst nightmare had begun in August of 2011, and by August of 2012 I was finishing writing the draft of my story. On Friday, June 8, 2012, while I was writing, I turned on the television as background noise to keep me motivated. However, the subject of the program caught my attention, and I had to stop writing and watch the entire hour. It was a show hosted by Diane Sawyer and dedicated exclusively to the abduction story of Jaycee Lee Dugard. The girl had been abducted at age eleven and held captive for nearly two decades by Philip and Nancy Garrido. I cried and felt the pain Jaycee's mother had gone through. Despite the safe return of her daughter, she was still in pain and angry for all the time and memories that had been stolen from her. After the program ended, I could not go back to writing and decided to go to bed. This story haunted me for days. I knew there had been a message for me and a purpose that led me to turn the television on at that time and tune it to that station. Nothing was a coincidence, and the message finally became clear: in many ways, what those people did to Jaycee was no different than what Karen did, and continued to do, with Miranda. Karen had stolen many years of beautiful memories from Nadia, Miranda, and me. Karen might not have physically abused Nadia and Miranda in a way that would subject her to legal punishment, but she had abused us all emotionally. Sadly, there is no legal punishment for that. How will Nadia and Miranda deal with obstacles in their lives? Are they going to run away as they saw their mother do time and time again? I have faith that my story will open many eyes and begin conversations toward preventing this type of unethical abuse.

CHAPTER TWENTY-SIX
· ·

Epilogue
(And Prologue to Whatever Comes Next)

As I wind down the writing of my story, I am hoping for a pleasant turn of events or a call from one or both of my daughters to make a "happy ending." I am not planning to force any events just to have a positive story, being confident enough that everything runs on divine timing. I know I missed celebrating Miranda's seventeenth and eighteenth birthdays, being with my girls on both Christmas 2011 and 2012, and many of Nadia's birthdays, but at this point of writing, I am somewhat optimistic that I will see them and make up for lost time. I am confident that our relationship will be stronger than ever. I come back to this big beautiful empty home that I built for our daughters. I have placed poster sized pictures of my daughters in their empty rooms and often visit them and talk to them full of tears. After the passing of nineteen months, I still cannot believe that any mother can do that to her children. What has happened is nothing short of evil work from someone who never misses attending church. I often think of Karen's family and why they have not attempted to change Karen's mind. They are all church attendees and supposedly believe in God. I recall an old tradition that I believe goes back to my ancestors called "breaking bread." I have cooked and welcomed Karen's family and we all "broke bread" many times. To this day and during the years of our marriage, not even one of them ever tried to ask for my version of the story.

I went around visiting all the trees I had planted throughout the years and talked and connected to God and the angels. I affirmed that I did not own the land or the property but that it belonged to God, as I did. I said that I was no more than a steward whose job was to take care of God's property. I said I thought I had been a good steward all these years and said to God that if he approved of my work, I would like to continue to do it. But if God had another plan for me, I was at peace to serve wherever he wanted me to serve. I had always felt the connection with all the trees I had planted and was aware of the existence of the elements around the house supporting me. I felt peaceful after this conversation with God and stopped worrying about what would happen with the house.

As I was concluding my writing, I could not help but think and rethink about what Deborah King had told me when I called her during the online class on prayer. If you recall, I had asked Ms. King about what she saw blocking me from writing. Her answer was, "Absolutely nothing is blocking you. All you have to do is open your laptop and begin writing. The angels will be helping you write." I was very thrilled, of course, but wondered how exactly they would do that. I knew that nothing would be written if I did not start, so how were the angels going to help with that? The answer to my question did not come as a prophecy or someone showing up in my life to tell me what to write, but throughout my writing, the angels helped me in ways that I never expected. The fact is, I had never written notes or journals in my entire life. In fact, I never even liked writing. Since the beginning, I liked math, physics, and science and never cared to do anything literary. With that kind of background, I did not know what I would remember about the events in my life, but I was determined to write whatever I could remember. I was not worried about writing many details regarding my childhood, as my memories were not very clear except for events involving Nadia. My mission was to be detailed about what I had gone through after arriving at my new home and after getting married. So I began writing.

I usually spent an hour or two in life review at each writing session. I found out that I could not write except when I was at home. I would save my work each time, moving randomly from one event or year to another at the next opportunity. I was often surprised by the emergence of long-forgotten events that belonged to a time period I thought I had finished writing about. I was getting these thoughts and visions while driving or just while sitting and doing my daily work. I often found myself opening my writing document and quickly writing a reminder note to myself to include the new material. I even had to resort to a portable recorder to quickly record the visions while I was driving. At first, I thought that this was very normal, but from the way in which these visions came to me and the frequency with which they happened, I had to tell myself that the angels were working in mysterious ways to help me. The angels did not exactly write for me, but in many ways, they did. I wrote down every received thought or vision, because I believed the angels were reminding me for a reason. They were all divine thoughts and visions.

For example, I had always remembered the "act of kindness" my mother taught me by cooking and having us deliver food at night to people whom she knew did not have enough to eat. I never forgot that lesson, but other things, like my mother telling me to "squeeze my nose," had been forgotten. Apparently the angels had not forgotten, however, and they were the ones who reminded me in visions. How and why am I telling you, the reader, about this of any importance? I truly do not have the answer to that, but I feel that I have been guided to record that event, as I was for many other events throughout this book.

These multitudes of messages or visions began as soon as I started to write. But I will have to think very hard to distinguish between the stories that were on my mind versus the ones to which I was guided or given a vision about. They seem at this point to be interwoven. All of these visions were accurate and happened the way I described them, concerning events forgotten until the vision reminded me of them. The only vision that did not reflect a memory, because it was of the future, was the one I had driving home from Walmart when Dr. Wayne Dyer challenged me to say something. I mentioned it because it happened, and I am hopeful that it will become a reality.

After what I thought was the completion of my writing and the beginning of the editing, I was guided and reminded by the angels about a few more things that were fairly important to me and to my life and thus, worth mentioning. One was my love for music in general and my desire to learn to play the guitar. My guitar love has not diminished, and I have always kept a guitar or two around, even though I still have not taken the time to learn to play it. And though I loved listening to Abdel Halim Hafez and Nagat, I also listened to foreign music. One song that has always stayed with me is "Tell Laura I Love Her." I had a forty-five of this song and loved playing it over and over. Much later, I tried to find this song and realized that I had not memorized the name of the singer. I finally found out that it was Ray Peterson and was recently able to purchase the song on CD and, at last, hear it again.

One especially vivid vision or image I was given was of the time in my childhood when I was bored and just trying to kill some time flying my kite in the midst of a curfew. Though this was a non-event to me at the time, I knew I was given the vision after so many years for a reason, and I had to describe it as it happened. Did the shooter truly miss me from sixty or seventy feet, or did the angels, or Archangel St.

Michael, make me move a few inches to prevent my little head from being shattered by the bullet? The vision was very strong and was almost as if I were watching myself on a videotape.

I would now like to look back over my entire story and share some general reflections.

As to my brushes with death ... a single event like this might not be considered very unusual and called just a stroke of luck. However, when one realizes that there were four of them—especially given the fact that Insiah told me that Archangel St. Michael had not only saved me one of those times but had also sent me to see her, which ultimately led me to the angels and all my spiritual mentors—well, I cannot possibly ignore these events any longer. I am a firm believer that there is a much bigger reason and message here for me. One of the messages I received from a dear friend recently was, *"You lived in Atlantis in that golden age and were a wise teacher ... bring forth that knowledge ... written in your book."* I do not claim that I have all the answers, but I am trusting that everything will happen in divine timing and divine order.

The first person I want to look at is my older brother. I grew up with him and saw him disrespect our own father and later my stepmother. He tried to control everyone, and when my father finished building our last big, beautiful home, my brother occupied half of the entire second level without even discussing it with my father. My brother was the one who locked the door to the roof and prevented me from feeding my pigeons and later almost killed me when I tried to climb to the roof to feed my innocent pets. Even with all that knowledge about my brother, I took him under my wing for many years and spent most of what I had to send him what he needed for gifts. Did I truly expect him to all of a sudden change when I joined him in Minot, North Dakota? Not really. I was hopeful but not very confident. Despite the way my brother treated me after rejoining him, I always respected him as my eldest brother, but with very little in return. Today he is living in Sweden and has not made many attempts to reach out to me, his brother. I have reached out to him and his family many times when I was guided to do so. I have remained the person I always was.

The next important big thing is the story of Denise. It was clear that I was attracted to Denise from the beginning, and apparently she was attracted to me also. Despite my attraction, I honored my love to Nadia and never attempted to date Denise. This I am very proud of and I would not have done anything differently. Later, when I reconnected with Denise in Minnesota, it was nothing other than divine purpose. Was this a test for me? I have no idea, but if it was, then I passed. I remained as a good friend and did everything I could have ever done, including being in her wedding and taking the videotape for her to remember for the rest of her life. Why did Denise decide to cut her connection with me? Was it Karen? Was it Rob, her husband? I am not clear about that. But I have decided to continue acting ethically. The last attempt from me to reconnect was when I sent her daughter gifts when, in reality, I was not even on the shower invitation list. I finally decided to stop trying, because regardless of her motives, I still feel that I deserved, at minimum, an explanation. Will Denise appear in my life again? I have no idea, but if she does, I will be acting as honorably and ethically as ever but with new boundaries.

Regarding our Minnetonka neighbor, Dee Dee, I said earlier that I considered the day we had to move out of our first house one of my worst days; because I was being forced out of an area I had loved so much. I knew that this woman's constant police calling had evoked little but compassion from the officers, and they were feeling very sorry for us, but for various reasons they could not do anything. Dee Dee was not breaking the law, but she was taking things to their extreme, and the officers knew that. For years, I did not see the full potential of the area to which I had moved because of the long commute and the mobile home problems. But once I settled into my new country home and my young seedlings started to grow right in front of my eyes, that is when I started to realize that I had just created "heaven on earth" for myself and my family. So many times when I came across a nest near the seedlings I had planted, I got teary eyed, knowing I had helped these ducks or other birds to establish their own families. That is when I truly realized the gift Dee Dee gave us by forcing us to seek this "heaven on earth." To this day when I walk to the mailbox and see the mature trees on both sides of my driveway, I often say, "Thank you God and the angels, and thank you, Dee Dee."

How important to me was becoming a U.S. citizen, which was my very first citizenship? How about my graduation from college with a computer science degree, only days after my first citizenship? How can I explain what the U.S. citizenship meant to me? Would my working so hard as a youngster just to listen in total secret and fear to the radio programming of Voice of America tell you the magnitude in my mind of becoming a U.S. citizen? There are truly no words that could ever describe my joy at this achievement. I had always connected my mother's promise of sending me to the United States and becoming a U.S. citizen as a single goal. I know my mother was smiling on that day.

Am I totally happy that I am living in the United States as a person with Middle Eastern looks and background? For the most part, the answer is yes. I do get frustrated when there is bad news from the Middle East region and some people feel the need to take it out on me. I often find even so-called educated people falling into the same trap as the less-educated population. And I often find myself in discussions of something that has nothing to do with politics ending with a statement like, "*Well, this is America.*" When I hear something like that, I immediately know exactly what they are referring to, and it is very sad to hear. Oh how many times I wanted to say *"Yes, indeed this America. Something I fought very hard and gave up many things just to be part of and you were born and taking everything for granted."* I usually elect to just move on without arguing. My BS in computer science in 1985 was not a degree in engineering, my dream degree, but after what I had gone through, my graduation still symbolized my determination to achieve my goals, regardless of the circumstances. I could have easily gone on to pursue that dream later, but I elected to convince myself that because that degree had not worked out for reasons beyond my control, it meant that I was not supposed to pursue it. I have never questioned or said "what if" on that score.

Another important person in my life was my cousin, Tony. I have always enjoyed my cousin when he has no drama around him. I never gave up on him and always sought him out. But Tony had issues and perhaps hatred toward my father dating from his childhood and sometimes displayed this hatred, especially when drinking. He often blamed my father for not helping his father, because he thought my father was so well off. He had two children with his first wife but ended up divorcing her. He recently divorced his second wife also, with whom he also had two children. He has pretty much ignored the children from his first marriage. I have an issue with him in that regard. I have not heard from or seen Tony for several years. I love my cousin. I just do not like his lifestyle, and I have elected to keep my distance. I will always welcome him back into my life if he ever decides to grow up and realize that there is more to life than drinking beer.

Next, I would like to talk in general about Saddam Hussein: his rise and eventually his demise. Was Saddam Hussein evil? Did he serve any purpose? Of course, Hussein was neither the first person nor the last to prefer evil work instead of God's work. I believe that he was definitely following Satan's footsteps. Hussein killed many innocent people for little or no reason. In his younger days, he was given a second chance at life after his failed attempt to kill Iraq's first president. He could have easily thanked God for the second chance and changed his life around, but instead he became even more evil and had no regard for God's creation, either human or animal.

The images of the people hanging by their necks at the forced rally when I was in high school are still vivid in my mind. Hussein killed and gassed and buried alive many people. He is behind the destruction and deportation of my own family and the killing of at least two of my brothers. Was I happy to see the first American intervention after Hussein sent his troops to invade Kuwait? Of course I was, and I also volunteered my services to several government agencies to help. I was never taken up on those offers, but nevertheless, I was very happy to see the world without Saddam Hussein.

On the other hand, I did not like or approve of the second invasion, because too many lives were destroyed in the process. I would have preferred to have seen Hussein killed in battle instead of being chased down to where he was hiding in a hole. I definitely did not approve of the way Saddam Hussein was hung and then viewed by millions. As much as I thought Hussein was evil and needed to go, I did not approve of hanging him and videotaping the whole thing. I think every soul deserves some respect. I wonder how we could possibly have lowered our morals to his level. Is Iraq better off right now than before the invasion? I believe that only the people who lost their loved ones or whose lives have been destroyed should answer this question. I have to say that I totally agree with my mentor, Dr. Wayne W. Dyer, when he says, *"We cannot go on thinking in militant ways if we want to bring peace to our world."* (Twitter, Wayne Dyer Quotes @WayneDyerQuotes)

Next, I would like to revisit my relationship, problems, and heartbreak with Karen and her family. First, I would like to make it clear that I would never, ever, under any circumstances, claim that I was always an "angel" and never said anything bad to Karen. That is not the case at all. When people argue and get into arguments, they often do and say things that they do not mean. I am very positive that I said many regrettable things in the heat of the moment. One thing I am sure of, however, is my total dedication to my family, including Karen. Was she sent into my life for a purpose? I am very convinced that was the case, and I will share some insights on this issue shortly. The fact is that I was not in love with Karen before the marriage in the way I loved Nadia and later Denise. Karen did not make it easy to fall in love with her after the marriage either. I believe that she did have issues beyond my analysis, and she never opened up so that I could help her.

To start, Karen never gave me any sign that she was interested until she read the article in the *Red & Green* in which I indicated my desire to move to Minnesota shortly after my graduation from Minot State. I think that was what made her all of sudden warm up to me. Without that sign, I would most likely have moved to Minnesota without even remembering her. Then, once I made the mistake of getting engaged, I went through with the marriage solely because I was acting honorably and could not see myself breaking the engagement. My morals and sense of honor got the best of me, for sure.

Should I have questioned the absence of Karen's oldest brother from the wedding? I honestly believe that I should have and also demanded a good reason. There was clearly something there that I never became aware of, even to this day. Why did Karen's family go along with letting me marry their daughter when, in fact, the color of my skin was an issue to them? Should I have divorced after the *Not Without My Daughter* comments? I am one hundred percent sure that I should have divorced without question at that time. Karen had absolutely no basis for comments like that. I had no place to escape to with my daughter, even if I had wanted to. Why didn't I divorce then? Again, it was because of my morals and thinking it was the best for my daughter, which proved to be wrong.

Should I have divorced after Karen's operation that prevented her from having more children against my will and desire? Again, I am one hundred percent positive that a divorce would have been the only answer. Again, I did not divorce, thinking I was doing the best for my daughters. As to the restraining orders, I am not ashamed of having put up with everything I suffered to protect my daughters. It was all based on my understanding—even though that was later proved to be wrong. Regardless, I feel that I did the most honorable thing for my daughters and for Karen.

There is one rather astonishing detail that has only now come to the surface that concerns my dealings with a former business partner, Kim. She opened another salon in her house against the contract we had, and we had many other disagreements. When she found out about my difficulties with Karen, she obtained copies of the police records (which are a matter of public record), went to the salon when I was at work, and showed these police records to my stylists. That was the real reason I was not able to keep many stylists. After selling the salons, I decided to seek an attorney who could help me to expunge these records, meaning they would still be there, but the public would not have access to them as easily as Kim had. I had actually sought the expungement more than a year before filing for the divorce. However, this was a lower priority process for the attorney I had hired and he was taking his time and he was not at any rush nor was I.

Unfortunately, the expungement case came in front of the court and the judge after I was already divorced. The reason I say unfortunately is not because the request was denied, as it did not mean all that much to me, but because I found out that Karen had taken the time to see the judge and object to the expungement. The judge cited this in his reasoning to deny my request. Before I filed for divorce, I was thinking of Karen's well-being and working with a real estate person to find her a home to live in after the divorce. That is how I operated—out of love—only to find out that Karen had taken time from her work to deny a simple request. That by itself explains how we both operated throughout the years we were married. I cannot control what my readers will think, do, or say. I only can control myself and must remain honest and tell everything without being selective about the events. Besides Karen, I would like you, the reader, to guess who else might have objected to my expungement case. Believe it or not, even after more than four years of selling the salon and after not owning any business in Buffalo or elsewhere. The Buffalo police chief did not waste yet another opportunity to cause me harm. The Buffalo police chief took the time to influence the judge's decision and deny my request. Can anyone with that type of personal vendetta serve in a public office especially when his duties are to "protect" the public?

I could go on and on about all the restraining orders and the jealousy and all the rest. I did not divorce even then, thinking it was for the best, and I kept thinking that Karen would eventually recognize and appreciate everything I did for her. None of it worked, and now I have only two choices: 1) blame myself for the rest of my life and feel guilty, or 2) tell myself that I was honorable and did my best.

My life was always filled with guilt about various things. For years, I felt guilty about making it to the United States while my family was deported. I began to learn not to feel guilty only when I connected with my parents through Kathryn Harwig. I have come to the conclusion that I am not going to feel guilty. I am trying to find the lessons that I was meant to learn from these experiences and share them with others to help them avoid making the same mistakes.

Having said that, I would not be totally honest if I said I have *no* guilt. I feel guilty because I brought into this world two beautiful daughters who had no reasons to go through what they went through. Actually, sometimes I have unbearable amounts of guilt. I constantly pray to God and the angels that my girls will be safe and do not repeat their mother's mistakes. I miss them dearly and would love to talk to and see them. It is no longer about their birthdays, Thanksgiving, or Christmas. It is far more serious than that.

Why do I still feel guilt? I often wonder about the amount of guilt my daughters carry for not contacting me and succumbing to their mother's wishes. I miss and love my daughters more than anything else in life. I want to hug them and take them into my arms. I have never blamed them, and I have told them that they do not need my forgiveness because they have not done anything to me. I believe they will eventually recognize the truth, and we will reconnect. I only have one fear that I cannot do anything about. I am afraid of dying before seeing my daughters. I am, in general, not afraid of meeting my creator, and in many ways, I welcome the day. I just do not want to leave behind two beautiful daughters who will feel guilty for the rest of their lives. But I have decided that I will surrender this fear to God our creator.

The last person I would like to look at here is Amy. Amy, as you might remember, is the coworker about whom I was receiving angelic messages to help. Was she brought into my life for a purpose? I think I answered that earlier—it was clearly to "wake me up." But having recognized that, why was Amy not grateful for my good gestures? I honestly do not understand how anyone could be so ungrateful unless Amy's ungratefulness was part of the master universe plan also. This is still a mystery to me, because she was educated and definitely was not blind. Expressing gratitude to someone does not imply an intention to have a romantic relationship.

I have no remaining questions about Amy's nature. I did not sense a grateful bone in her body. The salon confirmed that she did use my massage gift certificate, and I am happy that she did. Will Amy ever show up in my life again? She might, but I do not expect to fall at her feet and try to win back her friendship with gifts. If she does show up, I will deal with her as I do with everyone—with respect and integrity.

There is more one thing that I must mention about Amy to be complete. If it had not been for Amy and the way she behaved toward me, I would not have responded to Insiah's email and sought Insiah out for An intuitive reading. Remember, I had been told that Amy needed my help, and I did not know what to make of that because she was not open with me. Because of Insiah, I became aware of the archangels, especially Archangel St. Michael. My angel knowledge led me to Doreen Virtue, Dr. Wayne Dyer, and many others. In truth, my own sense of myself as a spiritual being was ignited as a result of Amy coming into my life. For that, I am forever grateful to her, wherever she might be.

This discussion about Amy is a good segue to the summary of my spiritual views. As I noted when writing about my early years, I grew up seeing members of all three of God's major religions (Judaism, Christianity, and Islam) living together, respecting each other, and most importantly, respecting each other's beliefs. I grew up exposed to all three holy books, though I never mastered any of them. My mother's teaching to help people and her example of cooking all day for others was not from a specific religious base, but it was the principle of all three religions.

God is simply God, regardless of what we call a religion. My mother taught me that the only important thing was that God knew what she was doing. She did not use the special names of Almighty God the Father, Jesus, or Allah. I learned early on that God is each one of those, and God is me and you. My mother passed away in a hospital where Mother Mary greeted all visitors, and she was laid to rest in the holy Muslim shrine of Najaf, Iraq. What does that tell you? That was my background, and I am very proud of it. I know that all three of these world religions originated from my home area, and I am thankful that I never succumbed to any of the political messages that said one religion was good and the others were not.

When I was in West Germany, I did not have enough contacts to check out religious life in that country. I wish I had taken the time to attend a few services there. In North Dakota, I went from church to church without regard to denomination. Deep down, I did not think there was need for any divisions when, in truth, we were all talking about the same God. Translations and interpretations should not be the basis for divisions, especially when we are talking about God. I will never force my opinions on anyone else, and I often get puzzled about how other people act when it comes to religion.

Karen took our children away from me time and time again just to hurt me, but never missed going to church even during those times. I often wonder if some people think that mere attendance at church, mosque, or synagogue to worship is good enough. What about practicing it? When I began to read about and follow Archangel St. Michael, Karen started to go to Bible school because she said that I "brought the devils home." The notion of a Catholic calling Archangel St. Michael a devil was very puzzling to me. I wondered if she had ever been taught that in the Book of Revelation St. Michael leads God's armies against Satan's forces.

At the end of the day, regardless of what we practice as a religion and what we look like, our family trees ultimately take us to one father and one mother.

When I was told that the archangel was the one who had saved me, his name was not new news to me, as I was aware that he is mentioned in all God's books. I was very blessed and thankful. In truth, this was a new beginning for me. When Insiah told me that there was a huge gap in spiritual levels separating me from Amy, I did not know what to make of that, because I had never looked at myself as spiritual. Insiah's words were, *"You don't know who you are."* In truth, I did not know who I was. I still don't know who I am exactly, and I am searching for me. These words were repeated later in Hawaii when the Asian-appearing lady stopped me and asked me why I was walking the way I was walking, followed by the question, *"Do you know who you are?"* And only a few minutes before that encounter I had met the couple who told me, *"I see God in you."* These are a few dots that I have connected so far. I am hoping for a few more dots to connect to solve this amazing puzzle. Was I being motivated to put this story out as part of my bigger picture? I know that one day I shall find out.

I am also still wondering about something else. When I initially bought many books to learn about Archangel St. Michael, why did I single out the ones by Doreen Virtue? Was it because she was better than the rest? I truly cannot answer that, as I never gave the others a chance. My intuition and guidance tells me that the others were "just books and authors." None of the others were doing what Doreen was doing in terms of classes and appearances. Of course, initially when I purchased the books, I did not know this fact about Doreen Virtue. This is how intuition and gut feelings work.

And what was behind my getting the email about the "I Can Do It" conference in Vancouver? This was also planned by divine guidance, and I followed my intuitions in the midst of a terrible situation at home. The way it worked out in Vancouver that Dr. Dyer was nowhere to be found on Saturday was also in divine order for me. If he had been there on Saturday, I would not have had the chance to be guided by angels to meet him on Sunday. I believe that the two nicely dressed people who guided me back to see Dr. Dyer were Archangel St. Michael and Archangel Gabriel. This is my own intuition. I was told to trust my intuition, and I am learning to do so.

I have met Dr. Dyer one more time since that magical angelic intervention day, and of course, I have met Doreen Virtue several times also. I have taken the time to be certified as an angel therapy practitioner by Doreen Virtue. Does being certified give me an edge on anything? I personally do not think so. I believe that God and the angels are there for all of us regardless of any certifications, and they will hear us regardless of how we talk to them. It is just that I believe that if I had not become an Angel Therapy Practitioner, I would have missed something important for myself, which is the birth of my own spiritual awareness. So I am grateful that I did what I did regardless of how I feel about Doreen now, her overwhelming number of appearances, and her mass production of books, oracle cards, and her personal relationships circle. I have since come to know many spiritual mentors, like Deborah King. In fact, I am currently working on manifesting a meeting with Ms. King, as I am guided to follow her footsteps. She was the one who finally ignited my creativity and started me writing.

Since my early childhood, I have taken care of animals without ever really knowing why. I rehabilitated and set free many sparrows, spending my allowance to save sparrows from the destructive hands of other children. Later I grew to love pigeons. I took care of them and watched them fly high and return to their homes. This gave me a lot of joy. My first brush with death involved pigeons. Later, when Karen and I had our first home, I took the chance to get my first dog and have continued with dogs to this day. At one point, dogs even kept us from renting a home, but I never considered giving them away and saw them as part of the family.

I can never forget one incident a few years ago when I was looking for a particular kind of dog. One day I announced to Karen and both my daughters that on the upcoming weekend I would be going to South Dakota to get a puppy. Both girls wanted to come along, and I was really happy to share quality time with them. It was a six-hundred-mile round trip. Karen decided to come along, which was fine by me. We had a great time on the way back, stopping for lunch and breaks at many small towns and playing with the puppy. The following week we bought all the puppy supplies, and then suddenly, out of nowhere, Karen began to voice displeasure, saying, *"I never wanted the puppy in the first place."*

I replied, *"Why did you not say that earlier? And why did you come with us on the trip to get it?"* She always had her own stubborn take on everything, and I could not ever reason with her. I think it was just that she knew how much I loved animals and dogs, and she wanted to strip everything I loved away from me.

What role does my love of animals, birds, and human beings have in my existence as a spiritual being? I believe it is my nature and how and why I came to this world. What role do animals play in my future life's purpose and mission? I do not see any changes coming in the way I am. I will always want to be the voice for God's creations, especially the ones without a voice.

Another common theme through my life has been that I have always been in situations where I felt I was doing the best anyone can do but never received any gratitude. Why have I spent my life running toward betrayals? Why is it when I extend my hand to help someone, they usually find a way to hurt me? Deep down, I know I have always been ethical and acted with integrity. I am not sure exactly where I was going wrong. These thoughts often created the feeling of self-blame and added to my depression.

Besides these feelings, I have always wondered why I could not be with the few people I loved in my life. It seems I have had to leave them all for one reason or another. This was true about Nadia, then Denise, and some others, and yet the ones whom I do not want in my life somehow end up there. What was it about me?

I was finally guided to participate in a four-part online class with Deborah King that finally answered this question. The first part of this class took place on October 30, 2012. It was about the Book of Life, or the Akashic Records. These records hold the plans or lessons we have chosen to experience for the growth of our souls and show how those plans are part of everything that's happening in our lives. The class taught us to access our own records. When I signed up, I did not know anything about these records. I only signed up because it was taught by Deborah King.

In the beginning of the class, Ms. King went over the records in great detail. At some point she mentioned that "all of us," by which she meant all the people who had signed up for the class, had not appeared by accident and that "we all intentionally chose to reincarnate at this particular time to help the transition from the fourth world to the fifth world." The fourth world, she said, is ending on December 20, 2012, and the fifth world is starting the following day, December 21, 2012.

I finally got through to her on the phone and asked her, "Deborah, how is it possible that I had intentionally chosen this time? I had to leave my big, happy family for almost thirty years without seeing them. Some of my family died, some got killed by Saddam, and the rest are living in pain, deported, without my being able to help them. I left my family and worked hard to educate and establish myself, only to have a terrible marriage that ended in divorce, and I have not seen my own children in some time. Everyone seems to turn against me, so how is it possible I chose this time?"

She tuned into my energy and said, "I am seeing your records very clearly. This is a hugely spiritual transformative period for you, and that pain you have suffered is your entrée into the next kingdom. You already have one foot in the fifth world. You are truly stepping up, so you are one of the Light Bearers. All that was just to take away from you anything that might keep you from moving into the Light. It seems very odd, but I am going to throw you a historical example that might not be helpful to you from your background, but I am thinking about how Jesus left his family and said to them, 'I have no family, I have no mother, no father, no sister, no brother.' You know some of us have to actually leave our families or be stripped of them in order to step into the Light, and I believe that is your challenge. And it appears to me that you have already met it."

The message from the rest of the call was that I had to see all this pain, suffering, and betrayal as a push into what I am doing now. I was taken to the point where I could not sleep that Tuesday night. I was asking myself, "Who am I to make Deborah King give me an example such as Jesus to compare myself to?" I truly could not sleep from joy, but also from sadness. What is my mission in life? It is clear to me that there is a mission that I have yet to see. That night, I could not help reviewing Insiah's comment, then the Vancouver series of incidents, the couple by the poolside in Hawaii, and finally the Asian lady. I was very tired in the morning but went to work regardless, waiting for the recording of the first class, which included my phone call.

The timing of this class and the urge to call, getting through to talk to Deborah, and getting the amazing message proved to me once again that nothing happens by accident. Everything is happening in divine order and timing. The trick is to be open to receive these messages. It is clear that in a time when I was going through financial difficulties, I still wanted to take part in a class such as that one. I don't want to give you the impression that this class was expensive, because it was not, but for my situation, everything was expensive. I was clearly guided to take part in this class, and I responded.

After this phone call, I started to put all my life events into a new perspective. I began to think that I personally did not have anything to do with what had happened to my own family. I did not have anything to do with what Saddam Hussein did to many innocent people, and I did not betray Nadia and always had her in my heart regardless of the miles and the passing of time. I went on and on to review all my life events, including Karen, Amy, and Denise, and believed that I had followed the honorable road. I started to forgive everyone, knowing that everything had transpired according to a divine plan. I began to see the light and transcend the pain and my heavy heart into a state of gratefulness for each and every one who had been part of the journey. Everyone was following the master plan, and I must not be angry, hateful, or resentful toward anyone.

Do I consider what Deborah King told me more moving or important than what was said to me by the couple by the poolside? I can't say I do, as both were very moving and emotional to me. What Ms. King did for me was help me to finally put all my experiences, encounters, and everything else into prospective. Why didn't Doreen have nearly the impact on me, spiritual development, and my moving forward like Deborah King did? I truly cannot answer this question knowing how hard I scarified my time and money even in my toughest times just to see her and how hard I tried to be part of Doreen's loyal messenger.

The one thing with which I am still working toward peace is the idea of Karen using our children as a hostage or pawn to deal with me. It has been very difficult for me to forgive Karen for what she did over eighteen years, regardless of who is to blame. Recently my intuition has stepped in on this issue. Since I do believe that when we use the words "I am," we are talking about God, I have to also say that "I am forgiveness," and so I now know that I must forgive her. I am very at peace with the fact that I was always there for my daughters; I always wanted the best for them and their education. I do not want to say that I sacrificed my own happiness for the sake of my children's well-being, as that might inflict some unneeded pain on them. I did what any honorable man would do for his children, but was handcuffed by Karen's acts.

I have always liked to use many quotes in my daily life, but two of them have risen to special service and apply to me now more than ever. I learned both of them from my mentor, Dr. Wayne W. Dyer, as quoted in his 2007 book, *Inspiration, Your Ultimate Calling.* They come from different sources. The first is from Vivekananda:

"A man may have never entered a church or a mosque nor performed any ceremony; but if he realizes God within himself, and is thereby lifted above the vanities of the world, that man is a holy man, a saint, call him what you will . . ."

I am not claiming to be a holy man or saint at all. I am what I am, and going along with whatever is the plan for me. It is just a quote that I have always liked. The second is from Ramakrishna:

"Saints are like big steamships, which not only cross the ocean themselves but carry many passengers to the other shore. May you too be like those big steamships—but if you're not, then by all means allow yourself to be one of those lucky passengers."

Of course, I would like to see myself as the big steamship, but if not, I would still love only to be one of those lucky passengers.

In closing, let me say that I was born into a proud family with a very proud heritage and distinguished ancestors. Events and many turns and twists led me to leave my family in search of my life's purpose and calling. I did not look at my journey as such in the beginning, but I do now. During the early days of this journey, I pumped gas, picked up garbage, and cleaned floors to make an honest living instead of waiting for a handout from anyone. I never went around saying that I was above this or that, and I was willing to do anything for mere minimum wage without feeling that I was not being fair or honest to my heritage and my family's status. When the pharmacist in Minot wanted to keep our friendship secret because she did not want to be seen with a maintenance person, I acted as my true self and did not want any part of that relationship. I never looked at my pride as something based on my work or position. My pride was within me, and my wage or job was not going to change that. I heard the term *Auslander* (foreigner) applied to me many times when I was Germany. Did that take away from my pride? Hardly. When one is sure of himself or herself, words like that will not change anything. Later, during the Gulf War and beyond, I heard many ethnic-based jokes from strangers and friends alike. None of that changed my mind about myself. The phone call from Karen's sister after the horrible events on September 11, 2001, and the *Not Without My Daughter* comments proved to be very poisonous and hurtful, but did not take away from my pride or heritage.

Did all the restraining orders and issues with the law take away from my pride? Not at all, even though at the time they did demoralize me to the point of depression. You can say that they bent me, but they did not break me. Was all of that the "price of entrée," as Deborah King stated? If so, then I am happy I had to go through all of that and would not have asked for anything different.

Did I go through a lot of difficulties? Of course I did, starting before I graduated from high school. In the short time I had with my mother, her early promise to send me to the United States ignited me and acted like a torch to lead me and guide me through the deserts of western Iraq, surviving snakes and scorpions, and on through the difficulties of West Germany. This is why I called my book *Guided by Divine Love*. This title is not just a "pretty" title but is, in fact, the essence of my book and my message. *I am always guided by my mother's divine love.* My mother's promise was not just to lead me to the United States. In many ways, it was the guide that saved my life. If not for that promise, I would have easily stayed in Iraq, possibly married my first sweetheart, and been killed by Saddam Hussein along with my brothers and thousands of other innocent people. Was I so special that I was saved from these horrific acts of violence? I cannot answer this question, and all I have to say is that time definitely will tell.

I might not be very clear yet about my life's purpose or mission, but I am confident that with everything I have been through, including the many brushes with death, I do have one.

As I neared the end of writing my story, I had a few questions to myself that wanted immediate answers. One was this: "David, do you really want the whole world to experience the kind of abuse you put up with? Not to mention all the restraining orders and the police records?" After thinking very hard, I figured there would be two different groups of readers with two different reactions after they finished reading my story. The first group will want to find me and kill me for being such a coward and putting up with all of that s—— for so long. The second might understand my point and try to do something to bring this issue into public awareness.

I took the question to my mentor, Deborah King. Her response was short and to the point. "David, have you read my book, *Truth Heals: What You Hide Can Hurt You?*" I said I did have the book, but hadn't read it yet. She responded, "Once you read it, you won't be asking a question like that." From that point, I let the issue rest and trusted the Divine.

I knew there might be other issues and concerns that would obviously be out of my control once I published my story, such as "Will my readers conclude that I am painting myself as a victim?" I thought and meditated very hard about that too, in relation to every single life event recounted here. The only answer that came to me was as follows: "This is my story, my true story. I never intended or wanted to paint myself as a victim or seek any kind of sympathy. When I left my home and my love Nadia behind, I was planning to be faithful to her and contact her once I was established to find a way to reconnect. Not in my wildest dreams did I ever think I would lose all connection to my roots. Telling this sad story does not make me a victim. I cannot imagine anyone telling a Holocaust survivor, "You sound like you are painting yourself as a victim." The true victims are my brothers who were killed for no reason, my entire family who were deported to Iran and had everything, including their home, taken away from them. I do not want to be looked at as a victim. I learned from my father to trust people, and I did. All these things really happened, and I have had to deal with them and move on.

I often think that someone might ask me if I played any role in all these events. Of course I did. If I had never left my homeland, none of these events would have taken place. Using this same analogy, we can say if President John F. Kennedy had not visited the state of Texas when he did, he would not have been murdered. Nothing will be accomplished and no new technologies will be discovered if we all fear failure. Mr. Neale Donald Walsch said, and he was correct, "Don't worry about 'mistakes.' Rather, worry about being afraid not to make them."

Earlier I mentioned how I began writing after I had signed with Balboa Press, but they are not who you see as my current publisher. I stayed faithfully with Balboa through several phases and finally submitted everything for the final design phase. Without going into any details, I unfortunately came to realize that Balboa was not exactly right for me. I do not have a big ego when it comes to this book, and frankly, even if my daughters are the only two readers, I will feel that my mission was a complete success. I will be very grateful if anyone besides my daughters get to read my story. I am also very grateful to Balboa for the motivation they instilled in me to begin and finish writing this story.

So, for now, I will say that my purpose is to ignite awareness. The first awareness is the importance of education, illustrated by what I did for myself. The other thing I learned is the importance of keeping children out of any personal games.

And from now on, I am planning to follow my guides to wherever they might lead me next.